THE POST-TRUTH ERA

Chancing It: Why We Take Risks

The Courage to Write: How Writers Transcend Fear

The Height of Your Life

The Innovation Paradox: The Success of Failure, the Failure of Success
(coauthored with Richard Farson)

Is There Life After High School?

"Nice Guys Finish Seventh": False Phrases, Spurious Sayings,
and Familiar Misquotations

Sons on Fathers: A Book of Men's Writing

Timelock: How Life Got So Hectic and What You Can Do About It

We, the Lonely People: Searching for Community

The Wit and Wisdom of Harry Truman

The Wit and Wisdom of Oscar Wilde

The Writer's Book of Hope: Getting from Frustration to Publication

THE POST-TRUTH ERA

Dishonesty and Deception
in Contemporary Life

Ralph Keyes

St. Martin's Press
New York

www.stmartins.com

Library of Congress Cataloging-in-Publication Data

Keyes, Ralph.
    The post-truth era: dishonesty and deception in contemporary life
/ Ralph Keyes.—1st U.S. ed.
      p. cm
    Includes bibliographical references (p.) and index.
    ISBN 0-312-30648-2
    EAN 978-0312-30648-9
    1. Truthfulness and falsehood.   I. Title.

BJ1421.K49 2004
177'.3—dc22   2004049030

First Edition: October 2004

10 9 8 7 6 5 4 3 2 1

For Bill Phillips,
the friend and supporter
every author dreams of

Contents

I

Honesty's Decline

One

Beyond Honesty

"Truth" has been displaced by "believability."
—DANIEL BOORSTIN

During years of studying deceptive behavior, psychologist Robert Feldman has made some intriguing discoveries. The older children get, the more deft they grow at lying. Popular teenagers are better liars than unpopular ones. We're more likely to lie when our self-esteem is threatened. Such findings haven't surprised the psychologist. Nonetheless, even Feldman was startled by what transpired when he gathered 121 college students to engage in ten-minute conversations with someone they had just met.

Most of the subjects carried their assignment off with aplomb. Feldman then asked them to watch videotapes of their brief conversations and tell him when they'd said something that wasn't accurate. Most assured him that this wouldn't be necessary, because everything they had said was accurate. That's why the students were so surprised to see one lie after another emerge from their mouths on instant replay. During their ten-minute exchanges, members of this group told an average of three lies, or one every 3.3 minutes. Despite a few whoppers (one young man who couldn't even play guitar said he was in a rock group that had just signed a big recording contract), most of their fibs were petty. There were just a lot of them. In conversations with Feldman afterward, few subjects seemed concerned about the lies they'd told. Lying is just part of everyday life, they told the University of Massachusetts psychologist. "Everybody does it," they said. If this is the case, where does that leave the expectation that we can depend on each other's basic honesty? "I think most of us assume that during the course of the day we are hearing the truth almost all the time," Feldman concluded. "But I think the reality is very different."

A Whole Lotta Lyin'

Many have already reached that conclusion on their own. There is a growing suspicion that more lies than ever are being told. To paraphrase the great social commentator Jerry Lee Lewis, a feeling is widespread that *there's a whole lotta lyin' goin' on.* Until fairly recently there was little data to confirm or deny this hunch. Now, studies such as Feldman's are putting it to the test. Preliminary results are disconcerting. One researcher after another has confirmed that lying has become as common as scratching itches.

When they had several hundred subjects record every lie they told in the course of a week, California sociologists Noelie Rodriguez and Alan Rygrave were as surprised as Robert Feldman was by the sheer volume of lies recorded. Even those who had assured the researchers they were truth tellers turned in journals filled with falsehoods. One woman promised a friend that she'd watch him play basketball when she had no intention of doing so. Another assured her husband that their tedious lovemaking was terrific. A mother told her child that they couldn't go swimming because the pool was closed when it wasn't. A healthy young man had his mother tell a friend he was too sick to go to the movies as he'd promised. Another said he'd help a friend move, then pretended he couldn't because of a previous engagement. What struck researchers and subjects alike was how casually these lies were conveyed. Few were planned in advance. They slid into the conversational flow as easily as a car merging onto an uncrowded freeway. Based on their findings, Rodriguez and Rygrave speculated that during any conversation at all it could be that "lying is not only a possible action, but a preferred one."

I think it's fair to say that honesty is on the ropes. Deception has become commonplace at all levels of contemporary life. At one level that consists of "He's in a meeting" or "No, that dress doesn't make you look fat." On another level it refers to "I never had sexual relations with that woman" or "We found the weapons of mass destruction." High-profile dissemblers vie for headlines: fabulist college professors, fabricating journalists, stonewalling bishops, book-cooking executives and their friends the creative accountants. They are the most visible face of a far broader phenomenon: the routinization of dishonesty. I'm not talking just about those who try to fib their way out of a tight spot ("I wasn't out drinking last night; I had to work late") but casual lying done for no apparent reason ("Yes, I was a cheerleader in high school").

Ludwig Wittgenstein once observed how often he lied when the truth would have done just as well. This Viennese philosopher has many modern disciples. The gap between truth and lies has shrunk to a sliver. Choosing which to tell is largely a matter of convenience. We lie for all the usual reasons, or for no apparent reason at all. It's no longer assumed that truth telling is even our default setting. When Monica Lewinsky said she'd lied and been lied to all her life, few eyebrows were raised. Our attitudes toward lying have grown, to say the least, *tolerant*. "It's now as acceptable to lie as it is to exceed the speed limit when driving," observed British psychologist Philip Hodson. "Nobody thinks twice about it."

The tattered condition of contemporary candor is suggested by how often we use phrases such as "quite frankly," "let me be frank," "let me be candid," "truth be told," "to tell you the truth," "to be truthful," "the truth is," "truthfully," "in all candor," "in all honesty," "in my honest opinion," and "to be perfectly honest." Such verbal tics are a rough gauge of how routinely we deceive each other. If we didn't, why all the disclaimers?

Most of us lie and are lied to on a regular basis. These lies run the gamut from "I like sushi" to "I love you." Even though we're more likely to deceive strangers than friends, we save our most serious lies for those we care about most. Many have to do with sex. One priest said he rarely hears a confession that doesn't include some element of sexual deceit. A colleague of his said it's a rare day that a parishioner doesn't confess to telling lies, sometimes with figures in hand ("twenty times to the same person, Father"). He couldn't believe that they actually keep track.

A regard for honesty or disdain for lying has not disappeared altogether. Quite the contrary. Pollsters detect rising concern about falling ethics, especially among older cohorts. Surveys in the United States and elsewhere confirm that truthfulness is still one of our most highly valued traits. As the new millennium began, for only the second time in half a century those polled by Gallup put ethics and morality near the top of the list of problems facing Americans. An earlier poll of citizens in ten western European countries found that honesty headed the qualities they most wanted to instill in children. (Confounding stereotypes, Italians were the least tolerant of lying, Belgians the most.) The problem is that a commitment to honesty in principle too often goes hand in glove with routine lying in practice. In biannual surveys conducted by the Josephson Institute of Ethics in Marina Del Rey, California, the vast majority of thousands of middle school, high school, and college students express satisfaction with their ethics and character. Yet nearly three-quarters admit to being "serial liars." Most say they'd lie to save money, almost half to get a good job. Nearly all of the students are confident they can get away with telling such lies. Granted this is a young, cocksure cohort. But, as institute head Michael Josephson has pointed out, these students cannot have been raised with much ethical rigor. And as they enter the workforce, their problem will become our problem.

Like Josephson's subjects, when it comes to honesty we're caught in a chink between our values and our behavior. Most believe that lying is wrong, at least in principle. Few consider themselves unethical. Nonetheless, if research on this subject is credible, nearly all of us tell lies, and far more often than we realize. Once this is called to our attention, it's hard not to wonder how often others lie to us.

How often do we lie and get lied to? All sorts of figures get bandied about. I've seen estimates that range from two hundred times a day to once. One study concluded that we tell thirteen lies a week on the average. Another found that some form of deception occurs in nearly two-thirds of all conversations. If this sounds far-fetched, bear in mind that the most frequent lie of all is "Fine" (in response to the question "How are you?"). This fib is so ubiquitous that deception researcher Bella DePaulo excused subjects from recording it in records they kept of every lie they told in a week's time. DePaulo's group consisted not just of seventy-seven University of Virginia students but seventy residents of nearby Charlottesville. During their week of self-scrutiny, the two groups combined recorded 1,535 lies. Charlottesville residents averaged about a lie a day, UVA students two. (This finding may have been skewed by the fact that students lied nearly every other time they talked to their mothers.) One student and six townspeople got through the week lie-free. Among those who didn't, 70 percent of the entire group said they'd tell the same lies again. Neither group expressed much remorse about their dishonesty.

No one has paid more attention to the issue of contemporary dishonesty than Bella DePaulo.* Over more than two decades' time the psychologist has assessed from many different angles how often we lie, to whom, how, and why. The more eager we are to make a good impression, she has found, the more likely we are to tell lies. We're more prone to lie to those we like than to those we dislike. Attractive people are more likely to trim the truth, more likely to get away with it, and more likely to be lied to. Extrapolating from her studies, DePaulo has concluded that the average American is dishonest at least once a day. During all the years DePaulo has spent investigating this topic, only one of her subjects claimed he always told the truth. She thought he was lying. Occasionally a student of DePaulo's has tried to go for a week without telling a lie. Few have succeeded. "Lying is a routine event," DePaulo has concluded. "It has become part of the fabric of our lives, almost a necessity of social and professional life."

The actual rate of lying or how it's determined is less revealing than the fact that such observations raise so few eyebrows. To the contrary, they confirm what many suspect already: we live in fib-friendly times. Deceiving others has become something of a leisure activity. We're of two minds about this: excusing our own lies at the same time that we're appalled by the prevalence of dishonesty.

---

*Although DePaulo conducted many of her studies in conjunction with colleagues, for the sake of simplicity, when discussing her work I use her name alone. The names of DePaulo's collaborators, along with citations of sources of information used throughout this book, can be found in the notes section.

(Put somewhat differently, my lies are understandable; your lies are contemptible.) At the very least we're intrigued by this subject. Plots of movies and television shows are routinely based on lying. Newspaper and magazine feature stories regularly cover dishonesty. Lies and liars have become a popular book topic. Some note a looser approach to dishonesty in the postmodern world. As Jeremy Campbell wrote in *The Liar's Tale*, "it is a creeping assumption at the start of a new millennium that there are things more important than truth."

There have always been those who considered honesty overrated. Oscar Wilde defended the aesthetic and moral value of lies. Friedrich Nietzsche thought the well-told lie was a sign of greatness. "A liar in full flower," wrote Ernest Hemingway, "is as beautiful as cherry trees, or apple trees when they are in blossom." Nonetheless, in cultures old and new, lies have generally been considered the antithesis of truth, and on balance best not told. Society would collapse if dishonesty became the norm. Most sense that. That's why concern about lying is rising in conjunction with its prevalence.

Whatever Happened to Honesty?

This book is not meant to be a jeremiad against all lies and every liar. (By "lie" I mean a false statement made knowingly, with intent to deceive; by "liar" I mean one who knowingly conveys false information, intending to deceive.) Rather, it's an expression of concern about casual lying, its effect on how we deal with each other, and on society as a whole.

As long as human beings have had words to say, they've said words that weren't true. At the same time, most societies have had some variation of *Honesty is the best policy* as a norm. What concerns me is the loss of a stigma attached to telling lies, and a widespread acceptance of the fact that lies can be told with impunity. Lying has become, essentially, a no-fault transgression. "That's okay," we say of those who are caught dissembling. "She meant well." "Who am I to judge?" And the clincher: "What is truth, anyway?"

Nearly everyone trims and embroiders the truth and hopes for the best. I've been known to round down how many miles an hour I was driving, and round up the size of audiences at my lectures. I also get lied to a lot, big lies and small lies, stretchers and whoppers, fun lies and devious ones, petty fibs and felony lies. Who doesn't? Not that I wring my hands and gnash my teeth when I'm deceived. Like most people, I've come to accept dishonesty as commonplace, even routine. Perhaps it would be better if we didn't.

The obvious cause of dishonesty's rise is ethical decline. From this perspective, moral compasses have broken down. Our sense of right and wrong has gone into remission. Conscience is considered old-fashioned. Conviction has been replaced by cynicism. Restoring prayer in schools, some argue, would be a giant step toward renewed morality. Or hanging the Ten Commandments on walls of public buildings. Nonsense. There is no evidence that early Americans were more moral than their descendants. It's doubtful that former-day Americans—the ones who broke treaties with Indians, enslaved Africans, and exploited child labor—had better ethics than current ones. Nor was antebellum religious faith as devout as we like to imagine. Two centuries ago church membership was far lower than it is today, involving less than 10 percent of all Americans.

There never was an ethical nirvana in America or anywhere else, only a time when it was harder to tell lies, and the consequences were greater if one got caught. This book's premise is that we may be no more prone to making things up than our ancestors were, but we are better able to get away with deceiving others, more likely to be let off the hook if exposed, and in the process convince ourselves that no harm's been done. As we'll explore, the mobility and anonymity of contemporary life facilitate dishonesty. So do deceit-friendly intellectual trends, the many celebrity role models of self-invention, and repeated instances of high-profile dissembling that desensitize us to its dangers.

Decades of official lies about Vietnam, Watergate, Irangate, and Iraq (to name just a few such events) have left us morally numb. Early in the new century, a Pew Research Center poll found that three-fourths of those surveyed said they believe people are not as honest as they used to be. Can this be proven? Those who have taken a serious interest in this subject say that would be hard. Nonetheless, they have little doubt that more lies are being told today than were told in our grandparents' era, or even our parents':

There is no scientific data, but I think people probably lie more now.
—CHARLES V. FORD, PSYCHIATRIST

There is a general consensus that deception, unethical acts, and cheating increased dramatically over the past several years.
—DAN O'HAIR AND MICHAEL CODY, PSYCHOLOGISTS

Lying in everyday life is more widespread than had previously been assumed.
—RICHARD WISEMAN, PSYCHOLOGIST

It seems to me that lying has reached epidemic proportions in recent years and that we've all become immunized to it.
—BEN BRADLEE, FORMER EDITOR OF THE *WASHINGTON POST*

Although Sissela Bok could not determine that more lies are being told today "per capita," in the preface to her updated classic *Lying* Bok did conclude that "we are all on the receiving end of a great many more lies than in the past." Even if the relative proportion of deceptive messages that we get today is no greater than ever, because we get so many more messages of all kinds—via cell phones, e-mail, instant messaging, the Internet, talk radio, and cable channels—the actual volume of lies we hear is up, way up. Although it would be hard to establish statistically that we tell more lies than ever, my concern is that lies are being told so routinely that we don't always realize when we're lying, let alone when we are being lied to.

In the Reagan-Clinton-Bush era we're so accustomed to being deceived that we forget what a stunner it was in 1960 when Dwight Eisenhower admitted that government officials hadn't told the truth when they said that a U-2 spy plane shot down by the Soviet Union had been doing weather research. As recently as the early 1970s we could still get outraged about Richard Nixon's serial deceits. Jimmy Carter was elected in part because he promised never to tell us a lie. By the time of Monica Lewinsky and weapons of mass destruction, the mood had changed. Now our attitude seemed to be: Everyone lies, especially our leaders. What's the big deal? Dishonesty has come to feel less like the exception and more like the norm. Along with our acceptance of lying as commonplace we've developed ingenious ways to let ourselves off ethical hooks.

Post-Truthfulness

Even though there have always been liars, lies have usually been told with hesitation, a dash of anxiety, a bit of guilt, a little shame, at least some sheepishness. Now, clever people that we are, we have come up with rationales for tampering with truth so we can

dissemble guilt-free. I call it *post-truth*. We live in a post-truth era.*
Post-truthfulness exists in an ethical twilight zone. It allows us to
dissemble without considering ourselves dishonest. When our behavior conflicts with our values, what we're most likely to do is
reconceive our values. Few of us want to think of ourselves as being unethical, let alone admit that to others, so we devise alternative approaches to morality. Think of them as *alt.ethics*. This term
refers to ethical systems in which dissembling is considered okay,
not necessarily wrong, therefore not really "dishonest" in the negative sense of the word.

Even if we do tell more lies than ever, no one wants to be considered a *liar*. That word sounds so harsh, so judgmental. Men in
particular are extremely careful to avoid giving other men any opportunity to say "You callin' me a liar?" Once those fatal words are
spoken, it's hard for dialogue to continue without fists being
thrown, or worse. The word *lie* itself is both a description and a
weapon. According to the *Oxford English Dictionary*, this term "is
normally a violent expression of moral reprobation, which in po-
lite conversation tends to be avoided." That's why we come up
with avoidance mechanisms: rationales for dishonesty, reasons why
it's okay to lie, not nearly as bad as we once thought, maybe not so
bad after all. The emotional valence of words associated with deception has declined. We no longer tell lies. Instead we "mis-
speak." We "exaggerate." We "exercise poor judgment." "Mistakes
were made," we say. The term "deceive" gives way to the more
playful "spin." At worst, saying "I wasn't truthful" sounds better
than "I lied." Nor would we want to accuse others of lying; we say

---

*Much as I would love to say this phrase is mine, it isn't. I first saw it in a 1992 *Nation* essay
by the late Steve Tesich.

they're "in denial." That was sometimes said even of Richard Nixon, the premier liar of modern times, who went to his grave without ever confessing to anything more than errors of judgment. Presidential aspirant Gary Hart admitted only to "thoughtlessness and misjudgment" after reporters revealed Hart's dishonesty (not only about his sex life but about his age). When, during a primary debate, John Kerry referred to a nonexistent poll that put his popularity well above Hillary Clinton's, an aide later said Kerry "misspoke." And it isn't just male politicians who parse words this way. In the course of writing *The Dance of Deception*, Harriet Lerner asked women friends what lies they'd recently told. This request was invariably greeted with silence. When Lerner asked the same friends for examples of "pretending," they had no problem complying. "I pretended to be out when my friends called," said one without hesitation.

A direct admission of lying ("I lied") is rare to nonexistent. Those willing to make such a bold statement cast doubt on anything they have said in the past and anything they will say in the future. This is why, rather than open the floodgates and accept lying as a way of life, we manipulate notions of truth. We "massage" truthfulness, we "sweeten it," we tell "the truth improved." Britain's cabinet secretary Sir Robert Armstrong once created an uproar with his droll admission that he'd been "economical with the truth" (a phrase he borrowed from Edmund Burke). Since then, all manner of creative phrasemaking has been devoted to explaining why lies are something else altogether. My favorite depicts a liar as "someone for whom truth is temporarily unavailable."

When *Trump: The Art of the Deal* was published, Donald Trump claimed that 200,000 copies had been printed, that *The Today Show* planned to interview him five times, and that the issue of *New York* magazine with an excerpt of his book was its biggest seller ever. In fact, 150,000 copies of *Trump* were printed, *Today* interviewed him twice, and *New York's* sales figures were not available at the time he made his claims. In his book, Trump called this kind of braggadocio "truthful hyperbole." After *The Apprentice* became a hit, Trump claimed his television show was the season's ratings leader (when it was actually #7) and said he was America's highest-paid television personality. A *Fortune* reporter who debunked these claims, and many others, concluded that Trump's boasts about himself were, at best, "loosely truth-based."

Euphemasia

Dishonesty inspires more euphemisms than copulation or defecation. This helps desensitize us to its implications. In the post-truth era we don't just have truth and lies, but a third category of ambiguous statements that are not exactly the truth but fall short of a lie. *Enhanced truth* it might be called. *Neo-truth. Soft truth. Faux truth. Truth lite.* Through such aggressive *euphemasia* we take the sting out of telling lies. Euphemasia calls up remarkable powers of linguistic creativity. In addition to golden oldies such as "credibility gap," "reframing," and Winston Churchill's "terminological inexactitudes," consider the following examples of post-truthful euphemisms:

Lies

poetic truth
parallel truth
nuanced truth
imaginative truth
virtual truth
alternative reality
strategic misrepresentations
creative enhancement

nonfull disclosure
selective disclosure
augmented reality
nearly true
almost true
counterfactual statements
fact-based information

To Lie
enrich the truth
enhance the truth
embroider the truth
massage the truth
tamper with the truth
tell more than the truth
bend the truth
soften the truth
shade the truth
shave the truth
stretch the truth
stray from the truth
withhold the truth
tell the truth improved
present the truth in a favorable perspective
make things clearer than the truth
be lenient with honesty
spin

Eventually euphemisms themselves develop connotations and
spawn progeny. As an executive tells employees in a *New Yorker*
cartoon: "I'm not spinning—I'm contextualizing."

Ledger-Book Morality

Honesty was once considered an all-or-nothing proposition. You were either honest or dishonest. In the post-truth era this concept has become more nuanced. We think less about honesty and dishonesty per se and more about degrees of either one. Ethics are judged on a sliding scale. If our intentions are good, and we tell the truth more often than we lie, we consider ourselves on firm moral ground. If we add up truths and lies we've told and find more of the former than the latter, we classify ourselves honest. This is ledger-book morality. Conceding that his magazine soft-pedaled criticism of advertisers, one publisher concluded, "I guess you could say we're 75 percent honest, which isn't bad."

In terms of values, this approach denotes a significant shift. Previous generations tended to think you were virtuous or you weren't. Morality was not assessed by tallying assets and debits on a spreadsheet of virtue and hoping to come out ahead. Another analogy would be that we have shifted from set menu to buffet-style ethics: picking and choosing which ones to abide. This approach allows for the "compartmentalizing" at which Bill Clinton was said to excel. Abraham Lincoln would not be impressed.

Rising dishonesty has less to do with declining ethics than with a social context that doesn't place enough emphasis on truthfulness. There has never been a shortage of unscrupulous people. Wherever there are those who think they can get away with lying, there will be liars. The question is: What circumstances foster getting away with telling lies? Apart from sociopaths who make no real distinction between truth and lies, most of us are more honest in certain circumstances, less honest in others. Circumstances that condone dishonesty have risen while those that nurture honesty are in decline. If we do lie more—and I believe we do—it's because the context of contemporary life doesn't do enough to penalize dishonesty. At times our culture seems to do just the opposite. Lies pay off, the truth pays a penalty. Whistle-blowers get reprimanded, those on whom whistles are blown get promoted. The army's chief of staff was rebuked, then hounded out of uniform after his prescient observation that many more troops would be needed to occupy Iraq than to invade that country. A government actuary was threatened with dismissal for suggesting (accurately) that the overall cost of a Medicare prescription-benefit program would be far higher than the figure propagated by the White House. By contrast, known liars such as Monica Lewinsky, Geraldo Rivera, Oliver North, Mike Barnicle, Jayson Blair, and Joe Klein were rewarded with television or radio programs, book contracts, and magazine columns. Being notoriously deceitful can make the deceiver famous, a celebrity even. On our media-driven scale of values, celebrity trumps honesty.

Any Psychology 101 student knows that reinforced behavior is likely to persist. We get the society we pay for. In this case, that means a post-truthful one. Even if more lies are being told than ever, I don't think there's any greater human propensity to tell lies. What I do believe is that an age-old willingness to deceive others is being facilitated in new ways. To get a better handle on the prevalence of dishonesty today, let's first take a brief look at the history of lying.

Two

A Brief History of Lying

Some level of truthfulness has always been seen as
essential to human society.

—SISSELA BOK

The tendency to tell lies is a natural tendency . . . ,
spontaneous and universal.

—JEAN PIAGET

Three decades ago, a number of primates were taught to "speak," using a modified form of human sign language. They included a year-old gorilla named Koko who learned to sign under the tutelage of psychologist Penny Patterson. Soon after she and Koko began to converse, Patterson noted how often Koko used signs to deceive her. After breaking a toy cat, Koko signed that a colleague of her trainer was the actual guilty party. When apprehended eating crayons, she pretended to be using them as lipstick, signing "lip." Koko later used a chopstick she stole from the silverware drawer to poke holes in a window screen. Caught in the act and asked what she was doing, the gorilla signed "smoke mouth" (for a pretend smoking game she liked to play with sticks). When her ruses were pointed out to her, Koko signed "Bad again. Koko bad again."

Patterson's experience mirrored that of colleagues. Others who taught simians to sign soon found them signing deceptively. Although some have questioned whether such episodes demonstrate actual, conscious deception, the trainers themselves had little doubt that their pupils were deliberately putting them on. Furthermore, the more signs these primate Richard Nixons learned, the more "lies" they were able to convey. This suggests that lying comes as easily as truth telling to our evolutionary ancestors. Is the same thing true of *Homo sapiens?*

The Liar's Edge

As the only species that can actually talk, *Homo sapiens* is the only one that can lie out loud. This capacity gave early human beings a major evolutionary edge. They'd already demonstrated their mastery of the deceptive arts by hunting prey with artfully hidden traps or by tricking them into running off cliffs. As the human capacity to speak developed, so did our ability not only to trick prey and deceive predators but to lie to other humans. This too could be advantageous. Those who could persuade members of a rival tribe that a westward-moving herd of caribou had migrated east won a battle in the war for survival. Verbal deceitfulness gave early humans such a survival advantage that some evolutionary biologists believe the capacity to speak and the ability to lie developed hand in hand. Words made lying easier, while lying called for ever more words.

At the outset, human speech was probably not much different from the grunts, clicks, and shrieks of a chimpanzee. Early on there was little need for anything more complex. Wanting to tell others about important events ("Lion chased me!") probably took language to a higher level of complexity. But the real creativity of language only blossomed when—like Koko—we wanted to deceive others. Once words could be used to depict the world around us, why stick to the facts? This was especially true when we had something to conceal. As philosopher Karl Popper observed, "the moment when language became human was very closely related to the moment when a man invented a story, a myth in order to excuse a mistake he had made."

Imagine an early human who is sent off with three spears to catch some fish for his tribe's evening meal. While wading in a river he stumbles and drops his spears. They float downstream. What is our poor fisherman to do, not just to feed his flock but to save his face? This dilemma would call for great powers of imagination to come up with a credible-sounding story about the enemy tribesmen who ambushed him on his way to the river but whom he was able to fend off, thank goodness, although they did steal his spears.

Some see in such early falsehoods the birth of human creativity. A capacity to lie allowed us to depict not only what *is* but what *isn't*. To fictionalize, in other words. Our hapless fisherman with his ability to spin a yarn might have been Mark Twain's earliest ancestor. The need to tell lies required bigger vocabularies and expanded cognitive powers. The demands of inventing and selling falsehoods helped *Homo sapien* brains develop new synapses.

But that was hardly the end of the story. Once early human beings grasped their capacity to say what isn't as well as what is, they undoubtedly realized that some form of regulation was necessary. When was it permissible to tell lies and when not?

Early Ethics

One of the less appreciated dimensions of Darwin's revolution was his suggestion that nature didn't care a fig whether spiders, chimps, or human beings were honest. Her only concern was whether such a trait was adaptive. Darwin's own conclusion was a mixed bag. Like most naturalists, he noted that the natural world was full of hustlers, hoaxers, con artists, and swindlers. This was as true of human beings as it was of Venus flytraps. Honesty, Darwin believed, was a learned, not an innate, virtue.

I agree with Darwin that we have no more inherent will to tell the truth than we do to tell lies. It's a matter of context. All human beings have competing urges to deceive and be truthful. Depending on the circumstances, both tendencies improved our odds of survival. A capacity for deception enhanced one's ability to hunt prey, evade predators, and thwart enemies. Closer to home, the picture was quite different. Stable human groups can no more incorporate those who routinely hoodwink each other than banks can manage money with an open-vault policy. It doesn't take much reflection to recognize that the capacity to deceive which gave early *Homo sapiens* an edge outside the tribe eroded their bonds within. This realization must have been one of the earliest ethical impulses of our distant ancestors.

From that insight grew a nearly universal emphasis on honesty. At the outset this emphasis was not based on any need to speak accurately or to do the right thing. All that mattered was a need for trust among those who lived together. Trust is hard to sustain among those who lie to each other. That's why pressure to be honest has always been more social than spiritual, more outer than inner. The Buddha himself warned that lying not only degraded the liar, but destroyed the atmosphere of trust within society.

Darwin agreed. Even though he believed we have no inherent will to be honest, this did not mean that ethics could be thrown into the dustbin of history. For human survival, *fidelity*—keeping faith with our own—was essential, far more important than honesty per se. But fidelity requires honesty. As Darwin wrote in *The Descent of Man*, "There cannot be fidelity without truth." If fidelity is what spawns honesty, it stands to reason that truthfulness is a virtue only among those who feel attached to each other.

This perspective can be seen in our very words. Historically, terms signifying truth and truthfulness have had more to do with Charles Darwin's concept of fidelity to our own than with Immanuel Kant's conviction that we should never lie, or even with the scientific need for factual accuracy. The Moroccan term *haqq* signifies not just "truth" or "reality," but "duty" and "obligation." In German, *wahr* refers to that which is factual, while *treu* refers to a kind of truthfulness that's based more on loyalty. For English speakers, the word *truth* does double duty. Just as the word *sound* can refer both to something we hear and to someone who's dependable, the word *true* has multiple meanings: reliable, on the one hand, factually accurate on the other.

Like *wahr* in German, the Old English word *trouthe* signified loyalty, fidelity, and reliability. The strong social bond suggested by that term could even include marriage ("I pledge thee my troth"). A person who was "true" was someone who could be counted on, whose word was good. In time the concept of truthfulness came to signify that not just your *word* but your *words* could be counted on—that they were "true." Finally, *truth* became a synonym for veracity itself. Although we still sometimes use the word "true" in its original sense—as when the Beach Boys exhort us to "be true to your school"—more often today *true* is synonymous with *accurate*.

For most people for most of time, however, this term was used more in the Beach Boys sense than in the scientific or ethical version. This is not merely a matter of semantics. Speech reflects values. As anthropologists routinely discover, among indigenous peoples whose lives resemble those of our early ancestors, the concept of truthfulness emphasizes social cohesion far more than factual accuracy. Among the Tiv of Nigeria, for example, honesty refers primarily to reciprocal obligations. "'Truth' in Tivland," observed anthropologist Paul Bohannan, "is an elusive matter because smooth social relationships are deemed of higher cultural value than mere precision of fact." Bohannan's colleague Ethel Albert discovered the same thing in Burundi. To those whom Albert studied in this small central African country, the worst sort of liar was not someone who made things up but one who broke a promise—to do a favor, say, or give a gift. Ethel Albert was also well versed in the ways of the American Navajo. Lying, she found, was condemned among the Navajo less because it was wrong and more because it was likely to disturb group harmony. Traditionally, this tribe had two standards for proper behavior, a less stringent one involving common decency toward everyone, and another involving strict obligations toward fellow Navajo. The Navajo even used different words for lies told outside the tribe (not that big a deal) and those told within (an extremely big deal).

Those who have studied the ethical systems of tribal societies have found common elements. They include an emphasis on honesty among kinfolk combined with an acute awareness that everyone has an impulse to lie; a distinction between playful deception and malevolent lying; and, most important, a sharp distinction between ethical obligations to outsiders and ethical obligations to insiders. "When I read what the white man has written of our customs, I laugh," commented a member of the Tiv, "for it is the custom of our people to lie as a matter of course to outsiders, especially the white man."

The Insider's Guide to Honesty

Social groups historically have had a fundamentally different attitude toward telling the truth to insiders and telling the truth to outsiders. Few moral systems wasted time fretting over lies told outside the primary group. According to philosopher Bernard Williams, most incorporated the thought that "some people deserve more in the way of truth than others." That could be man's oldest ethical principle: honesty for insiders, whatever works for everyone else. Because truthfulness was seen primarily as a tool for keeping social bonds in good repair, the need to be truthful did not apply to those outside one's society. Deceiving an outsider was considered little different from deceiving a hyena, say, or a cheetah. Tricking strangers was considered no more sinful than tricking a bison into running off a cliff, or luring a fox into a trap. Traditional Bantu parents even warned their children not to tell the truth to strangers for fear of subjecting their family to witchcraft.

To this day, outsiders are considered fair game for prankish lies. This can lead to serious misunderstanding. In his book *The Russian Mind*, Ronald Hingley speculated that the tendency of tourists to dismiss Russians as hopelessly dishonest was based in part on the fact that they themselves were such an easy target for blarney. Lie as prank is commonplace throughout the world, each society having its own twists, turns, and terms for this practice. Among some Muslim Lebanese, the word *kizb* refers to the common leg pulling engaged in by residents. Afghans call their own capacity for hyperbole *laaf*. The Greek term *psemata* refers to whoppers that only an outsider would take seriously. Samoans call their version *taufa'ase'e*. *Taufa'ase'e* may be what Samoan maidens were engaged in when they told Margaret Mead about their lusty love lives. Sixty years after Mead completed her fieldwork for *Coming of Age in Samoa*, one of her subjects told an interviewer, "As you know, Samoan girls are terrific liars when it comes to joking, but Margaret accepted our trumped-up stories as though they were true."*

One reason indigenous peoples welcome anthropologists into their lives is that they provide fresh, gullible targets for put-ons. During her fieldwork among the Saami of Lapland, ethnographer Myrdene Anderson found herself the target of repeated deception. A remarkable number of her hosts introduced themselves to Anderson as "shamans." Others claimed to own nonexistent reindeer. "Lying, bluff, secrecy, and espionage are all coordinated into their dealings with non-Saami and nonhumans," wrote Anderson of those she'd come to study. The size of their reindeer herds was a particular source of hyperbole, vastly underestimated for tax collectors, wildly inflated to other outsiders (sometimes by a factor of ten). Being able to pull the reindeer hide over others' eyes was a source of Saami status, Anderson found. It wasn't enough just to be an effective trickster, however. No society, least of all that of the Saami, could survive if any and all lie telling was considered acceptable. The challenge, wrote Anderson, lay in ensuring that one's reputation as "a humorous, clever and sporty deceiver exceeds that as an excessive, trivial, or malicious one."

Although nearly all cultures condone some form of recreational lying (we call ours "practical jokes"), a clear distinction is usually

---

*In the two decades since anthropologist Derek Freeman charged that Mead's findings were based on unreliable reports from Samoan subjects, with compelling evidence based on his many years in Samoa, these allegations have remained a subject of unresolved controversy among his colleagues.

made between playful deceptions and ones that are mean-spirited. Russians distinguish between malevolent lies they call *lozh* and the put-ons they call *vranyo*. To be caught pulling someone's leg while engaged in *vranyo* is no big deal. To be revealed as a liar peddling *lozh* is. One practice is considered playful and benign; the other, loathsome and despicable.

Every society regulates honesty in its own way. Some are relatively flexible, others more unbending. The Incas put liars in prison. Ancient Greeks put their lying gods on pedestals. After reviewing accounts of visitors to scores of different tribes, philosopher-sociologist Herbert Spencer compiled an extensive list of societies that strongly emphasized truth telling and others that displayed more tolerance of dishonesty. What all shared was a recognition that social systems must take account of the fact that when left to their own devices, human beings are prone to tell lies.

Lie Regulation

All societies must reconcile the fact that lying is socially toxic with the fact that nearly all their members engage in this practice. Every belief system does its best to regulate dishonesty with taboos, sanctions, and norms. Few such systems claim that every lie is always wrong. This would put them too far out of synch with facts on the ground. Therefore a major task for all belief systems has been to determine when it's permissible to tell a lie.

Those participating in this search have usually taken three basic approaches: (1) lying is wrong, period (Augustine, Wesley, Kant); (2) it all depends (Montaigne, Voltaire, Bacon); (3) there is something to be said for a good lie well told (Machiavelli, Nietzsche, Wilde).

Greek gods were celebrated for their skill at deceiving humans and each other. In *The Odyssey*, Odysseus the dissembler is a far more intriguing character than Achilles the truth teller. When Athena, no slouch herself in the deception arts, approaches Odysseus upon his return to Ithaca in disguise, she is favorably impressed by the persuasive yarns he spins about himself. "Crafty must be he," Athena tells Odysseus, "and Knavish, who would outdo thee in all manner of guile."

Even early ethicists who warned against telling lies seldom did so on absolute terms. Plato, who condemned lying on general principles, nonetheless thought it was crucial for the guardians of his ideal republic to propagate "noble lies" so that the masses would accept their place and not disturb social harmony. Across the Adriatic, Cicero's *On Duties* emphasized the need for truth telling among free men. In Cicero's world, lying to a slave was not considered dishonest.

Most societies leave the question of determining which lies are justified to their clergy. Over the millennia theologians of all stripes have occupied themselves with explaining why some lies are worse than others. Even though the fourth of Buddhism's five precepts admonishes the faithful to abstain from lying, Buddhists distinguish between major lies (such as feigning enlightenment), minor lies (making things up), and lies told to benefit others (as when a doctor conceals the truth from a patient who is dying). The latter in particular are not considered much of a problem.

Like Buddhism's fourth precept, Hindu ethics proscribe lying. The seminal text *Laws of Manu* admonishes Hindi never to "swear an oath falsely, even in a trifling matter." That seems clear enough. In its next passage, however, Manu's laws advise that "there is no crime in a [false] oath about women whom one desires, marriages, fodder for cows, fuel, and helping a priest."

This is how it goes in most theology. Admonitions not to lie are followed by a list of circumstances in which lying is permissible.

Muhammad said his followers should always be truthful, except when a lie was necessary to preserve domestic harmony, save their life, or keep the peace. The Talmud also notes a need to keep peace as justifying falsehood. According to Judaism's civil and religious laws, a pious scholar is always to tell the truth except when asked about his marital relations, or to avoid sounding boastful, or when telling others how well he has been hosted might burden his host with too many other guests.

Both Testaments of the Bible, and the Old Testament especially, combine condemnations of dishonesty with admiring accounts of successful deception: Abraham claiming that Sarah was his sister, not his wife; Jacob passing as his brother Esau to win his father's blessing (and inheritance); Egyptian midwives rescuing Hebrew children by telling Pharaoh that their mothers were so vigorous that—unlike Egyptian women—they gave birth before the midwives arrived. The most admired biblical liar of all was Solomon, who pretended he would dismember the baby two women claimed was theirs. In *The Concise Book of Lying*, Evelin Sullivan characterizes the Old Testament attitude toward deception as "a pragmatic acceptance of lies as part and parcel of life in the world, necessary or even commendable at times, understandable always."*

Even though the circumstances in which lies were permitted varied with each religion, on one point most agreed: lies told to believers were far worse than ones told to nonbelievers. Although strictures against lying were clearly part of Judeo-Christian ethics, even there the insider-outsider dichotomy kept rearing its head. Truthfulness was reserved for one's dealings with God, and his cho-

---

*I am indebted to Evelin Sullivan for her through assessment of Biblical attitudes toward lying in *The Concise Book of Lying*.

sen people. When God told Moses that members of his flock should not steal, deal falsely, or "lie to one another," it wasn't clear that this extended beyond the Israelites themselves. Believers were admonished not to bear false witness "against thy neighbor." Presumably this did not include the Canaanites.

Admonitions not to lie grew more frequent and more direct in the New Testament. There, Satan was portrayed as "the father of lies." Liars now were worse than tribal norm breakers; they were disciples of the devil himself. Since Jesus said to always tell the truth, oaths no longer needed to be sworn. These proscriptions get closer to the concept of *conscience*, the notion that lying is wrong because it is sinful, not just because it breaks the rules.

It took Saint Augustine to establish this ethic without equivocation. A promiscuous liar as a young man, Augustine laid down the law on lying with the clarity and zeal of a convert. In many tracts written during the late fourth and early fifth centuries, Augustine assessed this issue in terms we have no problem understanding even today. One of the dilemmas he posed—whether it was right to tell a perilously sick father that his son just died—is still used in contemporary considerations of honesty. Augustine rebuked contemporaries who felt that telling lies was not sinful so long as one kept the truth firmly in one's heart. He took special pains to refute the notion that it was acceptable to deceive strangers as if such people were "not our neighbors in the community of truth." That community was the only one to which we owed our allegiance. This denoted an important shift away from loyalty to one's kin and toward loyalty to a principle. Augustine considered lying to anyone—not just to one's own kind—wrong.

This was an awfully strict standard to meet. Should those suffering religious persecution tell the truth to their persecutors? That dilemma confronted the devout of many faiths. Shia Muslims be-ing persecuted by Sunnis found justification for hiding their true beliefs in the Islamic doctrine of *takiya*. According to a verse in the Koran, "Whether ye conceal what is in your hearts or reveal it, Al-lah knows it." A medieval Koranic commentator took this to mean that "if anyone is compelled and professes unbelief with his tongue, while his heart contradicts him, to escape his enemies, no blame falls on him, because God takes his servants as their hearts believe."

This is remarkably close to the concept of *mental reservation* de-veloped by Reformation-era Catholics who were being persecuted by Protestants. According to this concept, one might mislead per-secutors with half-truths, retaining the more important half in one's heart. Thus, if a priest incognito was asked if he was a priest, he might reply, "No, I am not," while thinking to himself "to such as you." If asked whether he'd performed Mass, he could say, "I swear I didn't," then murmur to himself "today." This is the theo-logical counterpart of a child's crossed fingers. To those facing hot irons and fingernail removal, the moral relief of the mental reser-vation is understandable. In time, however, it became an easy way to rationalize all manner of prevarication. Ultimately this dispen-sation morphed into a form of license, permitting a chicken thief, for example, to say, "I didn't steal a chicken," while thinking, "to-day," so God would know that he might be a thief but at least he wasn't a liar.

Upright Protestants saw such sophistry as one more example of Catholic venality. A key grievance of the Reformation was that the church had gone overboard with its many dispensations for liars who invoked the mental reservation. An echo of this concern can be heard when elected officials and new citizens of the United

States take their oaths "without any mental reservation."

In response to what they saw as flaccid morality among Catholics, many Protestant reformers took a doctrinaire stand against dishonesty. John Wesley considered lying "an abomination," and endorsed what he called "that saying of the ancient Father, 'I would not tell a wilful lie to save the souls of the whole world.'" The concurrent rise of science during the Enlightenment placed new emphasis on truthfulness. Scientific inquiry depended on an ethic of accurate testimony. So did the emerging rule of law. This ethic also contributed to the rise of capitalism, with its need for reliable data and personal trust. Max Weber thought that was why Protestants, with their stern emphasis on probity, did so well in free-market economies. "Honest as a Huguenot"—a term in common use during the seventeenth century—had both religious and economic overtones. The unusual success of Quaker merchants was due in part to their reputation for integrity. Even Benjamin Franklin's puritanical creed of "Honesty is the best policy" had economic significance. Without such a policy the extension of credit would have been impossible.

Honesty's market value is too little appreciated in the history of ethics. Truth telling underlies not just individual reputations but the health of society as a whole. Immanuel Kant's case for absolute honesty was based in part on the fact that legal contracts assume truthfulness. The rule of law could be established only among those whose basic honesty could be counted on. That was why Kant felt so strongly that members of a healthy society couldn't pick and choose which truths to tell. Like Augustine before him, Kant challenged the notion that truth was reserved for those who deserved it. "For a lie always harms another," wrote the German philosopher; "if not some other particular man, still it harms mankind generally, for it vitiates the source of law it-self."

Civil Society

The larger and more complex society grew, the greater was the need for ethics that shifted the moral locus from outer norms to in-ner conviction. Tribal mores could no more build the trust among strangers required by civil societies, scientific inquiry, and free-market economies than donkey carts could ship their goods. "Un-der modern conditions," wrote sociologist Georg Simmel, "the lie, therefore, becomes something much more devastating than it was earlier, something which questions the very foundations of our life. If among ourselves today, the lie were as negligible a sin as it was among the Greek gods, the Jewish patriarchs, or the South Sea is-landers; and if we were not deterred from it by the utmost severity of moral law; then the organization of modern life would be simply impossible; for, modern life is a 'credit economy' in a much broader than a strictly economic sense."

Victorian Englishmen put their own spin on this issue. Using Cicero's *On Duties* as a handbook, and tapping their own heritage of chivalry, upper-class Englishmen were expected never to lie to one another. (Lying to a French peasant, or even a cockney fish-monger, was not considered any big deal, any more than lying to Indians or slaves was thought to be a problem among colonial En-glish gentlemen such as George Washington.) During Darwin's time, "scrupulous adherence to truth" (in the words of one) was taken for granted among gentlemen of good character. Presumably the security they felt in their social position obviated any need to embellish the truth. "Christian gentlemen" were thought to be too self-assured to have to lie. In fact, an upper-class Englishman was considered so immune from any tacky urge to dissemble that his word alone was taken as proof in a court of law. This commitment to scrupulous honesty did not occur in a vacuum, however. As Robert Wright points out in *The Moral Animal,* most residents of Victorian-era England lived in the equivalent of small towns. They kept an eye on each other. Even if their sense of class and Christian duty did not promote honesty among English gentlemen, the fact that they might get caught did.

Three

The Honesty Connection

People are more likely to value and practice honesty when they see
themselves tied personally to their communities.

–ALAN WOLFE

All community is continued by Truth.

–THOMAS BROWNE

In "Ambéli," a pseudonymous Greek mountain village where she
spent several years, anthropologist Juliet du Boulay found both a
strict code of honesty and frequent attempts to violate this code.
What made such attempts difficult, however, was the intimate fa-
miliarity Ambélians had with each other. "Villagers read the lives
of others from signs and indications much as a hunter tracks an animal by its prints," reported du Boulay. Their curiosity about each
other (i.e., nosiness) made it hard for residents to conceal their vi-
olations of Ambéli's moral code. Even cover-ups that seemed foolproof were invariably revealed, if the lie in question was of any
consequence, and on a matter that interested enough townspeople.
In the end, du Boulay concluded, it was the gossip of Ambélians
more than any code of ethics that made their dishonesty "self-
limiting."

In our search for sources of an increasingly casual attitude toward honesty, we might look less to theology and more to sociology. Because it is so much bigger, more complex, and more mobile, postwar life facilitates guilt-free duplicity. The most basic sources of post-truthfulness are not moral breakdown but interstate highways, U-Haul vans, and For Sale signs on front lawns. Deceit's rise is rooted less in the decline of ethics and more in the breakdown of community.

Community

Community is the place where we feel known. Among those who know each other, dissembling is problematic. There is a limit to how many lies we can feed those whom we see on a regular basis. Routine deception requires a backdrop of people who aren't familiar enough with deceivers to expose them, and who see no reason to search the Internet for evidence of their chicanery. Those who are well acquainted don't need technological aids. Much gets conveyed between the lines. Longtime acquaintances who pay attention to each other—in the best and worst sense—are organic lie detectors. One woman noted that a relative would invariably raise a hand to her mouth and clear her throat before telling a big one. A friend of hers always rubbed his hands together while making things up. In Burundi, an elderly man observed by Ethel Albert usually telegraphed his intention to lie by swearing that he always told the truth (as was well known to his fellow tribesmen).

No lie detector can compare to people who know each other well. Those who interact regularly over time are well equipped to note, or even just to sense, when someone is not being truthful. Knowing so much about each other—their family, their ancestry, their relationship with their spouse, their behavior patterns—also gives them a database with which to evaluate assertions.

Community has been defined as a place where residents cannot alter their age. It's impossible to credibly add or subtract years in a setting where your birth was once announced. A Harvard degree is hard to claim when the local mail carrier never delivered any letters with Cambridge postmarks to your parents' home. One can hardly brag about spurious combat heroics among those who didn't see you march off to war.

Knowing how hard it is to peddle such fictions, community members are less likely to lie, more because they fear exposure than from any ethical rigor or love of their neighbors. It's a misconception that those who enjoy a sense of community are honest because they care about each other so deeply. Often it's just the opposite. Many can't stand each other. Yet this doesn't preclude a sense of caring. Members of small communities are intensely conscious of the ambivalence that characterizes the way they feel about many fellow members. As Juliet du Boulay discovered in Ambéli, "the villager can accommodate without difficulty a deep understanding of the reality of the commandment to love his neighbor with the fact that very often he hates him."

Regardless of how community members feel about each other, there is no question that close, regular contact keeps them honest. We're far less likely to lie to those we see often than those we see seldom. To test this hypothesis, Bella DePaulo compared frequency of lying with frequency of contact among University of Virginia students and residents of Charlottesville. The psychologist found that members of both groups told fewer lies per interaction to those with whom they had the most contact and—among the townspeople—those they had known longest.

If we were more honest in our dealings with each other in eras past, as I believe we were, it was not so much because we were more conscientious, but because so many of our interactions took place among familiar faces. Those who know each other well may be no less prone to tell lies than their disconnected cousins, but hesitate from fear of the consequences. There are two basic reasons to avoid lying: (1) because it's wrong and (2) because we might get caught. Where there's little consensus about what "wrong" refers to, fear of getting caught is the most compelling reason not to deceive others. Yet the likelihood of that happening has declined along with any clear sense of right and wrong. With less face-to-face contact among those who are well enough acquainted to spot a lie, external reasons to be honest decline along with internal ones.

Although I don't believe that we have an instinct to be honest any more than we have one to be dishonest, I do believe that we have a will to gather in community. Communities are fertilized by truthfulness. Members remind each other regularly—in deeds more than words—that honesty has value.

While conducting interviews in eight American settings of various sizes, sociologist Alan Wolfe found the greatest emphasis on personal integrity among the 3,155 residents of Tipton, Iowa. Although this emphasis was expressed in moral terms, a little probing revealed that its real basis was more pragmatic. To Tiptonites, honesty was tied intimately to reputation. A good reputation depended on being known as an honest person. Without such a reputation, life could get awfully sticky in a town like Tipton—particularly for those in business. "People catch on right away if you're not a straight shooter," one resident told Wolfe. "When you look someone in the face, it's harder to lie," said another.

This doesn't mean that community members are slavish truth

tellers. The point is not that members of closely knit communities don't try to deceive each other. They do, all the time, but usually in ways that are considered socially acceptable. Most cultures condone some form of put-on lying. Like the Saami and the Samoans, many indigenous people delight in trying to pull each other's legs. Some even designate "tricksters," who have license to lie. But such in-community lying usually happens in ways that everyone understands. Those who belong to communities usually have an inbred sense of when it's okay to lie, and who is likely to do so. "Everyone knows the rules," said Ethel Albert of the frequent falsehoods exchanged among Burundians. "Everyone plays the game of matching wits through verbal parry and thrust." This is a far cry from the post-truth society, in which anything goes and it's each man and woman for him- or herself when trying to determine what's a lie and who's a liar.

Situational Dishonesty

My friend George characterized the memories of townspeople in his rural Kentucky hometown as "longer than a credit card record. The community knew everyone who lied, drank, or slept with a neighbor." After moving to Manhattan, George continued to deal with others as he had back home: assuming their honesty could be counted on because of social scrutiny. When he tried to buy a co-op apartment from an affluent young executive whom I'll call Woodruff, however, this man proved to be unscrupulous in nearly every aspect of their negotiation. George mentioned his experience to colleagues of Mr. Woodruff whom he knew, at the corporation where he worked. They expressed surprise. On the job, Woodruff was known for his integrity. For him, his office was comparable to George's hometown: the place where he was known. To be caught lying there would have been devastating. Selling property to a stranger was another matter. Mr. Woodruff wasn't altogether dishonest. He just had different standards of honesty for different settings.

Think of this as *situational dishonesty*. It is practiced by those who are known partially in many places but fully in none. That allows them to convey varying amounts of truth, depending on whom they're dealing with. Belonging to a wide range of communities makes it possible to have a wide range of ethics. In the absence of a strong connection with others who share common values, our ethical standards are determined in settings where we do feel a sense of belonging: raves, say, chat groups, or as vicarious members of talk shows and soap operas. Members of place-based communities are permitted only one set of ethics. In such gatherings a single standard of honesty is reinforced by family, school, church, and the Lions Club. When a sense of common purpose and common values erodes, as it has in our time for so many of us, agreed-upon standards of conduct are replaced by 57 varieties. This is ethical segmentation. We can have one set of ethics at home, another with friends, a third for colleagues, perhaps one for church, or at a support group, yet another online, and, finally, one for rank strangers.

This doesn't mean that in the absence a strong sense of community we will take every opportunity to deceive others. Nonetheless, feeling disconnected certainly reduces inhibitions about being deceitful when we're so inclined. This notion is not necessarily unappealing. One reason so many of us can't wait to leave the suffocating embrace of our respective Gopher Prairies is to enhance our capacity to be many things to many people. That wish needn't be unhealthy, but can become so. Those suffering from pathological psychiatric syndromes are more likely to be found in the isolation of urban settings than in suburbs, which in turn have more members of this population than towns do. One study of those suffer-ing from "antisocial personality"—of which lying is a prominent symptom—found nearly 6 percent of an inner-city group fit that profile, compared with just over 3 percent of those in an inner sub-urb and 2.5 percent of small town residents.

Just as mushrooms grow best in dark basements, dishonesty flourishes in anonymous settings. We're far more likely to try to put one over on a Wal-Mart clerk than on Wally of Wally's Market. "Liars feel less guilty when their targets are impersonal or totally anonymous . . . ," observes psychologist Paul Ekman in *Telling Lies.* "It is easier to indulge the guilt-reducing fantasy that the target is not really hurt, doesn't really care, won't even notice the lie, or even deserves or wants to be misled, if the target is anonymous."

When it comes to post-truthfulness, the fraying of human con-nections is both cause and effect. Not feeling connected to others makes it easier to lie, which in turn makes it harder to reconnect. Eroded communities foster dishonesty. Dishonesty contributes to the further erosion of communities. As communal bonds wither, unfettered self-interest is unleashed. Truth trimming feels more permissible, or at least less reprehensible. This isn't to say that members of small communities aren't motivated by self-interest; only that this motivation is tempered by a sense of obligation to other members.

From the perspective of English ethicist Jennifer Jackson, the "wrongness" of lying has less to do with the harm it inflicts on a lie's target and more to do with the damage inflicted on human communities. Our oldest motivation to be honest was not taboos so much as an awareness that the best way to get others to honor their obligations to us was to honor our obligations to them (e.g., not tell them lies). Reciprocal obligations were a far stronger source of ethical behavior than conscience. Anthropologist

Charles Cooley believed that an emphasis on truth telling among our most distant ancestors resulted less from a need to be accurate than from "a sense of the unfairness of deceiving people of our own sort, and of the shame of being detected in so doing." To feel shame when caught telling a lie, one must be part of a group whose eyes could judge us. Most people for most of time belonged to such a group: tribe, clan, community.

If the best guarantor of honesty is living among familiar faces, next best is a set of ethics that promote truth telling among those who aren't so well acquainted. The ideal is to combine a strong sense of connectedness with a robust sense of right and wrong. We have the worst of both worlds: a declining sense of community and eroding ethics. This means we must live among semistrangers, with little assurance of their verisimilitude, and with no reliable way to detect their lies.

Ethical Memories

In large, complex societies, honesty takes on added weight because so many transactions take place between strangers. At the same time, we're descended from those who felt little need to tell the truth to those they didn't recognize. As we saw in the last chapter, for most of human history, lying to outsiders was not only condoned but sanctioned. Integrity helped us deal with our own, duplicity with outsiders. As a result, the will to deceive unfamiliar human beings may be one of our genetic memories. Paradoxically, a will to be honest may also be an inherited trait. Darwin himself believed that because it strengthened communal bonds, truthfulness had survival value. Members of tribes that emphasized honesty were most likely to have heirs. Us. From our distant ancestors we have inherited complementary urges to be honest and dishonest. Depending on the context, both tendencies helped us survive:

honesty for our own kind, deception for everyone else. Just as dealing with familiar faces promotes a tendency to tell the truth to this
very day, so may contact with a stranger trigger an ancient impulse
to lie. This bifurcated heritage is reflected in the variable ethical
standards that are still commonplace. Subjects in one of Bella De-
Paulo's studies said they lied during 28 percent of their conversations with friends, 48 percent with acquaintances, and 77 percent
with strangers. Even in Tipton, Iowa, Alan Wolfe found an insider-
outsider ethical dichotomy alive and well. The strong emphasis
residents placed on being honest with each other weakened when
questions arose about telling the truth to those who lived elsewhere, or to large corporations, or the IRS. "The moral instinct of
Tiptonites is to value honesty more when the recipient of one's
honesty is a close neighbor or friend," Wolfe discovered, "than
when it is a stranger."

If it is true that dealing with people we don't know, or don't
know well, triggers a tendency to deceive inherited from our ancestors on the savanna, then as more and more of us deal with a
rising numbers of strangers (or those who feel like strangers), an
urge to tell lies is increasingly unleashed. At the very least our inhibitions about being dishonest are lowered. On the receiving end,
anyone we meet could be lying at any time about anything, and we
would have no way to know. (As we'll see in a later chapter, the
human capacity to detect lies is quite limited.) Paul Ekman—who
has devoted his career to studying deception—believes it is unwise
to trust one's assessment of another person's honesty without having some knowledge about that person. One proven enhancer of
lie-detection accuracy is knowing how a suspected liar has behaved
in two or more situations.

Ekman has an interesting theory about why most of us can't detect lies very well. In our ancestral environment, he speculates,

there was not much opportunity to deceive one another. We lived cheek by jowl in groups where consequences for being deceitful were severe. As a result, there was little incentive to be dishonest, or opportunity to unmask those who were. Lies would not have been told often enough for lie catchers to hone their skills. In such a context the adaptive value of a lie-telling talent or a complementary ability to catch liars would be low. The context in which most of us now live is just the opposite. Opportunities to lie are constant today, the means to disguise lies plentiful, and the penalties for being caught meager. At worst, those revealed as liars can simply move on—to another place, a different spouse, new friends, who have no idea that they are known liars.

One could hypothesize that the looser human ties are in any social context, the more likely it is that those who live there will deceive and be deceived. And even if we aren't being hoodwinked in such settings, it is easy to suspect that we are, because we *just don't know.*

Impression Management

An attractive woman I'll call Tammy, whom I met in San Diego, told me she was a former model who had written articles for *Glamour,* published short stories in literary magazines, and recently signed a book contract with Random House. I never saw Tammy's byline anywhere, however. When I asked mutual friends who had known her longer about the discrepancy, they laughed. "Tammy didn't do any of those things," they explained. "She just tells people whatever she thinks will impress them."

Among strangers and semistrangers, what sociologists call *impression management* kicks in. Deception is an integral part of that effort. According to students of dishonesty, one of the leading motivations to tell lies, especially about ourselves, is wanting to "make a good impression." This isn't necessarily malevolent (though it can be). Unlike sociopaths who lie compulsively, or Machiavellian personalities who lie to manipulate others, those who are overly concerned with how they're coming across tell lies so they can appear to be whom they think other people want them to be. "Image is everything," they're prone to say. "Whatever it takes" is another popular saying. Fusing the two justifies creating a deceptive image based on manipulated evidence.

In the absence of personal knowledge about each other, symbols of rectitude take on added importance. When dealing with strangers or near strangers, appearances do matter. We search for signs of veracity among those we don't know but want to trust. Psychologists talk of the "assessment signals" we transmit and measure in others: our clothing, our accoutrements, our résumé. This can be problematic. One may feel a sense of kinship with someone whose cap says he shares a commitment to the New York Knicks or whose tote bag indicates she's a fellow NPR listener, but this hardly constitutes evidence of rectitude. Those signals are easy to manipulate. Good con artists know what articles of clothing inspire trust among which marks. They are artistes of impression management. One grifter said he always carried a can of dog food in grocery stores to inspire confidence in any potential dupe he might bump into in the aisles.

The less we actually know about each other, the more we depend on clothing labels, shoe style, purse brand, handshake, and eye contact to tell us whom to trust. Most such assessment signals are ethically useless. Accomplished liars tend to be firm handshakers who gaze steadily into other people's eyes. They know better than anyone how much others rely upon such signals as evidence of trustworthiness. A former Soviet spy said one thing he learned in espionage school was how to lock his eyes on those of anyone he wanted to deceive. Studies consistently find that liars make better eye contact than truth tellers. Many of those who were lied to by Bill Clinton cited his steady gaze as the reason they believed him. When Clinton told the Reverend Robert Schuller that he'd never had sex with Monica Lewinsky, Schuller later recalled, "he did it with such passion, and with his eyes locked on me."

If it's true that we're more likely to deceive and be deceived by strangers (or those who feel strangerlike), then the United States of America is unusually fertile ground for deception of all kinds. Americans seldom know each other well enough to sense when wool is being pulled over their eyes. Too many of its citizens are professional outsiders—A Nation of Strangers, in the memorable title of Vance Packard's book. This is important to consider not only in its own right, but because American culture provides the template for so many other cultures around the world.

Four

Whistler's Druthers

To have a history in America, one had to make it up oneself.
—JAMES ATLAS

In his seventh decade, James Whistler was confronted in a London restaurant by a fellow native of Lowell, Massachusetts. This man wondered why the artist claimed to be sixty-seven when they'd both been born around the same time and he was sixty-eight. "Ha-ha!" responded Whistler. "Very charming! And so you are 68 and were born at Lowell! Most interesting, no doubt, and as you please. But I shall be born when and where I want, and I do not choose to be born at Lowell, and I refuse to be 68!"

Myth America

America has always been a nation of blarney peddlers. Telling lies about themselves is as American as apple crisp. This country's very name derived from a tall-tale merchant, Amerigo Vespucci, who apparently made few of the trips to the New World that he claimed to have made. By rights America should be named Columbia after its actual "discoverer," Christopher Columbus. Columbus himself was an explorer of dubious character who kept two logs on his 1492 journey, one genuine, one faked to suggest to his anxious crew that they were not as far from home as they feared. The Italian adventurer was a man of many faces and names: Christoforo Colombo in his native land, Cristovao Colom in Portugal (where he lived for a time), Cristóbal Colón in Spain, and Christopher Columbus in the anglicized version historians thought would go easier on Anglo ears. Much of what we "know" about Columbus is apocryphal, owing less to the historical record than to a wildly popular, highly embellished biography written by Washington Irving in 1828.

America's bedrock parable of honesty—little George Washington admitting he'd cut down the cherry tree—was invented by another biographer, Parson Mason Locke Weems. Weems's best-selling biography of America's first president, in which his father told him "Truth, George, is the loveliest quality of youth," contained far more fiction than fact, including the fanciful story of Washington on his knees in prayer at Valley Forge during the supposedly severe but actually mild winter of 1777, and, of course, the one about the honest little boy caught redhanded next to a fallen cherry tree with a hatchet in his hand. Parson Weems, whose novelization of Washington's life went through multiple editions, himself claimed to have been "Rector of Mount-Vernon Parish." There was no such church.

Although humbuggery is hardly an American invention, America's citizens took this practice to breathtaking levels. The New World was a land of unlimited opportunities, including the opportunity to reconceive concepts of truthfulness. As historian Daniel Boorstin put it, in such a land, "the old boundaries—between fact and wish . . . no longer served." American speech changed continually to accommodate Americans' need to make things sound bigger, better, and more spectacular than they actually were. For a contemporary example, go no further than your local Starbucks, where the smallest cup of coffee is called a "Tall." Boorstin called this form of inflated expression "tall talk." Tall talk blurred the distinction between fact and fiction. It was "the language of the neither true-nor-false, the language of ill-defined magnificence," wrote Boorstin. A mid-nineteenth-century American didn't just sleep soundly, he "slept so sound it would take an earthquake to wake him." When angry he would "blow up like a steamboat." Davy Crockett was said to be able to "walk like an ox, run like a fox, swim like an eel, yell like an Indian, fight like a devil, spout like an earthquake, [and] make love like a mad bull." Like Columbus and Washington, Crockett benefited from biographers who were less than fastidious about facts. The so-called King of the Wild Frontier only began wearing a coonskin cap after a character in a popular play (*The Lion of the West*) did so. Crockett thought wearing this cap might help him get elected to Congress, as it did. He was notorious for making up his own legend, including the false claim that he had participated in a mutiny against General Andrew Jackson.

A striking number of America's historical legends are apocryphal in whole or in part. Many of our most stirring quotations—"Give me liberty or give me death," "No taxation without representation," "I have not yet begun to fight!"—were never uttered in the form they're remembered, at the time they were supposed to have been said, or by the person who was supposed to have said them. Historians seriously doubt that Pocahontas begged her father to spare John Smith's life, that Paul Revere made it to Concord, or that Betsy Ross sewed America's first flag. There is no recorded episode of two westerners ever facing each other wielding guns. The gunfight at the OK Corral was little more than a street brawl. Wyatt Earp was an obscure figure of dubious character who was reconceived as an upright lawman by yet another fictionalized biography, this one published in 1931. Far from being like Gary Cooper, many western lawmen such as Earp had second careers as thieves, poachers, and cattle rustlers.

Could citizens of any country face the truth about their own history? Clearly that's been a problem for those who live in the United States. If Americans ever fully confronted less attractive facts about their own history, especially the way its settlers treated Indians and African slaves, they might question whether God actually did shed his grace on them.

Like so many Americans of my generation, I was raised on the gruel that yes, slavery was bad, but, well, maybe not *that* bad. Probably most owners treated their slaves pretty well, right? When doing research about the Underground Railroad I discovered that the peculiar institution wasn't just that bad, it was worse: not only physically vicious but unspeakably cruel in complying with the pitiless market logic that impelled even benevolent slave owners to break up families so they could sell members separately to the highest bidder. In the course of this research, I was also struck by how much that we think we know about the Underground Railroad itself is dubious. Few participants ever dug a tunnel, built a secret compartment, learned a special handshake, or murmured code words in the night. Much of this romantic tall talk originated with the remarkable number of Americans who claimed to have been conductors on the Underground Railroad once the Civil War had ended.

Sojourner Truth was said to have been active in the Underground Railroad. That's unlikely. A lot of mythology surrounded this ex-slave, much of it due to her own efforts. Truth, whose adopted last name alluded to her reputation for rectitude, was an energetic self-promoter who embellished her own myth as she went along. According to biographer Nell Irvin Painter, this shrewd platform personality cultivated a persona of an uneducated, uncultured, dialect-spouting Negress that promoted her lecturing business and thrilled her audiences. Some pitched in on her mythmaking. Truth's signature line, "Ain't I a woman?" (originally "Ar'n't I a woman?") is thought to have been uttered by the former slave at an 1851 women's rights convention in Akron, Ohio. This bit of folk eloquence was actually concocted by a writer named Frances Dana Gage, who inserted it into an account of Truth's speech that was written more than a decade after the Akron gathering. According to Painter, Truth's famous four words were not anything she actually said; they are "what we need her to have said."

This pattern is repeated throughout American history. Too little of what we think we know about our past can withstand scholarly scrutiny. Why should that be? In Daniel Boorstin's opinion, a young country such as this one, hungry for legends, heroes, and stirring quotations, wasn't picky about their authenticity. Many legendary American figures benefited from imaginative historiography, their best quotations from posthumous ghostwriting. But the leading source of historical mythology was the subjects themselves. Not only swashbuckling figures like Davy Crockett, Daniel Boone, and Buffalo Bill but beacons of integrity such as Benjamin Franklin, Walt Whitman, and Henry David Thoreau stirred liberal dashes of myth into the reality of their identity. To this day Thoreau symbolizes a moral man pursuing an ethical life alone in the wilderness. Except the woods where Thoreau sought solitude were only a mile from his family's home. While communing with nature by Walden Pond, Thoreau went home almost daily. One biographer concluded that he merely "bivouacked" pondside. Had Winnebagos been available, Thoreau might have parked one there. During his year in the woods Thoreau was visited regularly by dozens of friends and hordes of curiosity seekers. He was little more than a camper engaged in creating a rustic legend about himself for an eager audience. *Walden* itself is a work of uneven veracity. Its author was a fine writer, creative thinker, and imaginative inventor of his own legend.

The Reinvented Self

Self-invention is a national pastime among Americans. "I reinvented myself," they're prone to say, with a little blush of pride. That process often involves dispensing with inconvenient old facts and replacing them with better new ones. This has been called "Marilynizing," in honor of the self-created Marilyn Monroe (née Norma Jean Baker). Today it might better be called "Laurenizing" or "Marthaizing" in recognition of Ralph Lauren and Martha Stewart, the quintessential reinvented Americans. The neo-aristocrat Lauren (né Ralph Lifshitz) makes little effort to disguise his actual origins. Stewart does. Long before she was convicted of lying about her investments, it was clear that truthfulness was not Martha Stewart's strong suit. Not that she agreed. In an early edition of *Martha Stewart Living*, Stewart wrote a tribute to honesty. After flaying public figures who misrepresented themselves and engaged in other forms of deception, she bemoaned the fact that truth telling no longer received the same respect it had in her childhood. Dishonesty was a thief of time, energy, and pride, Stewart advised her readers. Honesty helped one cope with fear. Truth tellers were admirable, liars cowards. No matter the immediate impact, in the long run being truthful obviated guilt and anxiety about truth coming out. "We must remember," Stewart concluded, "—and teach our children (and perhaps our political figures)—one essential: the truth shall make you free."

If that was true, she herself must have felt in bondage. Martha Stewart routinely misrepresented the type of family she grew up in, her father's occupation, whom she dated in college, where her roommate was from, what she earned as a model, the size of parties she threw, her husband's ability to father children, how much of her own writing she did, where her home was located (to avoid paying taxes), and why she sold her ImClone stocks. "Martha made stuff up all the time," a friend told biographer Jerry Oppenheimer. "The truth was never good enough," said her ex-husband. When Stewart's aunt was asked why her niece embroidered information so routinely, she responded, "It makes a better story." The most fantastic story of all, of course, was that this shrewd, unscrupulous businesswoman was a down-to-earth domestic goddess.

Puffery is an art form in the United States. This is for two reasons in particular: (1) it is a civilization of immigrants and their descendants who like to think they control not only their own destiny but their own identity, and (2) Americans are hypermobile, continually reintroducing themselves to others, often succumbing to the temptation to re-create their past in the process. Opportunities to touch up a self-portrait arise every time Americans move, as one in five do every year, and half do every five years. "For much of his life," memoirist Cyra McFadden wrote of her itinerant father, rodeo announcer Cy Taillon, "he was engaged in the game of inventing himself—adding to what was true and what was desirable, stirring counterclockwise and serving up the mix."

Obviously, deception about the self (and lots of other things) is not limited to Americans, or to our era. The wish to seem better than real is eternal and universal. Jacob, after all, wanted to be more like Esau. Odysseus made up a new identity for himself whenever an opportunity arose. The context of American life makes it easier to engage in this type of flimflam, however. It could hardly be otherwise in a country populated primarily by immigrants and their descendants. Excepting those who were already here and the ones brought in chains, America was settled by those shaking off Old World restrictions. Along with their previous lives, they left behind anyone who had known them in that life. Those who arrived in this country were in a position to wipe the slate clean. They felt free— duty-bound even—to re-create themselves, shedding inconvenient facts along the way like a snake molting old skin. Here Albert Einstein, a cold husband and indifferent father in Europe, could reintroduce himself as a warm humanitarian after arriving alone in New York. Occidental Petroleum founder Armand Hammer made up a personal past doing relief work with starving peasants and initiating business projects in Russia. Meg Greenfield's father successfully transformed himself from a first-generation son of Russian immigrants who grew up in a Philadelphia slum to something resembling a well-bred English gentleman. In her book *Washington*, Greenfield observed that "at least since Yankee Doodle tried his scam, Americans have been engaged in the business of personally reinventing themselves—enthusiastically, with varying degrees of fraudulence (or ingenuity, if you prefer), and often to perfectly good purpose."

Their penchant for mythmaking, and receptivity to each other's tall tales, doesn't make Americans less moral than those they left behind, simply more opportunistic. If no one around you knows your actual history, why be candid about it? Who was going to blow your cover? From the moment when immigrants Americanized their names at a port of entry, or had this done for them, how could it not occur to them that *this was a whole new ball game.* Gorodetsky a little hard to pronounce? How about Gordon? Shakishavili a bit of a mouthful? Try Shaw. If names could be changed that easily, what else might be changed as well? Age? Occupation?

Family origins? America was a land of unlimited possibilities, in many senses of the word.

Nearly half a century after he disembarked in Hoboken in 1939, Bruno Bettelheim could still remember how exuberant he felt while walking the streets of New York across the Hudson River. "It was a hot summer day," recalled the psychotherapist, "with blue skies; the sun was shining. At that moment, I felt . . . I would make a new life for myself very different from the old one." In the course of his research about Bettelheim, biographer Richard Pollak found out what he meant by this. The personal and professional self-portrait that this distinguished psychotherapist painted of himself was riddled with apocrypha. Bettelheim awarded himself degrees he hadn't earned back in Austria, inflated the number of patients he'd treated there, and even fictionalized parts of an account he wrote about his year in a concentration camp. To make matters worse, as Pollak recounted in excruciating detail in *The Creation of Dr. B*, Bettelheim also plagiarized more than a little of his prolific oeuvre.

A decade after Bettelheim arrived in Hoboken, Paul de Man came to the United States from Belgium. By the time he died of cancer in 1983, de Man had become a leading American literary light, a prominent member of Yale's faculty who was lauded not just for his intellectual precocity but for his personal integrity. "In a profession full of fakeness, he was real," said a colleague at the time of de Man's death. Four years later, a researcher discovered that de Man had left behind a past as a Nazi collaborator who engaged in shady business practices before fleeing creditors and abandoning his wife and three children when he left for the United States in 1948. There de Man claimed that his uncle was actually his father, remarried without divorcing his first wife, and introduced himself as a humane man of letters. This reincarnation was extraordinarily successful. De Man grew adept at deflecting questions about his past. When asked, the Yale professor suggested he'd spent the war years working as a translator in England, or studying in Paris, or as a resistance fighter in France. None of this was true. "De Man's triumphant American career seems either to dramatize something about our national capacity for amnesia," wrote biographer David Lehman, "or to illustrate the idea of America as a haven for those who want to bury the past."

Among the dissatisfactions that drove immigrants to American shores was dissatisfaction with the self. The very act of coming to the New World was an attempt at rebirth. Many hoped their self-doubt could be remedied here by becoming the person they wanted to be. If that proved impossible, they could at least claim to be that person. The vagueness of personal histories in this strange new land combined with its residents' penchant for tall talk created problems for descendants who wanted to learn something about their family's tree.

Roots?

According to family lore, my mother's great-grandfather Charles "Carl" Reiser was a wealthy civil engineer in Romania who helped build that country's first railroad. After leaving Romania for the United States in 1869, Carl ended up in San Francisco. There, his descendants were told, he had several wives, one of whom absconded with his money. This money came from the fleet of merchant ships Carl owned in California. He'd broken his leg while climbing a mainmast as an old man, and used a wooden one thereafter. When he died at 102, Carl was buried next to his amputated leg. Or so we were told.

While doing some genealogical research, my cousin Richard Reiser found an 1889 San Francisco Directory that listed Charles

Reiser as the proprietor of a secondhand-clothing store on Folsom Street. According to a gravestone Richard located south of San Francisco, Carl Reiser died on November 22, 1900, at the age of eighty-seven. No amputated leg was noted on the gravestone.

Carl's granddaughter, my grandmother Rachel, always told us she was the same age as her husband. After Rachel died we discovered that she was five years older than he was. This husband, my grandfather Jean, came to America as a young man, in 1906. Here he affected a French accent to imply that he was actually from Paris, France, not Sulina, Romania. Jean also said he came from a family of once-wealthy bankers. Four decades after her father died, my mother mentioned our bank-owning heritage to Jean's half brother Willy in Haifa, Israel. Willy snorted, "Bank *clerks* was more like it." Mimicking a teller counting bills, Willy added, "We *counted* money. We never owned any."

On the other side of the family, my father's grandfather Horace Scott was a druggist in Aberdeen, South Dakota. Horace said he hailed from a town named after his forebears: Scottsville, Vermont. That "town" is actually a block-square neighborhood, long ago absorbed by Danby (population three hundred). Horace also claimed to have been the richest man in South Dakota until the Depression wiped him out. I believed this claim until I read a stack of his letters that revealed the pre-1929 Horace Scott to be a moderately prosperous pharmacist and stock speculator who was not nearly as wealthy as he wanted others to believe.

When recounting their families' histories, high aspirations among Americans met great opportunity to improve the actual record. This penchant makes genealogy problematic for their descendants. During the Gilded Age, Tiffany's offered a genealogical service that helped customers prune unattractive limbs from their family tree and graft on more impressive ones. Such pruning and grafting frustrated ancestors who might rather have had an accurate record. But help was on the way. The growing interest in genealogy combined with sophisticated modern research tools has played havoc with many a family's legends. Based on DNA tests, more than one white genealogical explorer has discovered black ancestors. Others have found that they are not even related to those they assumed were kin (presumably because of concealed adoptions or out-of-wedlock births). Their presumed origins proved to be mythical.

Self-serving concoctions are part of almost any family's collective memory. With so much fudge clogging the gears, however, if trying to reconstruct a genealogy is demanding, writing a family memoir can be downright dangerous. While studying their origins, memoirists ranging from Geoffrey Wolff through Richard Rovere to Mary Gordon discovered that their fathers were not just petty fabricators but out-and-out frauds. Gordon's anti-Semitic Catholic father proved to be a convert from Judaism. After moving to America from France, Rovere's father had assumed a completely new identity, including a fantasy mother in New Orleans. Memoirist Clark Blaise developed a rule of thumb about his own Quebec-born father: any story that made him look good was probably a lie; the sad ones might be true. His father's tales of losing wealth, earning a Harvard degree, and being descended from French aristocracy turned out to be false. The ones about coming from a poverty-stricken family of twenty were largely accurate.

Geoffrey Wolff thought the social insecurity of Americans was what allowed such bunkum to be successfully merchandised. Geoffrey once listened as his father, Arthur "Duke" Wolff, told a Yale graduate that they were in the same class at Old Eli. (Duke Wolff had actually attended the University of Pennsylvania.) Far from expressing skepticism, this man apologized for his poor memory.

Geoffrey Wolff doubted that this would have happened in England. "Duke is it?" he thought an Englishman might have responded. "Duke of what, old man? Oh, quite, I see, Duke of nothing then, rilly. At Eton were you? What years? Then you know Bamber Lushington? No? Then you weren't at Eton, were you?"

Geoffrey Wolff based a bestselling memoir on his father's lifetime of lies: *The Duke of Deception.* Like so many other books about impostors, Wolff's intrigued reviewers and readers alike. One reason we're more fascinated than outraged when frauds like Duke Wolff get unmasked is that we identify with them. Most of us make up a little about our background and wonder what it would be like to make up a lot. Along the way we've struck an implicit bargain with each other: if you don't question my stories about myself, I won't question yours. As a result, so many of us have done ID makeovers that contemporary society is chockablock with members who are not, in ways large and small, exactly whom they appear to be.

Five

Great Pretenders

I was tired of being nothing but myself. To renew myself, to relive, to be someone else, was always the great temptation of my existence.

—ROMAIN GARY

God helps those who invent what they need.

—LILLIAN HELLMAN

When interviewing subjects for my writing, I've been lied to continually: about their age, their size, where they're from, even their adolescence. One actress told me in great detail about having been the captain of her high school's cheerleading squad, a member of its student council, and Lady Macbeth in the senior class play. When I located a copy of her high school yearbook, not a single activity was listed under the woman's senior picture.

Petty Fibbery

Ethically speaking, petty fibs such as these are akin to a little makeup, some eye shadow perhaps, a bit of blush to perk up the appearance. Telling them is an integral part of impression management. When we're in "image is everything" mode, it's hard to resist the temptation to sweeten that image a bit. One survey found that

90 percent of a large sample of Americans said they told little lies about themselves on a regular basis. Most often these fibs lower ages, raise incomes, bolster credentials, and enhance accomplishments.

For the most part, no harm done. Who cares if we gussy up our ID a bit? Such dissembling does pose problems for search committees, however, as well as for executive headhunters, and journalists. When an ex-boyfriend of filmmaker Barbara Kopple raised questions about her self-portrayal in *People,* the magazine discovered that Kopple was six years older than she claimed, and hadn't graduated from Northeastern University as she'd told their reporter. Based on information it got from Larry Ellison himself, the *New York Times* reported that Oracle's founder had B.S. and M.S. degrees in physics from the University of Chicago. Ellison has neither. Even wedding announcements aren't exempt from this kind of tall talk. After being burned once too often, the *Times* began checking information submitted by the soon-to-be-married. One woman canceled her wedding when the newspaper discovered that not just the master's degree but the Olympic medals she'd credited to her fiancé in their wedding announcement were imaginary.

Sprucing up one's background with dubious data has become as common as tucked tummies and transplanted hair. Its motivation dips from the same well: a desire to be better than real. Petty fibs allow us to wear psychic outfits beyond our means. They're a grown-up version of "let's pretend." Bs and Cs we got in college become As and Bs over time. The 200 game we bowled in high school creeps upward to 250. A retort we wish we'd made now is one we did. In his play *The Wild Duck* Ibsen called fibs such as these "life lies" (translated from *livslognen,* a term he coined). They're not white ones told to protect someone else's feelings or to smooth a rough social situation. These are unprovoked deceptions meant to make the deceiver look better.

It's a rare man or woman who doesn't inflate his or her height. Since so few of us are happy with our God-given feet and inches, the figure we report to the world tends to be a hodgepodge of fact, fantasy, and whatever we think we can get away with. After being told a fanciful height once too often by a subject, *Philadelphia Daily News* reporter Rose DeWolf said, "You think people lie about their age? Ha! Height is worse."

While promoting a book I wrote on this subject (*The Height of Your Life*), I was often asked how tall I was. Usually I'd round up a half inch to five feet eight. More than once a male TV interviewer who fielded this information calmly when we were sitting down grew ruffled after we stood up. "Hey, wait a minute," he'd exclaim. "Didn't you say you were five eight?" I had. "Well then how come we're looking each other right in the eye and I'm five ten?"

Among a group of job seekers who were measured *after* they'd recorded their height on an application, 100 percent—ten out of ten—had rounded up by an inch or more. And this is not just an oversight. Another study found that a group of women who were warned in advance that they would be measured reported their heights far more accurately than a second group who weren't warned but were measured.

In Hollywood, where height matters, one casting director made a practice of estimating how tall actors were as they walked through the door because she knew she couldn't trust the figure on their résumés. This document is where life-lying becomes art form. Résumés are not just a record of what we've done. They also tell the world what we wish we'd done.

A Matter of Degrees

Every year Milwaukee executive recruiter Jude Werra reviews several hundred résumés sent to him by candidates for top management positions. The proportion that include serious misrepresentation averages about 15 percent. Most such embellishment involves educational credentials. One job seeker gave Werra both a phony diploma and a forged college transcript. (There are Web sites that help job seekers create such material.) Another said his degree could not be verified because he'd earned it under an assumed name while in the Federal Witness Protection Program. Werra gave his "Lyin' King" award to a human resources executive whose position required him to verify other people's credentials, but who himself claimed an unearned B.A. The man had attended college for one year.

Personnel officers take it for granted that most of the résumés they read include some padding, and that as many as a quarter contain gross misinformation. From painful experience résumé scrutinizers have learned to be skeptical about everything from degrees earned through jobs held to place of birth. "People will do that even when they don't have to," said John G. Self, head of a Texas search firm. "The problem is more common than anyone admits."

Tracy Hogg, who wrote the best-selling *Baby Whisperer*, claimed to have a master's degree from the University of California Irvine. That institution could find no evidence that she was ever enrolled there. Bausch & Lomb CEO Ronald Zarrella said he graduated from New York University's business school when he hadn't. U.S. Olympic Committee president Sandra Baldwin relocated her undergraduate degree from Arizona State to the University of Colorado and claimed a Ph.D. from Arizona State that she'd never earned. Other prominent figures who granted themselves unearned degrees include Jeffrey Papows, the president of Lotus Development Corporation, MCG Capital's CEO Bryan J. Mitchell, Dartmouth's athletic director Charles Harris, Houston's Metropolitan Transit Authority president Shirley DeLibero, Milwaukee's Social Development Commission director Barbara Burke-Tatum, UCLA's body donor program director Henry G. Reid, and California's poet laureate Quincy Troupe.

One might imagine that those in the public eye would think twice before doctoring their credentials. Obviously that isn't always so. Candidates for highly visible management positions routinely prove to have embroidered résumés. A reference-checking firm in Toronto found that one-third of a thousand candidates for top management in Canadian corporations had misrepresented their qualifications or were hiding past performance issues. When Christian & Timbers, a leading American executive search firm, scrutinized seven thousand résumés for CEO, VP, and board of director positions, they found that nearly a quarter included at least some misrepresentation about past accomplishments, compensation, degrees, number of years in a job, or size of organizations managed.

Even those who are under intense scrutiny from voters and reporters have used dubious résumés. Until a reporter discovered that she had no degree at all, Mary Panzer, the majority leader of Wisconsin's state senate and cochair of George W. Bush's reelection campaign in her state, said she had graduated from the University of Wisconsin. Elaine Musselman, a congressional aspirant in Kentucky, dropped out of a Republican primary after it was revealed that she had neither of the two college degrees listed on her vita. In Connecticut, Ramon Antonio Serbia, the Republican candidate for state comptroller, withdrew when it turned out that he hadn't earned two degrees included on his résumé. Ronnie Few, the fire chief of Washington, D.C., resigned after his college degree and fire-chief-of-the-year award proved to be fanciful. When San Francisco's police chief Fred Lau said on his vita that he was an "alumnus" of San Francisco State, a college he'd attended without graduating, Mayor Willie Brown observed, "I don't know anyone who doesn't lie on their résumé."

Unearned degrees are the most common form of credential inflation. Needless to say, most come from prestigious institutions. UCLA exposes phony graduates on a regular basis. Yale keeps a file of several thousand Old Blue impersonators. (The late Hollywood mogul David Begelman was one.) Stanford is another popular listing on résumés. The vita of author–television personality Robert X. Cringely (né Mark Stephens) incorrectly said he had earned a Ph.D. at Stanford. Veritas Software's chief financial officer, Kenneth Lonchar, had neither the MBA nor an undergraduate degree he claimed that university had awarded him. James Baughman, San Jose's onetime superintendent of schools, put forged transcripts from Stanford in his personnel file.

An estimated half million Americans hold jobs for which their purported qualifications are spurious. An investigation by the General Accounting Office once uncovered twenty-eight senior federal employees with bogus college degrees. Three of them worked at the National Nuclear Security Administration. While writing this book I heard one story after another about this type of credential fraud. A friend who works at an Ann Arbor, Michigan, hospital told me that one year all job applicants at every level there—including professional medical personnel—were asked for permission to have information on their applications confirmed by Pinkerton investigators. Nearly a third took back their applications so they could "check dates" and the like. None returned them.

Falsified medical credentials are surprisingly widespread. The Humana Hospital chain once found that 5 percent of all physicians who worked there—39 of 773—had doctored their résumés. A survey of 650 Veterans Administration doctors who said they were board-certified discovered that nearly a fifth weren't. By one estimate as many as ten thousand Americans claim bogus medical degrees. Some haven't even graduated from high school. During Operation Desert Storm, a "doctor" treating Kuwaitis was exposed when TV cameras beamed his face back to those who knew him as a paramedic in California. When caught, phony physicians are usually prosecuted severely, as they should be. That hasn't reduced the practice. Nor can it account for the fact that the most stalwart defenders of many unmasked "doctors" are often their own patients.

What's striking about degree fakers in general is how talented so many are, individuals with more than enough ability to make it on the square. Biophysicist Stephen Kovacs, who invented one of the world's smallest artificial hearts, forged both his undergraduate and graduate degrees. A "geologist" named David Twedell who oversaw drilling at Love Canal and other toxic-waste dumps—and who appeared in court as an expert witness on that subject—turned out to have no degree at all. So what? one might ask. Who cares how people get hired? Did they do their job once they got it? That's all that matters. Americans have a long tradition of admiring Horatio Alger types who get hired by bluff, then strut their stuff. When actor Robert Urich revealed that he researched which plays were running where and when before listing them on his résumé, we chuckled with admiration at his initiative and moxie. "In the America we live in," said George O'Leary's brother Tom, "the willingness to lie on a résumé is an indication of how much you want the job."

When George O'Leary was relieved of his duties as Notre

Dame's football coach one week after being hired because of discrepancies on his résumé, many wondered if this punishment fit the crime. The phony athletic achievements and spurious master's degree he claimed were merely youthful indiscretions, they said. O'Leary's successful decades as a high school and college football coach more than compensated. That left an important question unanswered, however: What happened to the truthful job applicants who competed with O'Leary for the many jobs he'd won on the basis of phony credentials? This question must be posed to anyone who uses an embellished résumé to win a position. When Shirley DeLibero became the head of Houston's Metropolitan Transit Authority with two phony degrees on her vita, what honest applicants did she beat out for the job? By rewarding her, we punished them. Similarly, if a dissembling candidate for office beats one who's told the truth, was that election fair? In such cases we need to consider not only the dissemblers themselves but the many people who pay for their integrity in competition with those who had none.

The fake-it-till-you-make-it credo can have more lethal consequences. The man who oversaw maintenance of ValuJet airplanes at the time one crashed, killing 110 people, had falsified his credentials as an airplane mechanic. Before being unmasked, a man with phony engineering credentials approved construction plans at a nuclear-waste dump in Utah. Medical personnel with phony degrees have badly mistreated patients. They include a "Dr." Gerald Barnes in Los Angeles who has been arrested multiple times for impersonating a physician. Barnes, who has no medical degree of any kind, was sent to prison after a diabetic patient he was treating died.

Some pretenders don't stop with forging credentials. In the post-truth era some ask themselves, "Why stick to résumé doctoring? Why not do a more ambitious bio makeover?"

Imposeurs

While police chief of Gainesville, Florida, Wayland Clifton liked to boast about playing football for legendary coach Bear Bryant at the University of Alabama. When he ran for county sheriff, however, reporters couldn't verify this claim. To help them out, Clifton produced a 1960 clipping from the *Birmingham News*. According to this article, during an October 29 game against Mississippi State, "Buster" Clifton made nine tackles, recovered a fumble, and ran an intercepted pass back eighty yards. The clipping, complete with a picture of Clifton in his Alabama uniform (number 43), reported that he was named Southeastern Conference defensive player of the week for these heroics. In fact, no such article ever ran in the *Birmingham News*, no 'Bama player that year enjoyed the exploits it described, and none wore number 43. The clipping was a forgery. When this was revealed, Chief Clifton admitted his ruse. "It's probably the biggest bonehead thing I've ever done in my life," he said.

Clifton was part of the deception elite I call *imposeurs*. If lifelying is a form of psychic makeup, imposeurship is cosmetic surgery. Unlike impostors, imposeurs retain their basic identity but alter key elements. Their makeovers involve everything from homes owned to medals won. Imposeurs invent jobs they never held, touchdowns they didn't run, and spurious ancestors who aren't around to reveal the ruse.

Imposeurs are real-life Walter Mittys who download the fantasy selves in their heads and post them as if they were real. Ronald Reagan was a classic example. As president, Reagan was renowned for his indifference toward veracity about any- and everything, especially himself. Editor Michael Korda (who worked on Reagan's memoirs) compared him to the Woody Allen character Zelig in his tendency to place himself in the midst of events he'd only heard about. At one point Reagan talked movingly about helping film the liberation of concentration camps. In fact, Reagan never left Hollywood during World War II, but colluded with film studio publicists who suggested to the actor's fans that he was serving overseas.

Inventing stories about himself was a lifelong habit with Reagan. When I spent a few days at Eureka College interviewing those who knew "Dutch" Reagan as a student, his classmates and others told me that he'd dreamed up parts of the section about his Eureka days in his autobiography, especially a fanciful depiction of leading a student protest that toppled the college's president. Even after becoming the leader of the free world, Reagan continued to indulge in bio-enhancement. Nor did he see any reason why he shouldn't. After gently correcting someone else's mistaken memory of meeting him as a young actor, Reagan said, "You believed it because you wanted to believe it. There's nothing wrong with that. I do it all the time."

As the case of Ronald Reagan suggests, imposeurs are not necessarily pathetic losers trying to look like winners. Like him, many are distinguished, capable individuals who have no need to embellish their record. They include Chicago judge Michael O'Brien, who had a Congressional Medal of Honor cast on his own behalf; actor Burt Reynolds, who seldom got on the field as a Florida State football player but later portrayed himself as an all-conference running back who tried out for the Baltimore Colts; civil rights activist Jesse Jackson, who falsely claimed to have cradled Martin Luther King Jr.'s head in his lap as he died; playwright Lillian Hellman, who had no actual friend fitting the description of the Nazi-fighting "Julia" she described so vividly in her memoir *Pentimento*; and author Laurens van der Post, who concocted imaginary achievements for himself throughout his adult life. One curriculum vitae that von der Post wrote featured a childhood in which he didn't learn to speak until he was seven, a young adulthood in which he became familiar with every mile of African soil, a prewar life as a farmer in England, and combat duty during World War II as a member of the British Commandos and Special Forces. "Not a single word of this was true," concluded biographer J. D. F. Jones.

My own sampling of prominent imposeurs includes four judges, three police chiefs, several college professors, and quite a few businesspeople. Authors and actors galore show up in my files on this subject. So do dozens of politicians. A number of coaches are there, three high military officers, and Larry Lawrence, the late ambassador to Switzerland, whose corpse was dug up from Arlington National Cemetery after his claim to have fought in World War II was discredited. And these are just a tiny iceberg tip, the most prominent members of a vast army of imposeurs stationed throughout the world.

They are part of a proud tradition. Past practitioners of imposeurship have included Marco Polo; Baron Munchausen and T. E. Lawrence; explorers Richard Byrd and Robert Peary; the artist Pablo Picasso; and authors such as Hans Christian Andersen, Kahlil Gibran, André Malraux, Romain Gary, Ernest Hemingway, Patrick O'Brian, and Rebecca West. In years past those who developed fanciful personas were most likely to invent distinguished ancestors and upper-class origins. The nature of imposeurship has changed, however. If lying about one's pedigree is the norm in aristocracies, members of meritocracies are more prone to falsify degrees and achievements. In an egalitarian time, imposeurs don't just try to improve their social standing in status-seeking ways. Downwardly mobile entertainers such as Bob Dylan and Tom Waits have successfully transplanted their roots to the wrong side of the tracks.

(Waits, who grew up in a middle-class San Diego neighborhood, created a persona for himself as a world-weary denizen of skid row. Dylan implied that he'd grown up riding the rails like his role model Woody Guthrie, not riding his two-wheeler on the sidewalks of Hibbing, Minnesota, as he actually had.) Oracle's Larry Ellison, who was raised in a comfortable middle-class home, created a myth about pulling himself up from an impoverished childhood in a tough Chicago neighborhood. Gloria Steinem liked to suggest that a Toledo neighborhood where she lived as a girl was seedier than it actually was. Psychologist-author Dan Kiley (*The Peter Pan Syndrome*) told *People* magazine that he'd been raised on a hardscrabble farm where he slopped hogs and used an outdoor toilet. "It seems to us that Dan would have had to have been a pretty dumb kid to go outside to the toilet since we had two toilets inside the house," his parents later wrote to *People;* "the closest he got to slopping hogs was when he would polish off a half-pound of bacon before he went off to ride his pony."

The legends we create for ourselves are usually far more interesting than the truth (which is why we create them in the first place). Paradoxically, they are also more revealing. Therapists say that lies can reveal deeper truths about a person than actual facts. That's certainly true about the inventions of imposeurs. They cast laser beams on their deepest yearnings and feelings of inadequacy.

Fields of Unfulfilled Dreams

For men, unfulfilled aspirations most often focus on military and athletic glory. An occupational hazard of being a prominent athlete is that legions of wannabes claim to be you. The National Football League unmasks dozens of such imposeurs every year. Some are con men. More are just average Joes trying to get lucky. When a Boston Police Department employee was asked about athlete impersonators, he responded, "Like going into a bar and saying to a girl you're with the Red Sox? I do it all the time."

It is on the field of combat dreams that male imaginations soar. In Britain, "veterans" feign service in the Falklands, the Persian Gulf, or defusing bombs in Northern Ireland. Both Iraqi wars will certainly produce their share of ersatz warriors. Senator Lindsey Graham (R-SC), who was a National Guard lawyer based in South Carolina during the first Gulf War, once claimed on his Web site to be "an Operation Desert Shield and Desert Storm veteran." Jeffrey Papows, onetime head of the Lotus Development Corporation, said he was a marine fighter pilot in Desert Storm. Papows actually was a marine air traffic controller at that time, based in California and South Carolina. Spurious veterans of the subsequent war in Iraq are undoubtedly in the offing, eager to discuss their days of drama in Baghdad and Fallujah. They will be part of a long tradition. Feigning military service dates back at least to Odysseus, who pretended to have fought at Troy. In post-Appomattox America, a remarkable number of Union and Confederate "colonels" regaled others with dramatic tales of action at Bull Run, Antietam, and Gettysburg. A writer who investigated the last surviving "Civil War veterans" found that most were phonies, including all twelve of those who said they'd fought for the South. These were counterfeit Confederates. Few were even old enough to have taken part in the War Between the States.

Every war produces pseudosoldiers. The actor Tom Mix claimed to have charged up San Juan Hill with Teddy Roosevelt's Rough Riders. In fact Mix never left the United States during the Spanish-American War. After returning from domestic duty in World War I, William Faulkner limped around Oxford, Mississippi, for years, faking a battlefield injury. Senator Joseph McCarthy explained his limp by saying he'd been wounded as an airplane tail gunner during World War II when in fact he'd been a desk jockey whose leg was broken during drunken roughhousing on a ship taking him overseas.

The Korean conflict didn't spawn just ersatz combat veterans such as Oregon congressman Wes Cooley and evangelist Pat Robertson, but Darrow "Duke" Tully. During the seven years he spent as publisher of the *Arizona Republic* and *Phoenix Gazette*, Tully regularly donned a chestful of service ribbons to wow veterans groups with stories about his exploits as a fighter pilot in Korea and Vietnam. In one speech Tully told the American Fighter Aces Association that soldiers should avoid controversy. "I found this difficult in Korea," said the publisher, "and damn near impossible in Vietnam." Tully later admitted that he'd never even served in the air force, let alone fought in Korea or Vietnam.

Actual veterans tend to be circumspect about their combat experience. Some won't discuss it at all. The biggest tip-off that a "veteran" is a phony, real ones say, is that this person is eager to talk about his battlefield exploits. Other clues include dressing up in camouflage outfits, displaying medals, claiming to have been in elite units (Green Berets, Rangers, SEALs, etc.), and referring frequently to "secret" missions in which they took part. Frank Dux did such a convincing job of talking up the many medals he won during "clandestine" missions in Southeast Asia that his exploits became the basis of both a book (*The Secret Man: An American Warrior's Uncensored Story*) and a movie (*Bloodsport*). Like Wayland Clifton, Dux even forged a press account of his exploits. Research on these "exploits" conducted by *Los Angeles Times* reporter John Johnson and phony-veteran unmasker B. G. "Jug" Burkett revealed that Dux had been in the military for only a few months, didn't serve in Southeast Asia, and won no medals. His service records did indicate that Dux had been referred for psychiatric evaluation due to "flights of ideas and exaggerations."

All wars have produced their share of fraudulent veterans, but none so many as Vietnam. Thousands of combat pretenders from that conflict can be found at every level of American life. (Some are exposed on the Web sites phonyveterans.com cyberseals.org, ranger.org, and pownetwork.org.) They include not just Pulitzer Prize–winning historian Joseph Ellis but U.S. senator Tom Harkin (D-IA), actor Brian Dennehy, and onetime Toronto Blue Jays manager Tom Johnson. By comparing more than two thousand press accounts of such frauds with service records he acquired through the Freedom of Information Act, Jug Burkett determined that 75 percent of the "veterans" he investigated had misrepresented their military experience in whole or in part. Burkett, an actual Vietnam veteran, further estimated that perhaps 5 percent of all Vietnam-era military officers took undeserved credit for combat duty (including Admiral Jeremy Boorda, who committed suicide after it was revealed that he wore unearned Vs for valor on two service ribbons). Although he acknowledges that every war has produced its pretenders, and notes some in his book *Stolen Valor*, Burkett believes that Vietnam brought them out in unprecedented volume because the legend of that war's traumatized veterans gave those with disappointing lives a heroic way to explain them.

It's not hard to understand why those who lead disappointing lives might want to pose as someone they aren't. But why do so many distinguished, accomplished people puff up their biographies as well? Why, for example, did Joseph Ellis feel a need to pretend that he was not just a veteran of combat in Vietnam but an antiwar protester, a civil rights activist, and a high school football star?

Behind the Mask

The most common reaction to revelations about Joseph Ellis's apocryphal self was Why did he do it? When James Dickey invented a heroic combat record for himself, we cut him some slack. Poets are licensed to be creative. Nick Nolte's acting career wasn't hurt by the many bogus stories he told about his past. Actors act. But a respected historian? A custodian of the factual record? The best-selling author of *Founding Brothers*? And what about all the other fabulists we learned about in his wake, the politicians, jurists, athletes, and authors? Why would those with so much native ability and so many legitimate achievements feel a need to manufacture even more?

Alas, an ability to lie overlaps with ability in general. Among the talents many accomplished people enjoy is a gift for hoodwinking others. One review of a century's worth of research on chronic liars found their ranks filled with gifted, successful individuals. "We know from the literature that there are some highly functional, very creative people whose lives are almost entirely based on spectacular stories they spewed over the years," said Yale psychiatrist Charles Dike of this study (which he coauthored). Why they would do this is less clear. Perhaps it has something to do with wanting to make full use of all one's God-given gifts. Deception expert Paul Ekman believes that a small elite, perhaps 4 percent of us, are "natural performers" with an innate capacity to deceive. Ekman emphasizes that this doesn't necessarily mean gifted liars are more prone to lie, simply that when they choose to do so, they're very good at it. This is well known to those who specialize in this subject. Bella DePaulo once taped a group of experienced sales personnel fervently pitching one line of products they did like and another that they didn't. In several years of showing liar tapes to undergraduates, this was the first case in which viewers were utterly unable to distinguish truth from lies.

Especially good liars are common not just among sales personnel but poker players, actors, and, of course, politicians. Nietzsche thought that a capacity to deceive others was the basis of great leadership. Since he made this observation over a century ago, Nietzsche's contention has been tested empirically by Colgate psychology professor Caroline Keating. In a study of preschoolers, Keating found that those who could drink salted Kool-Aid, then persuade a group of grown-ups it was yummy were the ones who later emerged as leaders among their peers. This was true of boys and girls alike. In a group of adults Keating studied, the men who were best able to convince other men that they liked their briny drink were most likely to be chosen to lead groups of peers in a separate experiment. (This experiment brought together several groups of six same-sex adults who were asked to develop strategies for surviving a simulated plane crash in the Canadian wilderness. Most of those tapped to lead these groups had already shown themselves to be the best liars.) Keating found that an ability to lie was the single best predictor of male dominance. This led her to conclude that, among men at least, the same traits that make a convincing liar also make a good leader. Like Paul Ekman, Keating pointed out that this did not necessarily mean that talented liars lied a lot, simply that they were unusually competent when it came to deceiving others.

Few of us are skillful at telling significant lies about ourselves. Those who are often prove to have impressive skills in general. The gift of gab and an excess of charm seem especially valuable to imposeurs. "He was a very good communicator," said one employer who got burned by a consultant whose credentials proved to be spurious. "He would look you right in the eye, use technical jargon, good posture, and smiled a lot."

In Dayton, Ohio, a "Dr. Anthony Thomas" hired forty employees to staff his new company: NTS Machines. Thomas then persuaded a Dayton building owner to remodel a suite of offices for this high-tech research firm. The forty-three-year-old Thomas said he had both graduate and undergraduate degrees. When Anthony Thomas turned out to be a degree-free con artist named Anthony Holland, those working for him were dumbfounded. "That guy was great, believe me," said one. "I really take my hat off to the fellow. He had hired a lot of technical people and he had them completely snowed."

According to Jude Werra, those who score high in emotional intelligence include many credential fakers. As Werra explained, "they are so glib and so able to on first glance provide a wonderful credibility, sometimes a charisma, that people get so excited—they get this halo effect, and so they stop checking. And as a result people find it's very easy to get by with a fib, so they expand on it. And so yes, I played hockey, in fact I played on the 1980 team that won the gold medal. But maybe at best you played against one of those players in a scrimmage one day back in college. But you begin to find that nobody checks, so you can make it sound better."

Most of us have a public persona whose story lines have benefited from smoothing, rearranging, chronology shifting, and embellishing over time. If we think our stories still aren't interesting enough, we may even make up some episodes to give them some oomph. The more imaginative our personal myths become, the more "facts" we must create to make them work. We must be creative, in other words. Over time our stories can get away from us. It's easy to imagine Joseph Ellis in a playful moment allowing as how he'd fought in Vietnam. "Yes, I was there—101st Airborne.

Platoon leader. Rough situation. Very rough." The awe such an admission would undoubtedly elicit might have encouraged him to not just continue the ruse, but up the ante. Fighting in the war would lead to fighting against the war, for civil rights, and—why not?—running touchdowns in high school. Once Ellis realized what a complicated web he'd woven, there would be no turning back. Then he would have had to keep raising the stakes, buttress his lies, or throw in his hand—admit to being a fraud.

Lies once told can be retracted only if one is willing to confess to being a liar. "I have never been one of those people who can retract a lie," says a character in Suzanne Berne's novel *A Crime in the Neighborhood*, "who can explain that I spoke carelessly, that I hadn't meant what I said. Once I have lied, I've propelled myself into a story that has its own momentum."

Warner Communication head Steve Ross began telling others that he'd played football for the Cleveland Browns as a gag, goofing off among friends. Anyone close to the media mogul knew this was just tall talk. Others didn't, however, and in time the story took on a life of its own. Even Ross's wife and many of his coworkers believed he was an ex–football player. In a profile, the *New York Times* portrayed Ross as "a six-foot New Yorker who has a plate in his left arm to prove his honorable discharge from a short-lived career as an end for the Cleveland Browns. 'It was a lucky break,' he now says."

Even when they're forced to become involuntary truth tellers, imposeurs can be inventive in rationalizing their deception. A spokesperson for Condé Nast executive Steven Florio said his bogus claim to have played minor-league baseball in the Yankee system was simply part of a persona he'd created to motivate sales personnel. Lotus Development's Jeffrey Papows also said his imaginary record as a war hero was a valuable tool for pumping up staff, colleagues, and customers. Nancy Reagan justified the younger age she claimed by saying that because of an unhappy childhood she deserved a couple of bonus years. Connecticut state representative Robert Sorensen defended his spurious claim that he fought in Vietnam with the rationale that all Americans participated in that war vicariously if not directly, and all felt its pain. "So in a sense a part of us was there with every single person that fought there," said Sorensen. "So in a sense I was there."

Some wonder if those who rationalize their dissembling this way aren't deceiving themselves as much as anyone. The last line of self-defense for unmasked confabulators is to say they fooled themselves. I doubt it. Consider the case of Warren Cook Sr. A prominent Maine business executive and political adviser, Cook didn't just include an unearned master's degree on his résumé but said he was a member of America's 1968 Olympic ice hockey and had received the Navy Cross for valor in Vietnam. None of this was true. When his ruses were revealed, Warren Cook first tried an "I was considered for it" gambit with regard to the Navy Cross. When that didn't fly he resorted to an "innocent mistake" feint. Finally the Maine executive come clean: "It was a lie," Cook said of the high honor he'd awarded himself.

Then there's the case of James Dickey. Dickey loved to brag about his exploits as a fighter pilot in World War II. Until his father had to testify in court, the poet's son Christopher never knew if these accounts were true or, if they weren't, whether his father even realized he'd made them up. Under oath, Dickey described himself accurately as an intercept officer during the war, the number two man in a cockpit. He knew that his more colorful accounts were fantasies of his own making.

Self-deception among imposeurs is probably less common than we might imagine. Most realize perfectly well what they are up to.

They're not kidding themselves, only us. Studies by Bella DePaulo and others have found that liars usually know when they're lying. As sociologist J. A. Barnes observed in *A Pack of Lies*, only amateurs feel a need to believe their own lies.

This still begs the question of why. Why would those with so much going already feel a need to exaggerate their achievements? And what impels so many to tell one lie after another about themselves?

Six

Why Lie?

What am I doing when I lie?

–ELIZABETH KAMARCK MINNICH

Why?

Why isn't conscience always enough to keep us from telling lies?

Why are lies so often told when the truth would do just as well?

Why do so many smart, capable, seemingly sane individuals tell so many lies?

Some obvious reasons include, to get ahead, get an edge, get laid, make money, make time, wiggle out of tight spots, avoid embarrassment, avoid conflict, and smooth rough social situations. But there are many other, less obvious reasons to tell lies that reflect deeper needs.

Insecurity

After monitoring hours and hours of Lyndon Johnson's moans about this and groans about that on White House tapes, historian Michael Beschloss thought he'd finally hear a happy man on a recording made the day after Johnson's 1964 victory over Barry

Goldwater. Quite the opposite. Beschloss found it hard to believe that he was listening to someone who had just won the presidency in a landslide. Johnson sounded more like a loser: first grumbling that Robert Kennedy hadn't praised him enough, then complaining that the press had interpreted his election as a vote against Goldwater, not for Lyndon Johnson. "Nobody loves Johnson," the president whined at one point.

Not coincidentally, LBJ was also a great prevaricator. His nickname in college was "Bull" (short for "Bullshit") Johnson. Lyndon Johnson dissembled habitually about matters large and small, including his eligibility for a combat medal based on thirteen minutes he'd spent as an observer in a reconnaissance plane far from enemy fire during World War II. When historian Doris Kearns Goodwin asked him why he claimed his grandfather had died at the Alamo, the ex-president admitted that wasn't true. LBJ said his grandfather was actually killed at the more important battle of San Jacinto. Since few had heard of that battle, however, he'd simply moved his grandfather to one they had heard of. This sounded plausible, and the mildest of fibs. Goodwin subsequently discovered that LBJ's grandfather had died at home, in bed.

The most insistent self-embellishment occurs among those who combine a shaky self-image with great powers of imagination. They use their creativity to feed a hungry ego. Advancement per se is the lesser part of the equation. "I don't think it's primarily to get ahead," said Harvard psychologist David McClelland, who spent his career studying the psychology of achievement. McClelland thought that self-embellishment among the successful "comes out of a real uncertainty as to who you really are and out of a desire to create some kind of identity or authenticity for yourself—a deeper sense that you exist." As if to illustrate McClelland's point, Hollywood producer Brian Grazer once admitted that there was a time when he lied routinely, not in order to achieve anything but simply to boost his own morale, "to improve my self-image, to give myself the emotional apparatus so that I could continue to have hope."

It's an understandable mistake to assume that high achievers are unusually self-confident. Some are. But just as many are remarkably insecure. This hardly makes them unique. To a certain extent, to be alive is to be insecure. All this means is that the poised persona so many project does not always match the tremulous person hiding inside. One reason the Wizard of Oz has lasted so long as a metaphor is because so many of us see ourselves in him, anxious figures throwing up clouds of smoke and thunderous noise in hopes that no one will discover how insignificant we actually feel.

Whom we know ourselves to be generally has little to do with the person the world sees, no matter how impressive that person may appear. Deception can feel necessary to make a good impression. Studies of deceptive behavior have found that the more concerned someone is about the opinion of others, the more likely that person is to tell lies. This applies to public figures as much as anyone. Biographer Sydney Ladensohn Stern attributed Gloria Steinem's continual rewriting of her life story to the fact that "she was too insecure to trust her audiences to accept her as she was, contradictions and all." Biographies of wealthy moguls such as Armand Hammer, Steve Ross, and Larry Ellison portrayed their subjects as so desperate to impress others that they felt a constant need to buff up their backgrounds. Ross's biographer, Connie Bruck, attributed the executive's lifelong colorizing of his past to a gnawing sense that his life had been too "ordinary and monochromatic."

James Autry, former head of the Meredith Magazine Group, once observed that we should never assume apparently successful figures are as happy, secure, self-assured, or fulfilled as we imagine. In his book *Life and Work* he offered himself as Exhibit A. While Meredith's CEO, Autry had lunch with a friend who was a vice president at one of the country's largest companies. Midway through lunch, his friend asked abruptly, "Do you ever get the feeling that one day they are going to come into your office and say, 'Okay, Autry, we found out about you'?"

"Yes, yes," Autry replied without hesitating. He told his friend that he felt that way often. And him? The friend nodded. They both laughed.

"It's as if we're still the little boys playing with the big boys," Autry's friend said. "We don't really belong here, do we?"

Some call this "impostor syndrome." That much-studied phenomenon afflicts those on top at least as much those at the bottom of the status ladder. Public acclaim is no antidote to feeling like a fraud. Such acclaim contributes little to an inner sense of worth, and can even make us feel more fraudulent, as the gap between our outer and inner selves grows wider. As an old joke goes, if someone were to stand outside a hotel housing a CEO convention and yell, "Run! We've been found out!" the rooms would empty quickly.

It's always a bit of a shock to meet a prominent person and be subjected to an earful of boasting and dropped names. Why should those who have achieved public recognition feel a need to puff themselves so blatantly? Aren't they beyond the need for such blatant self-promotion? Apparently not. Apparently no amount of recognition can fill the hole they're trying to fill. Trying to understand the lifetime of lies that Laurens van der Post told about himself, biographer J. D. F. Jones observed that for someone like him, "lies are not so much a calculated attempt to deceive their hearers, as an effort to escape from themselves."

Many who achieve prominence do so because they are whipped

by the lash of self-doubt. The same gnawing insecurity that drives some to succeed can also cause them to make things up about themselves, both before and after they reach their destination. Insecurity seems to be an incurable disease. Achieving success doesn't automatically turn off the tap of self-doubt. In some cases it can actually increase its flow. When success is accompanied by fame, an inner sense of accomplishment can be that much harder to achieve.

According to psychologist Richard Farson, one of the first things therapists learn is that regardless of appearances, *nobody* has it made. "No one ever feels fully credentialed," says Farson, who is both a therapist and a management consultant, "even with a bona fide degree, a series of books, a distinguished professorship, and a Pulitzer Prize. Success such as that cuts two ways. It can make you feel secure in some ways, insecure in others. One of the findings about CEOs is that they often feel they have risen beyond their capabilities, that the bubble may burst, leading to their being discovered as the ordinary people they know themselves to be."

That seems to have been the case with Martha Stewart. Stewart's biographers portray her as engaging in outrageously insecure behavior throughout her adult life: belittling waiters, berating neighbors, abusing fellow passengers on airplanes, raging at anyone who didn't recognize her in public. The more prominent she became, the worse her tantrums grew. In *Martha Inc.*, Christopher Byron attributed his subject's bad behavior in part to "the work of putting on the *performance* of Martha Stewart," rather than simply being herself.

This pressure led Stewart to continually misrepresent herself and her origins. The cold, anger-filled home in which she grew up was transformed in her retelling into a warm Norman Rockwell–like one that left her with a passion for the domestic arts. Freud called this the "family romance." That concept refers to the practice of re-creating for public consumption, if not for ourselves, a fantasy family far superior to the one in which we actually grew up. Polishing up their origins this way is common among public figures. By Richard Nixon's account, his abusive, ne'er-do-well father was a stolid pillar of virtue, his cold, sharp-tongued mother a near saint. No amount of success and recognition could relieve this troubled man of his compulsion to appear better than he felt. It is well established by now that Nixon lied routinely: not just about Watergate and its cover-up or his plans for Vietnam, but about what he studied in college and how he met his wife. "To travel Richard Nixon's life," wrote biographer Anthony Summers, "requires, more than most subjects, a careful passage though a minefield of lies, lies of varying degrees of seriousness, lies self-serving but in the end self-defeating."

Apparently Nixon's lifetime of dissembling never won him the type of recognition he craved any more than constant prevarication made Lyndon Johnson feel more at home in his own skin. It couldn't have. Psychologist Arno Karlen suggests that the unquenchable thirst for attention (not love) among the many narcissists who crowd our headlines is what makes them say whatever they think will keep the focus on themselves, true or false. Left to its own devices, this compulsion has no remedy. "In talking about a person with a cancerous narcissistic personality," explains Karlen, "there is no such thing as enough. Only an outsider thinks that way."

An explanation for dissembling based on narcissism and insecurity can be taken only so far. I know plenty of scrupulously honest people who don't think much of themselves. I also know others who seem to have high self-regard but lie a lot anyway. For their motivations we need to look in other nooks and crannies of the liar's psyche.

Recreation

For years, market researcher Faith Popcorn told interviewers that her last name was adapted from that of her Italian great-grandfather: Corne. At Ellis Island, Popcorn said, he'd told immigration authorities, "My name is a-Papa Corne." In time their family name was Americanized to "Popcorn." Popcorn profilers dutifully reported this endearing story. But when a *Newsweek* reporter did some legwork, she discovered that Faith Popcorn was actually Faith Plotkin from New York's Lower East Side. Popcorn-Plotkin took the unmasking in good humor. She said that some called the put-on her "best piece of work."

This is the lying game. It's done for no better reason than horsing around. When we wonder why dishonesty is so ubiquitous, we might bear in mind that telling lies can be fun, fashionable, and far more entertaining than telling the truth. Even though he believed that the practice degraded those who engaged in it, Francis Bacon conceded that mixing lies with truths "doth ever add pleasure." André Malraux—no slouch at mythmaking on his own behalf—wrote with authority about this subject in his novel *The Walnut Trees of Altenberg*. Of its protagonist, Malraux observed, "he could perhaps have found some means of destroying the mythical person he was growing into, had he been compelled. But he had no wish to do so. His reputation was flattering. What was more important, he enjoyed it."

Telling lies is one of the few forms of mischief permitted grown-ups. The lying game is concerned less with advancing one's prospects or avoiding trouble than simply passing time in an amusing way. It is not done to bolster one's credentials, protect someone else's feelings, or wiggle out of a tight spot. Recreational lies are told simply as a leisure activity, an entertainment, and a challenging one at that. Any simpleton can tell the truth. Lying takes talent. Machiavelli, Nietzsche, and Wilde all made that point: the ability to lie well is a gift. Although Montaigne didn't agree, he did point out that the truth has a single face, its opposite a hundred thousand. Just as there is only one way to hit a bull's-eye but an infinite number of ways to miss it, so is the opportunity to lie a field without limit. That appeals to those who see no reason why they shouldn't enjoy the many creative opportunities presented by saying what isn't.

Boredom is the genesis of the lying game. The more bored people are, the more likely they are to fight tedium with dishonesty. Simple monotony is too little appreciated as a reason to tell lies. When our lives feel unexciting, as so many do, an exhilarating lie can stir things up, make life more exciting. Truth telling can be so tedious, so predictable. Its entertainment value is nearly nil. One student of deceptive behavior among police officers concluded that over time many didn't just grow morally desensitized to telling lies, but even came to enjoy it. "Lies often have an undeniably entertaining quality to them," concluded criminologist Carl Klockars. "Lies can be and often are intrinsically appealing, exciting, and attractive."

Recognizing the temptations of recreational lying, and knowing they must keep the practice under control, most societies provide for some form of playful deceit. The provisions they make usually assume that the butt of sanctioned leg pulling will be let in on the joke. Practical jokes mounted on April 1 are part of this tradition. Their culmination is "April fool!" when a prank is revealed to the dupe. The real fun of practical jokes depends on a prank's target realizing how hard his chain has just been jerked. The lying game is different. For one thing, those being lied to don't usually know the liar well enough to pick up cues that they might be getting snookered. Recreational lying that's part of playful inside jokes in more cohesive cultures is deceitful elsewhere. An inside joke presumes insiders. Few members of mass society feel like insiders. Also, there are so few agreed-upon norms in large, cosmopolitan societies that it isn't always clear when deceit is playful and when it isn't. Finally, recreational lying isn't always engaged in just for fun. This game can have a controlling, manipulative quality. For some that is part of its appeal.

Duping Delight

After he was fired from the *New York Times* for fabricating news accounts, then denying he'd done so, Jayson Blair seemed more delighted than despondent. "I fooled some of the most brilliant people in journalism," bragged Blair.

Paul Ekman calls the positive feeling some get from deceiving others "duping delight." "This comes from the pure thrill of getting away with something," Ekman explains. Psychoanalyst Ben Burstein concurs, but from a somewhat different perspective. Burstein's interest is in those who have what he calls a "manipulative personality." Unlike sociopaths, who lie reflexively and to no apparent end, manipulators derive great satisfaction from successful acts of deception. Influencing another person without some element of deception would not give them the same satisfaction. According to Burstein, a key trait of manipulative personalities is "the exhilaration of putting something over on the other person."

An urge to dissemble this way transcends any hope of tangible gain. For the recreational liar, getting away with something matters more than getting ahead. Successful duping is reward enough.

That helps explain why those with formidable credentials sometimes make them grander yet through subterfuge. An ad man I once knew used to include work done by others in his portfolio. He didn't need to. His own work was impressive enough. This man realized that getting caught could scuttle his career in advertising. He continued the ruse anyway. Why? Because the ad man enjoyed his little con. Wondering if he'd get caught gave his life an appealing edge. Succeeding made him feel powerful.

The lying game conveys a sense of control over those you're deceiving. You know you're lying to them; they don't know they're being lied to. Unlike leg-pulling lies, which succeed only once revealed, secrecy is at the heart of the power we enjoy when lying to others. We make them dependent on our version of reality, only they don't know it. When she tells someone a lie, observed philosopher Elizabeth Kamarck Minnich, "I decide, by myself and in secret, what needs to be said. I change other people's reality without their permission."

Needless to say this concept of power is rather childlike. It resembles the only type of power some children feel they can exercise: the power to deceive. "A friend of mine who lies a lot tells me she loves fooling people and making them act on knowledge that only she knows is untrue," wrote bell hooks; "she is ten years old."

Adventure

Most lying is a relatively low-risk game, more akin to riding a roller coaster than climbing a mountain. It is unlikely that fibs we peddle about ourselves will ever be exposed. That can happen, of course, especially when the fibber is a public figure. To a recreational liar, however, the risk of exposure is itself part of the fun. This heightens the sense of intrigue, of being a down-home double agent. Paul Ekman thinks delighted dupers enjoy this game most when a mark is hard to fool and the outcome of their ruse is in doubt. "The liar may feel excitement," explains Ekman in *Telling Lies,* "either when anticipating the challenge or during the very moment of lying, when success is not yet certain. Afterward there may be the pleasure that comes with relief, pride in the achievement, or feelings of smug contempt toward the target."

That sequence of feelings is little different from the one experienced by skydivers, rock climbers, and shoplifters. It's the high some get from courting danger. One commentator called the fabulism of so many prominent public figures their "drug of choice." This analogy was more apt than he may have realized. It might be a stretch to say that telling lies can turn you on, but not much. Lying doesn't just impart the thrill of adventure, it can arouse us no less than any other serotonin-releasing stimulus.

During an earlier project on risk taking, I found that deceiving others was a common form of "pot stirring," a miniadventure engaged in to move the day along. For the excitement-starved, a bit of casual deception can pump little drops of adrenaline. Not the least reason to tell a lie is the microdrama it creates. Can I concoct a good one? Put it over? Will I get caught? Or will I play the part of an honest person convincingly enough to live to lie another day? Lying for some is the most bold and creative act they engage in on a regular basis. Whether it is humane, moral, or even legal is beside the point. What is the point? Arousal. Adventure. Challenge. In a study of confidence men, Stanford psychologist Richard Blum found that risk taking motivated them more than moneymaking. All quickly lost the money they made by duping others—in gambling, spending sprees, crime, even by being duped themselves. The game meant more to them than the gain.

In their own minds, adventure-seeking liars see themselves as bold adventurers. Look at it from their perspective. Being honest presents no dare. Dishonesty does. Every time we alter the truth we throw our fate to the winds. In the lying game we challenge destiny by seeing how many lies we can get away with. From this perspective, truth telling is for wimps. Telling the truth takes neither skill, nerve, nor imagination. Lying does. Liars test themselves. They've got guts. Nietzsche thought one reason great men would rather lie than be truthful was because lying "requires more spirit and will."

Taking Charge

Determined pot stirrers told me that taking chances gave them a sense of control over their own lives. Doing something that could get them in trouble meant they were no longer passive life livers. They'd taken charge. The same thing is true of liars. Lying can convey a sense of mastery. When telling the truth we dance to honesty's tune. While telling lies we control the action. "A lie is at least a vigorous enterprise," observes a character in John Irving's novel *The Cider House Rules*; "it keeps you on your toes by making you suddenly responsible for what happens because of it. You must be alert to lie, and stay alert to keep your lie a secret. . . . When you lie it makes you feel in charge of your life."

It is generally accepted that lying can be a tool of self-preservation among those who feel oppressed. For slaves, prisoners, women dealing with some men, and children confronting most parents, lying may be the only way to establish any sense of control over their own lives. The more fully we feel in charge of our destiny, the less need we feel to tell lies. The less control we feel over our lives, the more we may use deception to take back the helm. When he compared reports of indigenous people who were known for being honest with those who weren't, Herbert Spencer concluded that the key difference lay on a continuum of power. Far more prevaricators were subject to coercive rule than truth tellers.

Lying can be symptomatic of feeling powerless. Fear is the essence of this feeling. "The liar lives in fear of losing control," wrote the feminist poet Adrienne Rich. "Her lies are a denial of her fear; a way of maintaining control." Rich addressed these words to women, to challenge their overdependence on deception as a way of life. In doing this she implied that there are differences in the ways men and women lie. Many have concluded that there is such a difference. Are they right?

Seven

Sex, Lies, and Sex Roles

Sure men were born to lie, and women to believe them!
–JOHN GAY

I also hate it when men lie to me. It's not becoming, and they're
rarely very good at it.
–CAROLINA GARCIA-AGUILERA

Is one gender more honest than the other? Opinions on that subject abound, but until recently, tangible information was scarce.

Historically, the men who have had most to say on this topic concluded that their sex was the more honest. As Chaucer wrote,

For half so boldely kan ther no man
Swere and lye as a womman kan.

Male Elizabethan poets thought women were far more deceitful then men, especially in matters of the heart. "Love loves truth," wrote the Earl of Essex, "which women hate." David Hume agreed, concluding that it was women who had "an appetite for falsehood." Devious women and honest men were a staple of English novels during the Victorian era. In Joseph Conrad's *Heart of Dark-*

ness, Marlow professes a widespread opinion that women have no capacity for grasping, let alone telling, the truth. As recently as 1970 a psychologist concluded that "as a rule, women tend to become more frequently and more deeply involved in lying than men."

Since these views were expressed, a body of actual research has explored truth telling by gender. Its results tell a far more complex story.

Sex Studies

In a classic psychological study, three-year-olds were left alone with a hidden toy and warned not to peek. Most peeked. When asked whether they'd done so, far more girls than boys said they hadn't. What's more, girls who peeked and lied were more persuasive than boys who did too. So can we conclude that little girls are more devious than little boys? Not necessarily. A replication of this study that added certain variables found more nuanced results. Girls, for example, were more likely to admit they'd lied when asked with a smile, boys when simply stared at. "Although there may be some stable gender differences in lying," the makers of this study concluded, "it is far more likely that such differences are variable and context-dependent."

In general this is the only safe conclusion one can draw about lying by gender: it all depends. Men are more prone to lie in some situations, women in others. When it comes to a tendency to deceive, gender is hard to distinguish from other contributing factors. This does not mean that gender doesn't matter, just that it's one of many situational influences on honest or dishonest behavior. More pertinent questions are How does a particular context influence deceitfulness in men and women? and Are those tendencies changing as contexts change?

According to social scientific studies, men and women lie at about the same rate. The nature of their lies does differ, however, in ways that reflect sex roles more than genetics. As sex roles change, so do the patterns of men's and women's lying.

In a late-1960s study of one hundred residents of a small industrial town, Stanford's Richard Blum found little difference in the overall rate of lying between men and women. Men in this mostly married group were more likely to tell lies at work, reflecting in part the fact that so many more of them had jobs outside the home. Their workplace lies were usually defensive (to cover up tardiness, say) or, less often, self-aggrandizing ones told in an effort to win a promotion or raise. Women, mostly housewives in Blum's sample, were more likely to lie about how much money they spent shopping. They were also four times more likely than men to admit they had covered up a transgression by someone else, usually their husband. In general, Blum concluded, the women he studied were more likely to protect others with lies, men to protect themselves—especially from valid suspicions of infidelity. Men were also more prone to use lies to resolve arguments and restore the appearance of harmony. One might think that avoiding conflict was more a feminine than a masculine trait, but apparently that isn't necessarily so. Muhammad permitted his male followers to lie for the sake of domestic tranquillity. As bell hooks once observed, "The men I have loved have always lied to avoid confrontation."

More women than men in Blum's sample said they'd lied to their parents as teenagers (70 percent of women, 46 percent of men). Perhaps they just had better memories. A subsequent study of sixty married couples in Ontario found that wives recalled episodes in their marriage far better than husbands did, but that husbands were more likely to embellish those episodes in the retelling. Those conducting this study concluded that women's more accurate memories might constrain them from making things up, while men were forced to fill the gaps in their hazy recollections with apocrypha. This is too charitable to men by half. I'd say husbands are more likely than wives to tell stretchers and whoppers simply to make themselves look better.

That could be why men are far more promiscuous résumé embellishers. In one sample of five hundred job candidates vetted by Toronto's Infocheck, those who got short-listed were about evenly divided between men and women. Two-thirds of those who faked their credentials were men, however. In general, Infocheck has found men are far more likely than women to lie about their qualifications for a job. "It's important to know" an Infocheck executive warned those who assess job candidates, "that the man sitting in front of you is twice as likely to lie about his past than the woman you just interviewed."

In the first chapter we looked at Robert Feldman's finding that college students told an average of three lies in ten-minute conversations. No significant difference was found in the rate of lying by gender in this study. There was a difference in content. Lies told by women were more often intended to smooth social situations, those told by men to impress others with dubious boasts. Like others who have studied this topic, Feldman found men are more prone than women to tell bald-faced lies, especially on their own behalf. Women's self-serving lies were based more on subtle exaggeration and omission (e.g., feigning agreement with statements with which they disagreed, saying they liked a movie they hadn't seen, or pretending to share someone else's enthusiasm for a class they hadn't even taken).

When it comes to lying, men and women clearly have different agendas. To oversimplify, men lie to impress, women to oblige.

Women are more likely to accommodate others with their lies, men to accommodate themselves. Men specialize in self-aggrandizing lies ("I just swung a big deal—huge"), women in charitable ones ("Love the dress") or fibs that are self-protective ("I eat mostly low-fat foods"). Their deceitfulness seems to be based on caring, perhaps too much, what others think of them. This reflects a broader psychological finding that women feel judged more on the quality of their relationships, men on the quality of their achievements.

No one has paid more attention to lying by gender than Bella DePaulo. DePaulo began studying this subject with a bias toward women's superior honesty. Because they are more "people oriented," self-disclosing, and supportive of others—"socioemotional specialists," to use her term—the psychologist thought female subjects would be less deceitful than male subjects. She could not have been more wrong.

Men and women DePaulo studied lied at about the same rate. There were clear gender differences in the lies they told, however. Men tended to distort information, ostentatiously "hamming" at times. Women deceived by withholding information and avoiding direct answers. Women were also better at feigning feelings, De-Paulo found, looking pleased, say, when given a gift they didn't like. In one study, DePaulo found female subjects not only were more likely to tell artists that they liked their paintings when they didn't, but sold this lie better than male subjects did. Such findings suggest that women may be more benevolent than men, DePaulo thought, but not more honest. As she put it, "other people's feelings matter more to them than the truth."

Let's examine the basis for this distinction a little more closely. Members of both sexes said they lied to women in order to protect them, but told men lies in order to one-up them. Why? Because, DePaulo explained, "they thought that the women to whom they told their lies would have felt even worse if they heard the truth instead of a lie." Isn't this patronizing? And what does it say about relative deceitfulness, independent of motivation? As DePaulo herself admitted, "At least some of the times when women are being protective of other people's feelings, they are simply lying. Men are less supportive in those ways, but also more truthful."

DePaulo originally thought this contrast reflected female supportiveness and male competitiveness. That was before she discovered how frequently women lied to each other. In same-sex interactions, they routinely told "kind" lies, "love-the-dress" lies. Women don't lie to spare other *people's* feelings, DePaulo found, so much as to spare other *women's* feelings. What's more, the least stressed of all her subjects were women lying to women. Women felt much greater distress when lying to a man. Men didn't feel quite so stressed about lying to women, and hardly stressed at all about lying to each other. Before assessing lying by gender, DePaulo concluded, one must first consider the gender of a lie's target. Men who routinely tell other men boastful lies switch to protective, other-oriented lies when dealing with women. Women's lies also change dramatically when aimed at the opposite sex. Then, self-serving deception becomes more common. In mixed groups, women are nearly as likely as men to concoct stories about their spurious achievements.

As sex roles change, mixed working groups grow more common, and women get more practice at telling self-serving lies, perhaps traditional patterns of lying by gender will change too. Traditionally, a stereotypical man who sees himself as a hunter, warrior, and breadwinner will be more tempted to spin fantasies about slaying a mastodon, winning medals for bravery, and making lots of money. A stereotypical woman who sees herself as attractive to the opposite sex, a good manipulator of men, and an all-around people

pleaser might allude to being sexier than she feels, more accommo-
dating of others, and able to handle men by grace or by guile. The
more women defy this stereotype, the more their styles of deception will change in the process.

Telling It Slant

Woman's role as devious conniver has historically been accepted by men and women alike. According to Sir Walter Scott,
woman "employs sincerity only when every other form of deception has failed." At one time this perception was based on a consensus that female deviousness reflected the gender's frailty. A
more likely explanation was that of Emily Dickinson, who advised
her gender-mates to

Tell all the Truth but tell it slant.

The concept of "telling it slant" was picked up by feminists and
others to depict what women, like any oppressed group, had to do
in order to survive. What was the alternative? "We have been required to tell different lies at different times," wrote Adrienne
Rich, "depending on what the men of the time needed to hear."

If women's lies have reflected their subservient social status, as
they attain positions of power once reserved for men, the nature of
their lying presumably will change. A friend of mine says that "I
used to be a model" is the spurious boast she's heard most often
from members of her gender. According to psychiatrist Charles
Ford, a common lie on women's résumés is that they were president
of their college sorority. Many a beauty contestant has padded her
vita, including a Miss New Jersey, Amy Fissel, an Atlantic Community College student who told contest judges she was a senior at
Rutgers; a Miss Virginia, Andrea Ballengee, who inflated her aca-

demic honors and said she was enrolled in a law school where she actually was wait-listed; and a Miss Mississippi named Kandace Williams, who listed Julius Caesar among her ancestors.

As opportunities increase to lie against type, women who want to swing huge deals may prove no less prone than men to say they did when they didn't. Even though the job candidates who inflate their résumés to vie for top positions are predominantly men, that doesn't mean women don't engage in this practice. Embellished vitas are one tool for breaking through the glass ceiling. As more women compete for better jobs in the marketplace, there is no reason to assume their credentials won't get puffier. Sandra Baldwin was not the only woman to win a prominent position (U.S. Olympic Committee president) with faked credentials. On the résumé she submitted for her job, Shirley DeLibero, the $254,000-a-year president of Houston's Metropolitan Transit Authority, listed degrees from two institutions of higher education, one of which was nonexistent, the other of which didn't admit women until years after the dates on her résumé. (DeLibero later refused on ethical grounds to hire a woman who falsely claimed to have a degree from Syracuse University.) Onetime Texas Railroad Commission chair Lena Guerrero was forced to admit that she wasn't really a Phi Beta Kappa graduate of the University of Texas, as she'd claimed. In fact, Guerrero had flunked six courses at Texas and never graduated. She resigned, as did Sandra Baldwin. Shirley DeLibero did not. A year after her ruse came to light DeLibero was given a substantial raise.

In the future, one can assume that imposeurs will no longer be primarily a gang of swaggering, bragging men. Following 9/11 poseurs of both sexes claimed to have been rescue workers at Ground Zero. As more women soldiers are put in harm's way, the ranks of phony combat veterans—Jessica Lynch wannabes—will undoubtedly include women, as will teams of would-be ex-athletes.

Until then, and until equal vocational opportunity is a reality as well as a goal, women's self-serving lies will continue to be weighted toward traditional areas: reducing weight and number of sex part-ners while exaggerating the quality of just-completed couplings.

Erotic Deception

Essayist Gene Weingarten once compiled the most common lies men and women tell each other.

> I love you. The earth moved. I have a headache. I read it for the articles. I will respect you in the morning. I am a virgin. I am not a virgin. I just need some space. It's just the right size. They're just the right size. I am getting a divorce. It's not the sex, it's the intimacy. I was not looking at her. I was not flirt-ing with him. I'll call you tomorrow. I had to work late. I never felt comfortable enough with anyone to do that before. She means nothing to me. Nice pants. Of course they are real. It's not you, it's me. I don't usually come to places like this. Yes, yes, yes, yesss.

Men and women save their biggest lies for each other. Most have to do with sex. This subject just seems to bring out the liar in us. One reason Americans were so tolerant of Bill Clinton's sexual deceits was because they felt vulnerable in this area themselves. "Everyone lies about sex," said Jerry Seinfeld at the height of Clin-ton's Monica mess. "People lie during sex. If it weren't for lies, there'd be no sex."

Shakespeare's women lied about this topic, and his men too, of-ten to each other:

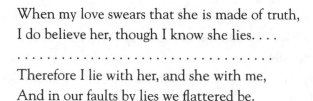

When my love swears that she is made of truth,
I do believe her, though I know she lies. . . .
. . . .
Therefore I lie with her, and she with me,
And in our faults by lies we flattered be.

Why is lying *with* each other such a routine occasion for lying *to* each other? Because the stakes are so high. Because the subject embarrasses us. Because we're ashamed of ourselves in this area, for what we do, what we don't do, even what crosses our perverted little minds. Sex pits our rational self against our primal self, and the rational self usually loses.

One way to resolve the consternation that ensues is by telling lies. The prevalence of sexual deception is a measure of this subject's gravity. Making love has to do not just with our prospects for leaving genes behind, but for being loved, and for being known intimately by another person. One reason we dissemble so insistently about sex is because we know that the act of intercourse is such a truth revealer. *"Veritas in coitu,"* historian Wendy Doniger called it. Whatever else may be said about copulating, it is seldom dignified. Appearances are hard to keep up in the sexual bed, backseat, or sleeping bag. Facades seldom survive the blast heat of lust. "Sex strips away identities it takes a lifetime to build," observed author John Hubner. "A naked aroused man is not a brain surgeon or a university president or a Methodist bishop. He is an animal with an erection."

For those to whom appearances matter—most of us—the only way to keep them up in the face of sex (or lack of sex) can be by dissembling. In the dry observation of one study, "Men report that they experience fellatio at a far greater rate than women report providing it." This common type of finding suggests one reason we have so little reliable information about sexual behavior. Even Alfred Kinsey's groundbreaking studies are now considered suspect because they were based on an unrepresentative sample of volunteer subjects whose veracity can't be confirmed. Kinsey himself seems to have taken liberties in reporting his findings while concealing his own rather bizarre bisexual practices behind a facade of detached scholarship. Apparently the deceptiveness that sex elicits extends to those who study it. Under fire for her own research methods, sexologist Shere Hite told Oprah Winfrey that the president of the American Sociological Association thought her methodology was great. When asked, the association's president said he'd never even read *The Hite Report* let alone endorsed its author's methodology.

As with their lies in general, there's a difference in men's and women's erotic deception. Women are more likely to cover up sexual activity with lies, men to boast with gusto about couplings that never happened. Psychiatrist Charles Ford thinks men's braggadocio about imagined sexual conquests might reflect an ancient impulse to establish dominance hierarchies. Their boasting could be little different than the chest thumping of silverback gorillas. More broadly speaking, Ford believes that sexual deception reflects long-standing sex roles and may even be part of our genetic memory. From this perspective, women routinely undercount previous sex partners to imply they'll be faithful mates, while men exaggerate their sexual prowess to suggest their potential as gene vehicles.

One study of sexually active college students found that a third of the 196 men said they'd lied to have sex. So did 10 percent of the 226 women. Sixty percent of the female subjects said they'd been lied to sexually (no surprise there) but 47 percent of the males said the same thing. Nearly half of each group—42 percent of the women, 47 percent of the men—were willing to understate their number of previous sex partners. In a similar study of 137 university students, 92 percent admitted that they'd lied to a current or prospective sex partner, most often about the number of their past partners. ("What a coincidence. We've both had the same amount!") The next most common lie had to do with how good a just-completed coupling was ("I've never had it so good!"), or how one partner felt about the other ("I love you"). Women in this study lied most frequently about having had an orgasm, next most often about their number of previous partners, next about the quality of the experience ("It was good"), next about how they felt about their partner ("You're the greatest!"), and after that about the relative size of their partner's sex organ ("You're the biggest!").

Sex researchers have long noted that women report having significantly fewer sex partners than men do. British men, for example, report thirteen partners on average, British women nine. Such figures have always created a statistical anomaly. (What happened to the extra four women?) Researchers usually explain this anomaly by assuming that men inflate their figures. Two American psychologists, Terri Fisher and Michelle Alexander, put this assumption to an ingenious test. In this test, 248 unmarried students at a midwestern college, aged eighteen to twenty-five, were randomly assigned to three groups, then asked to complete a questionnaire about their heterosexual sex experiences. Those in the first group were told their responses might be read by researchers. Members of the second group were promised complete anonymity. In the third group, participants had electrodes wired to their hands, forearms, and neck. These subjects were told (falsely) that the wires led to a contraption that would detect any lies they told. Here are the results: Women who thought their questionnaires would be read by others reported having an average of 2.6 sex partners. Those who were promised anonymity said they'd had 3.4

partners. But the third group, those hooked up to a "lie detector," admitted to an average of 4.4 sex partners. Since men who were wired up said they'd had an average of 4.0 sex partners (only slightly more than the 3.7 reported by those men who merely expected their results to be read), a question arose in the researchers' minds: Have men been more honest all along about their sex lives (at least when it comes to numbers of partners) and women more deceptive? That's exactly what they concluded. This certainly stood to reason, they thought. In a culture where sexually active women risk being labeled "sluts," lying about their sex life could be considered more prudent than prudish.

A final reason we lie about sex is to raise the stakes. One would think these stakes were high enough already, but that's not true for everyone. Sex and danger are inextricably linked. Fear can be a form of foreplay. As any couple knows who have ever craved each other after watching a horror movie, riding a roller coaster, or sailing a boat through a storm, shared jeopardy can turn them on. Risk taking in general is a well-known aphrodisiac. The danger of being caught dissembling can be as arousing as any other form of danger. One reason adolescent sex remains such an exciting memory is that it involved so much intrigue and deception: of parents, friends, and lovers.

Some consider erotic flimflam part of the sexual fun. Recreational lying is out in full force during the mating dance. This type of gamesmanship is the stuff of legends, stories, and novels. Saul Bellow once observed that you could no more have fiction without sexual deceit than you could have a circus without elephants. Bill Maher's novel *True Story* includes this exchange between a man named Dick and a woman named Tammi, whom he's just met while on vacation in Florida:

"What are you doing?" she squealed.

"I'm kissing you."

"Why?"

"Because I want to get to know you while I'm down here."

"Get to know me—does that mean go to bed with me?"

"No," Dick said, and felt his nose growing slightly longer. He thought about the first time he had lied to a woman in such a way, how it had excited him, and suddenly the metaphor of Pinocchio became clear. There was something so sexy about this game men and women played. . . . It just would be no fun without the bullshit, the drama, the chase.

Of course this is the perspective of a man, one engaged in the challenge of seduction. Since the average man is more intent on sexual conquest than the average woman, it's no surprise that men are more likely to lie to achieve this goal. Since they are also more likely to be unfaithful sexually, men are more prone to use deception to conceal their acts of adultery. Among the one hundred residents of a blue-collar town whom he studied, Stanford's Richard Blum found that the prospect of a spouse's infidelity mattered less to wives, who were routinely told lies about this subject, than to their husbands, who lied routinely about being faithful and assumed their wives did too. Obviously a bit of projection was at work there. On the other hand, male suspicions about wifely infidelity and lies told to conceal it are not just a matter of projection. Here's an interesting type of dissembling, long suspected by men, but only recently verified by modern biotechnology: based on analyses of couples' blood samples in France, England, and the United States, it seems that as many as 10 percent of all fathers may be helping raise a child who their partner said was his, but wasn't.

Relationships

Verifying paternity with DNA tests is one tool employed by the private investigators who are flourishing in the post-truth era. Much of their work involves verifying the background of potential mates at a time when deception has become a common mating strategy. ("Ever since I have started using my doctorate title," said a happy customer of a phony-degree service, "when I introduce myself to women, they find me irresistible.") One reason so many marriages fail is that they're based on false assumptions. These assumptions grow out of many deceits large and small that suitors feed each other. One study of couples in different relationship stages found deception most common among those who were dating. Another study found that liars of both sexes were especially good at gazing into the eyes of a suitor when telling their lies. The long-term prospects of any relationship built on a foundation of fantasy are not promising.

Along with private investigation, a thriving market exists for books with titles such as *When Your Lover Is a Liar*, *101 Lies Men Tell Women*, and *Romantic Deception: The Six Signs He's Lying*. Detecting lies is not that simple, however, especially among those who don't share much history. Those involved with each other over time are in a different category. They have a baseline of data with which to assess the other person's veracity—not just how he or she behaves when "normal" (i.e., not hiding anything), but how that person behaves when lying to others. One study found that any alteration of typical behavior triggered suspicion in a partner: change in eye contact, in length of conversational messages, or hand and foot movement. Those who don't know each other well enough to realize what behavior is out of the ordinary must listen more closely to what is being said. As the makers of this study put it, "relational intimates concentrate on the baseline while strangers concentrate on the story line."

These researchers also discovered that we're better at spotting lies told by friends than those told by spouses, presumably because married couples tend to ignore evidence they know might make them wary. The longer they're together, the better partners become at avoiding each other's hot buttons. In the process they discover that full disclosure isn't always the best policy. A study of couples in different stages of their relationship found that those who were married were more likely to deceive each other by omitting risky information, less likely to do so by outright falsehood.

Most husbands and wives tolerate certain kinds of deviousness in their relationship. They give each other latitude for deception by omission, avoid cross-examinations that might reveal information they'd rather not know, and don't maneuver their spouse into a situation where he or she must lie. Some even consider petty deception a necessary part of any lasting relationship. Those who want to stay involved with each other over time understand that all could be lost because of promiscuous truth telling. One wife found her deceptiveness escalating after she had children in her early thirties. The stakes were so much higher now, the need for marital harmony so much greater. "When you've got kids, you can't have a five-day fight," she explained, "or a big confrontation whenever you feel like it."

Candor grows more perilous over time. One could even say that the more we care, the more we lie. Bella DePaulo has found that the better her subjects liked someone, the more likely they were to deceive that person (to "spare their feelings"). By contrast, we are more likely to be told the truth, the whole truth, and nothing but the truth by those who have no reason to protect us. This doesn't include significant others. With someone we don't really care about, we might as well be honest. Even though it may be true that we feel less moral compunction about deceiving strangers, paradoxically, we can also feel better able to tell them truths precisely because we don't care enough to spare their feelings, and figure we may never see them again anyway. Great truths have been shared by strangers sitting next to each other on trains, and by authors addressing anonymous readers. Proust prized his contact with readers precisely because it was unencumbered by the lies friends felt obligated to tell each other. "Nor is there any deference," added Proust about the author-reader relationship; "we laugh at what Molière says only to that exact degree we find him funny; when he bores us, and when we have decidedly had enough of being with him, we put him back in his place as bluntly as if he had neither genius nor fame."

So far in this book we have looked at the rise of post-truthfulness in contemporary society, considered its origins (the breakdown of community especially), and shown how the American way of life facilitates deception, a fact that has relevance far beyond its borders in a world that takes so many cultural cues from the United States. Along the way we've examined motivations to lie that go beyond the obvious ones of saving face and getting ahead, and considered how those factors influence relations between the sexes. Opportunities to deceive are clearly on the rise, with no shortage of deceivers willing to take advantage. These opportunities will expand before they decline, for reasons to which we now will turn. They include the growing influence of lie-tolerant mentors such as therapists, lawyers, and politicians; postmodern intellectual trends in higher education; the increased emphasis on "storytelling" throughout society; the impact of electronic media, with their indifference to veracity; baby-boomer alt.ethics; and the growing amount of time we spend interacting anonymously online.

II

Enabling Dishonesty

Eight

Mentors and Role Models

Let us begin by committing ourselves to the truth, to see it like it is and to tell it like it is, to find the truth, to speak the truth and live with the truth. That's what we'll do.

–RICHARD NIXON

Without chiefs, shamans, neighbors, or extended families to give us reliable ethical guidelines, we seek guidance from therapists, lawyers, and politicians. Members of these professions have become moral mentors for a brave new ethical world. Such mentors model post-truthful behavior. They are primary practitioners of alt.ethics. In their line of work a certain amount of truth trimming is tolerated, even expected. That has been the case as long as there have been those who counseled patients, practiced law, or ran for office. We didn't use to consider them ethical archetypes, however. As their numbers and prominence grow, we do.

Therapists

On *Dr. Laura*, *The Oprah Winfrey Show*, and the Lifetime channel, therapists offer the type of guidance we used to get from parents and pastors. Dilemmas that were once assessed on moral grounds now get evaluated therapeutically. Ethical issues become ones of emotional health. Bishop Sheen gives way to John Gray, Norman Vincent Peale to Joyce Brothers.

Right and wrong were important concepts in early self-help psychology (which dates back to the mid-nineteenth century). Not until it cross-pollinated with Freudian therapy did this type of counsel adopt a nonjudgmental posture in which truth telling was considered optional. That perspective really took off after health plans began to pay for treatment of emotional disorders, therapists became television stars, and support groups grew ubiquitous.

Psychotherapy in its various manifestations has become our secular religion. Unlike an actual religion, however, many forms of therapy are at best neutral on the issue of dishonesty, at worst subtly encouraging of personal mythmaking. Lying is considered symptomatic of any number of emotional disorders (narcissism, hysterical personality, antisocial personality, psychopathic character, factitious disorder, mythomania, and Munchausen syndrome, to name just a few). In all such cases, however, dishonesty is treated as part of some broader pathology, not a cause for concern in itself. Nor is factual accuracy germane to counseling, necessarily. "The analyst is professionally disinterested in the difference between truth and lies," concluded Cambridge University historian John Forrester, the author of several books about psychoanalysis. A friend of mine discovered this when, in the midst of divorce proceedings, he suggested that his wife's therapist check out whether some of the things she'd said about him were accurate. The therapist responded that determining factual accuracy was not part of his job.

Few of his colleagues would have disagreed. "Most psychotherapists accept, without much question, the veracity of their patients' statements," wrote psychiatrist Charles Ford in *Lies! Lies! Lies!* "Doing so permits greater empathy, and the exact truth is often not regarded as important as what the patient feels at the moment." For the sake of a candid therapeutic hour, therapists take the moral onus off dishonesty. From their perspective, lies are nothing to be ashamed of. To the contrary, they are extremely useful therapeutic tools. Lies told by patients can be high-beam headlights leading therapists toward dark areas of denial, shame, and self-hatred. Charles Ford compared lies to dreams: data that reveal as much as they conceal. "Secrets, self-deception, and lies are facts of life," concluded Ford, "and, accordingly, must be the stuff of which psychotherapy is made."

One of the main challenges for early psychiatrists was breaking through the moral inhibitions of patients so they could free-associate without regard to veracity. Even when patients dissembled, observed psychoanalyst Jacques Lacan, they were operating in the realm of truth. This is not simply doublethink. To a therapist, lies can expose a patient's actual feelings better than statements which are factually accurate. Imagine a patient on the couch saying, "When I was carving a leg of lamb the other night my husband walked into the kitchen and I nearly carved his neck." That statement gives her therapist a better picture of his patient's state of mind than if she'd told him what really happened: "When I was carving a leg of lamb the other night my husband walked into the kitchen and I said, 'Hello, dear. How was your day?'"

Psychiatrists have always been as interested in the fantasy life of their patients as in their actual lives. Freudians put lying in the same category as slips of the tongue: an invaluable indicator of what's actually going on inside a patient. Analytically speaking, whether a given statement is true or false is irrelevant. According to psychiatrist Arnold Goldberg, dishonesty and honesty alike can characterize healthy or unhealthy behavior, depending on the circumstances. In Goldberg's opinion, "there is no particular biological or psychological reason to tell the truth, and a supposedly healthy superego allows a variety of deceptions, concealments, and white lies." An overemphasis on the morality of truth telling is "simplistic," Goldberg feels. Even a grandiose pseudologue, he writes, must be evaluated carefully to see if he is a compulsive liar or simply "someone for whom truth is temporarily unavailable."

In recent years, many therapists have concluded that their job is to help patients develop what they call "useful myths." Practitioners of narrative therapy encourage "reframing" or "reauthoring" one's life stories in more positive lights. Since objective reality is a mirage, these therapists advise clients, and memory is unreliable, "truth" is open to interpretation—and reinterpretation—with a counselor's help. "As if" is a big concept in this neck of the woods—behaving *as if* you were the person you'd like to be. Conventional notions of honesty and dishonesty don't apply. "I think the key distinction between this 'as if' talk and a lie is the person's intention," one advocate of this approach told author Gini Graham Scott. "If he is presenting himself in a certain way to cover up something or mislead somebody in some way, then that would be called a lie. But if a person is doing it for himself, such as to improve himself, by saying 'I'm very successful,' or 'My book is doing fantastically well,' I don't think they're lying. Rather, they're living in expectation—which is fine."

This concept is not as modern as it sounds. German philosopher Hans Vaihinger published a book in 1911 called *The Philosophy of "As If."* Vaihinger's book advocated creating myths about oneself, then acting as if they were true. One devotee of his philosophy was psychotherapist Bruno Bettelheim, who wrote about "the need and usefulness of acting on the basis of fictions that are known to be false." As we've seen, Bettelheim was true to this creed, fictionalizing his own credentials and professional experience, among other things. When biographer Richard Pollak called Bettelheim's record of deceit to the attention of his professional colleagues, many chuckled in essence and said, Oh yes, Bruno was quite the fabulist. We knew that all along. What's your point?

However useful it may be to blur the line between truth and lies during therapy, what happens when this accepting attitude ripples out? Tolerance of lying may be a sound counseling concept, but is it suited to society as a whole? Not questioning a client's honesty during a therapy session builds trust. Outside the therapist's office it does just the opposite. When we humor someone we think is lying, there is little basis for a genuine relationship. In a lasting relationship, actual honesty is as important as emotional honesty, if not more so. For those with longer-term commitments than therapist and patient, issues of trust matter more than ones of mental health. Even the deception-tolerant Sigmund Freud expelled Dr. Wilhelm Stekel from his inner circle because, as he wrote Stekel, "you had deceived me on a certain occasion in the most heinous manner." This is not necessarily inconsistent. I'm sure that if pressed on the point, Freud would have said that putting up with lies in a therapeutic relationship was not the same thing as putting up with them in a personal relationship, and he'd have been right.

Few therapists would argue that what works when counseling patients applies elsewhere, willy-nilly. But it's a hard conclusion to avoid. One reason we've lost our way in the ethical woods is that so many of us have adopted a therapeutic posture in which no one is held accountable for dishonesty, or much of anything. At best a nonjudgmental attitude toward lying promotes candor. At worst it becomes a free pass to deceive, guilt-free, with little sense of shame or embarrassment.

One setting where therapists have found a sympathetic audience for their ambiguous attitudes toward honesty is courts of law.

When testifying as expert witnesses, they sometimes explain the psychological roots of deceitful behavior by defendants. Judges and lawyers can be quite receptive to arguments based on the ambiguity of truth. They rely on that concept a lot themselves.

Lawyers

A Florida prosecutor once argued in one courtroom that a pair of teenagers had killed their father, and in another that a family friend was the actual killer. From a strictly legal perspective this was not inconsistent, but it certainly put a spotlight on the contrast between concepts of truthfulness within courts of law and those without.

If we wonder why notions of truth and falsehood have become more vague, more relative, more flexible, our legal system is an important influence to consider. For those who are not familiar with this system, taking part in a legal proceeding can be ethically breathtaking. At the heart of this shock is the realization that even though establishing truth and exposing lies is the stated goal, it is not only one. Nor are "truth" and "lies" understood to mean in court what they do on the street. From a legal standpoint, any lie that isn't told under oath is no lie at all. Legally speaking, truth is what evidence and testimony corroborate. If enough evidence and witnesses can prove that water is dry and dust wet, then legally speaking, dust is wet and water dry.

For all practical purposes, truth inside a courtroom consists of whatever a judge or jury decides is true. Whether legally established truths are factually accurate is beside the point. As any lawyer will tell you, legal truths do not always correspond to actual truths. There is even a concept in American jurisprudence called "legal fiction," which, according to *Black's Law Dictionary*, refers to "an assumption that something is true even though it may be untrue." In their own way, lawyers are no less indifferent than thera-pists to literal truth. Bill Clinton once observed that in their con-flicting testimony before the Senate, neither Anita Hill nor Clarence Thomas was a liar; each simply told the truth as he or she saw it. What a layperson might consider a lie, said Clinton, a lawyer such as he might see as simply an "alternative version of reality." Clinton's two terms as president were like an eight-year seminar in the difference between truthfulness as most people understand that term and truthfulness as a legal concept. The cul-mination was Clinton's assertion that his testimony denying he'd harassed Paula Jones was "legally accurate."

It is this type of comment that makes so many nonlawyers think that lawyers inhabit their own ethical universe. As one character in Linda Barnes's novel *Big Dig* says of another, "I wasn't sure about his honesty, but what the hell, he was a lawyer so it didn't count." This is a bum rap. It's not as though lawyers are born with defective honesty genes. Rather, they take part in a system of law that virtu-ally requires its participants to work at ethical cross-purposes. On the one hand, they are expected to engage in a search for truth, and not suborn perjury. At the same time, they must vigorously ad-vocate the case of clients even when this means manipulating facts, if not actually condoning lies. That forces lawyers to operate on a two-tier ethical system (assuming they are personally honest): one of their own, and a second on behalf of clients.

Early in his legal career, the dean of Yale's law school gave a speech in which he referred to "the indifference to truth that all advocacy entails." His major concern, said Anthony Kronman, was the destructive effect this indifference could have over time on the character of those who practice law. Law teachers needed to discuss this issue in their classrooms, Kronman thought, "because the craft they teach not only tolerates an indifference to truth but actively encourages it." Although he later modified this position, Kronman remained concerned about litigation techniques that employed "every device short of an outright lie, every form of dissembling, of evasion, or stonewalling and the like which can conceivably be used to advance the client's interest, irrespective of whether it serves the broad cause of finding the truth."

In defense of their all-out advocacy lawyers are fond of quoting Lord Brougham, who said, when defending Queen Caroline nearly two centuries ago:

> An advocate, in the discharge of his duty, knows but one person in all the world, and that person is his client. To save that client by all means and expedients, and at all hazards and costs to other persons, and, amongst them, to himself, is his first and only duty; and in performing this duty he must not regard the alarm, the torments, the destruction which he may bring upon others.

Few contemporary lawyers would disagree. A bedrock principle of legal counsel is that their job is to represent clients, not to judge them. Judgment is the job of the court. In an adversarial system of justice, it could hardly be otherwise. Standards of professional conduct put loyalty and zeal on behalf of clients way ahead of determining the actual facts of a case. Even if the Supreme Court did once rule that "the basic purpose of a trial is the determination of the truth," practically speaking the goal of good counsel is to vanquish the opposition. Trials typically resemble a bare-knuckle brawl more than a law-school seminar. "Much too frequently," observed Detroit lawyer Lamont Buffington of those in his profession, "our valiant gladiator uses his weapons in the courtroom not primarily in the quest for truth, but rather in an attempt to win." In theory, the rough-and-tumble of adversarial contests is most likely to reveal truths. As Sissela Bok points out, however, this hypothesis has never been tested empirically. No controlled experiments have ever confirmed that truth is the product or even the byproduct of courtroom combat.

Even though he and his colleagues liked to proclaim that a clash of adversaries was the best way to determine truth, federal judge Marvin Frankel wondered if they weren't kidding themselves. Frankel thought that a "great release from ethical inhibitions" was inherent in the notion that lawyers are meant to advocate, not judge: "What will out, we sometimes tell ourselves and often tell others, is the truth. And, if worst comes to worst, in the end who really knows what is truth? . . . There is much in this of cant, hypocrisy, and convenient overlooking."

In a unique critique of the adversarial system of justice, Frankel wrote that it was a rare trial in which anyone involved wanted the whole truth to be revealed. What's worse, Frankel added, "many of the rules and devices of adversary litigation as we conduct it are not geared for, but are often aptly suited to defeat, the development of the truth. . . . The process often achieves truth only as a convenience, a byproduct, or an accidental approximation." Frankel pointed out that an adversarial approach characterized no other profession that was committed to seeking truth (e.g., science, history, journalism), and few other systems of justice. Nor is justice by joust the norm in most countries. True, that is partly because some have arbitrary and corrupt legal systems. But the courtrooms of other countries—in Europe especially—place a search for truth far ahead of the clash of adversaries. Unlike our judges, who are usually chosen from the ranks of combative trial lawyers, their magistrates are professionals who are schooled in impartiality. These judges have far more leeway to question witnesses directly in an effort to establish facts, not just act as a referee between sparring counsel.

As long as Americans put their lawyers to work in a system in which winning is everything, they can hardly expect them to be Augustinian avatars of truthfulness. Although officers of the court are not to break the law or countenance fraud, clever strategies to obscure facts are considered part of the legal game and perfectly appropriate. According to Marvin Frankel, the yarn swapping in his colleagues' lunchrooms usually featured wily barristers who won the day with crafty subversions of the truth. These stories were shared with chuckling admiration.

Few lawyers would consider such ethical permissiveness a license to lie, but fewer still would argue that clever dissembling, half-truths, cover-ups, and discrediting of opposition witnesses aren't important weapons in their arsenal. Trial lawyers who wouldn't dream of presenting false testimony on a client's behalf think nothing of debunking the testimony of an unfriendly witness who they know is credible. Their commitment to vigorous advocacy is not one to cause them a lost moment of ethical sleep. Volunteering information that could serve the truth but hurt your client could even be construed as legal malpractice. That's why, as Supreme Court justice John Marshall Harlan once observed, in the discharge of his duties a lawyer "of necessity may become an obstacle to truthfinding."

Veteran defense lawyer Gerry Spence once said that in his long career he'd never taken part in a trial that wasn't laced with false testimony. Too many featured manufactured evidence, disreputable expert testimony, and outright perjury in support of "narratives" being presented. Spence thought that "storytelling" was the modus operandi in criminal trials more than any quest for truth. The yarns spun during trials might be based loosely on facts, said Spence, but were usually closer to fiction.

This is one reason that legal dramas, real and imagined, have become such a popular entertainment. Such dramas are one among many ways in which the legal value system has seeped out of the halls of justice and into society as a whole. Like therapists, lawyers have gone from being a small band of professionals with their own esoteric values to a large group of oracles who have many public forums in which to propagate these values. As the ranks of lawyers grow, along with the volume of cases they adjudicate— some before television cameras—their impact on everyday behavior rises. Best-selling legal novels by John Grisham, Scott Turow, and Lisa Scottoline (to name just a few lawyer-authors) have spread their profession's values into the many households of those who read them. So have movies based on such novels. Courtroom dramas on television have done the same thing for a much larger audience. Honesty may be the best policy, but you wouldn't know it from watching these entertainments. As a commentator observed in the *Toronto Star*, lawyer-based television shows "reinforce the message that . . . sometimes it's necessary to bend or bury the truth to save an innocent client's skin. As spectators, we become mesmerized by the performances and numb to the lies."

Politicians

The fact that so many politicians are lawyers reinforces their natural tendency to nibble around the edges of truthfulness. No one doubts that in trying to be many things to many people politicians routinely blow smoke in our faces. Nor do we expect ethical purity from our leaders. (One reason we were always a little dubious about Jimmy Carter was his unlikely claim that he'd never tell us a lie.) In cases of national security we cut government officials a lot of slack and don't hold them morally accountable for manipulating the truth. This side of Kenneth Starr, few Americans expect candor from politicians about their sex lives. Everyone expects a politician to try to wiggle out of sexual and other tight spots by dissembling.

But many politicians' prevaricating goes far beyond understandable dissembling into a realm of make-believe that's harder to comprehend, much less condone. As we've seen, studies have confirmed that a knack for deception is common among leaders. This can lead those in public life to embrace a certain vagueness about the concept of truthfulness. In my own contact with political figure, I've been struck repeatedly by how casually they twist facts for their own convenience. As F. G. Bailey points out in *The Prevalence of Deceit*, among politicians "Will it fly?" is considered a much more pertinent question than "Is it true?" This suggests a mind-set in which one might as well lie as not.

During an aborted run for the presidency, Democratic senator Joseph Biden said he'd garnered academic distinctions in college, attended law school on a full academic scholarship, won an international moot-court competition, and finished in the top half of his law-school class. None of these claims were true. Republican congressman Darrell Issa, who later engineered the recall of California governor Gray Davis, inflated five years of army duty to nine on his campaign biography, and transformed six months of service in a bomb-disposal unit to membership in an elite security detail that helped guard President Nixon during a 1971 World Series game (one Nixon hadn't actually attended).

Quite a few politicians from both parties have been unmasked as phony veterans. They include Democrats such as Iowa senator

Tom Harkin, who said he'd flown airplanes in Vietnam when he hadn't, and Republicans like State Representative Royall Switzler, who was a leading candidate for governor of Massachusetts until his claim to have been a Green Beret in Vietnam unraveled. Then-congressman Bruce Caputo, a onetime Republican candidate for the U.S. Senate from New York, was driven out of politics by the revelation that he hadn't served in Vietnam, or graduated from the Harvard Business School "with distinction," as he'd claimed. Al Gore, who did serve in Vietnam, later puffed his bio when he said he'd helped create the Strategic Petroleum Reserve (a process that began two years before Gore was elected to Congress); had been sung a union song as a lullaby when he was an infant (a song that wasn't written until Gore was twenty-seven); and that his mother-in-law paid three times the amount for the same arthritis medicine he bought for his dog (a figure Gore aides later admitted came from a congressional report, not his own experience).

Bill Clinton was a genius-grade practitioner of political flim-flam. This was not just about his history with marijuana, the military, and Monica. Clinton was also a petty prevaricator, as when he recalled his "vivid and painful memories of black churches being burned in my own state when I was a child." No record could be found of any black church being set ablaze in the state of Arkansas. The president's wife was apparently the more honest Clinton, but not upon closer scrutiny. Hillary Clinton may not have been a "congenital liar," as William Safire once charged, but like her husband she was prone to casual dissembling. After being introduced to Sir Edmund Hillary, Hillary told the mountain climber she was named after him. When Hillary Rodham was born in 1947, Sir Edmund was an obscure New Zealand beekeeper, six years away from becoming a household name for ascending Mount

Everest. Hillary Clinton subsequently talked of writing *It Takes a Village* longhand. In fact, this book was largely authored by an unacknowledged ghostwriter.

As we've seen, when it came to peddling blarney, Ronald Reagan was in a league of his own. "He could rearrange facts to make a good story better," former secretary of state George Shultz observed about Reagan. "Sometimes President Reagan simply did not seem to care that much about facts and details." The only problem was that when it came to more substantial matters, Reagan's ability to prevaricate did not cease. He fictionalized matters large and small with the aplomb of an experienced performer, then seemed surprised when his honesty was questioned. After it was shown irrefutably that, despite his denials, arms had been traded for the freedom of hostages in Iran, Reagan finally conceded the point, sort of. "I told the American people I did not trade arms for hostages," he admitted. "My heart and my best intentions still tell me that is true, but the facts and the evidence tell me it is not."

A propensity to dissemble characterizes politicians left, right, and center. This is more a personality trait than a political tendency. Former Nebraska senator Bob Kerrey thought the real source of political artifice was a craving to be liked. That and a hunger for attention. An uncommonly high proportion of narcissists can be found among those who run for office. (Theodore Roosevelt's daughter once said her father wanted to be the bride at every wedding, and the corpse at every funeral.) Indifference to truthfulness is a known narcissistic trait.

To politicians, most of their falsehoods are mere petty fibbery, lies of exuberance so insignificant that they hardly even qualify as lies. "Rhetorical excesses and leaps of faith," Al Gore called them. It's been suggested that Gore's well-known tendency to take liberties with facts was a result of growing up in a political family (his father was a longtime senator from Tennessee), where stretching the truth was not considered any great sin. Among themselves, politicians take a certain philosophical approach to matters of honesty. In their own minds this doesn't mean they lack this trait, simply that they define it differently than their average constituent does (alt.ethics again). By this ledger-book standard, if you tell the truth more often than not and are an upright sort of person, you're honest. Even straight-talking Harry Truman made a distinction between what he called "Political Truth" and "Real Truth." Real Truth, to Truman, included the admonition "A boy never lies to his mother." Political Truth, on the other hand, need not have any correlation with accuracy so long as the intentions of its disseminator were honorable, or at least not corrupt, and the statement was put across with enough conviction that it sounded true. One source of Truman's disdain for Adlai Stevenson was that Stevenson was such a bad dissembler. It was the contempt of a professional for an amateur.

During her many decades in the nation's capital, journalist Meg Greenfield saw the impulse to dissemble reach the point that politicians lost track of their genuine selves. The habit of saying one thing and thinking another was traditional among politicians, she conceded, as was the tendency to inflate their credentials. Some new factors made this practice ubiquitous, however. As Greenfield wrote in *Washington*, "for today's anxious, image-driven pol, there is no end to the subterfuge and hocus-pocus, no resting place, no designated, reachable destination, as there was for your basic impostor of yore." The wholesale self-invention of actual impostors, she thought, could hardly be as nerve-racking as "darting ceaselessly from identity to identity, political hairdo to political hairdo, reinvention to reinvention, as so many of today's public figures feel they must." In time, their real selves gave way to embellished versions. The result too often was that public figures ended up unsure of whom they thought they were supposed to be, "only that it is some unambiguously praiseworthy approximation of a human being that is pretty different from the one they really are."

A key source of this transformation is twenty-four-hour news cycles that put public figures always on call. The better looking and better spoken they are, the more frequently they're placed before cameras. With its penchant for politicians who perform well, TV gives the nod to those who are good at the deceptive arts. As a result, such politicians are a much bigger, more ubiquitous, and influential presence in our lives, not just on the Sunday news shows but 24/7 on cable news broadcasts, network talk shows, and even MTV.

When politicians double as celebrities we care less about their moral standards than their glamour quotient. A good head of hair can attract more votes than a sound set of ethics. (Quick: Who was the last bald president?) Winning smiles can impress us more than the truthfulness of words that emerge from those smiles. It is well known to those who study deception that the way we judge lies depends on who told them and how we feel about that person. In this sliding scale of judgment, the lies of liars we like are understandable. Those of liars we don't like are contemptible. The name Richard Nixon will go down in history as synonymous with loathsome falsehoods. Even his staunchest allies never claimed this man was appealing. Long after it was clear that honesty wasn't his strong suit, jaunty Bill Clinton remained far more popular than dour Bob Dole. We gave sunny Ronald Reagan one pass after another for making things up and passing them off as facts. The Gipper was just so gosh-darn *likable*.

The same thing is true of Arnold Schwarzenegger. Like Reagan, Schwarzenegger has a casual attitude toward truthfulness. Long before the bodybuilder-actor ran for governor of California, biographers discovered that much of what he said about himself didn't check out. His upbringing in Austria was middle-class, not poverty-stricken as he claimed. Schwarzenegger told conflicting stories about why he didn't attend his father's funeral, how he supported himself after arriving in America, whether he used drugs, and whether he participated in group sex. Even his official height—six feet two—was inflated by several inches (to the astonishment of smaller people who met the "big guy" eye to eye). When the many discrepancies in his background were made public, rather than contest them Schwarzenegger explained that most were simply concoctions he'd made up to promote his acting career. "Sell statements," Schwarzenegger called them, "a lot of outrageous things to get the headlines." Apparently this made sense to California's voters, who elected Arnold Schwarzenegger their governor by a substantial margin. After being elected, Schwarzenegger ignored his promise to investigate the many charges of sexual harassment leveled against him. His early success as governor and toothy charisma apparently made that unnecessary.

Politicians such as Schwarzenegger as well as lawyers and therapists as a group have not only become our moral role models. They are primary oracles of post-truthfulness. Are there counterweights, groups whose members are holding fast for high standards of honesty? How about colleges and universities? Can we count on those who teach and study in institutions of higher education to be stalwart defenders of truth telling? In a word: no.

Nine

It's Academic

The easiest rationalization for the refusal to seek the truth is the denial that truth exists.

—SIDNEY HOOK

One might think that those on campus hew to a higher standard of truthfulness than those off campus. Presumably a strong respect for truth is taught along with physics and philosophy. That isn't necessarily so. Few people outside the academy realize how far esteem for truthfulness has fallen within academic walls. Many who teach there consider tolerance for deception a sign of intellectual dexterity. Because this is where tomorrow's leaders are being incubated, it's important to evaluate the state of honesty in institutions of higher education, among students, faculty, and administrators alike.

On Campus

One campus after another has been rocked by classroom cheating scandals. That shouldn't surprise us by now, but it does anyway. Aren't those who are being highly educated not just our best and brightest but our most ethical and honorable? Apparently not.

Even at MIT, 80 percent of the students polled in a survey said they'd cheated at least once during their college career. A similar survey found that 75 percent of Duke students who were queried admitted to cheating. Twenty percent of first-year students at the University of Toronto falsified their first-term grades to get summer jobs. In a broader sampling of college students, 95 percent said they would lie to get a job. Forty-one percent admitted that they already had.

Two cheeky midwestern professors once compared the stated ethics of students enrolled in eleven MBA programs (including Harvard's) with convicted felons at three prisons. To the professors' surprise, there was little difference between the two groups. In some cases the inmates' declared ethics were actually higher. This paralleled Bella DePaulo's finding that University of Virginia students lied twice as often as residents of Charlottesville, who averaged one lie a day compared to two for the students. UVA students told lies in one out of every three interactions, on average, townspeople in one out of five. Though she couldn't explain the discrepancy, DePaulo declared herself "intrigued by the fact that by every measure of rate of lying, the community members seemed to lie less often than the college students."

It is true that students are a young cohort in a state of transition who have less to lose by being dishonest. But other factors come into play as well. A greater facility with words can facilitate lying among the highly educated. "Education gives some people the vocabulary and confidence to deceive," Bella DePaulo observed. (This suggests that the better educated we become as a people, the more lies we'll be able to tell.) DePaulo has also found that those telling lies are less likely than others to refer to themselves, but more likely to use the passive voice. ("Mistakes were made.") Such techniques characterize most academic discourse. This hardly means that academics are disposed by nature to be deceitful, but their preferred way of expressing themselves makes this easier when they choose to do so.

And some do so choose. A Northern Arizona University instructor was brought up short by the outcome when graduate students in a course on research methods debated this topic: "Resolved: We should lie with research." Those arguing for the affirmative won the debate handily. Key points made by these aspiring professors included the following: all quantitative research is more or less a lie anyway, its results a product of biases and predetermined conclusions; since other researchers lie, you must too, in self-defense; and, as their teacher reported, "It helps your career and there's no downside. It's almost impossible to get caught. And if you do get caught you can bog it down in nitpicky debate and avoid punishment. No one uses findings for any practical purpose so it's a victimless crime."

Anyone who has spent time at an institution of higher education is aware that the ethical standards of those who work there are, to say the least, variable. Ethics on college campuses may be somewhat better than those in the private sector, but they're not nearly as much better as higher educators themselves might like to believe. Anthropologist F. G. Bailey thought that many of his faculty colleagues, especially those who become administrators, could benefit from the example of indigenous peoples who at least make no bones about their love of clever deception. "The academic arena, too, is populated by deceivers," observed Bailey in *The Prevalence of Deceit*, "whether sporty or malicious or obsessed with triviality, public-spirited gamesters enjoying their politics." What's worse, he added, they were prone to "practice deceit while being enthusiasts for truth."

Although I know of no actual research on the ethics of faculty or administrators, anecdotally we have plenty of evidence that honesty isn't all it might be among those employed by institutions of higher education. Without even considering the moral fog surrounding intercollegiate athletics, there is no shortage of such evidence. In the cutthroat world of college rankings, those who do the ranking are routinely supplied with dubious data by those being ranked. The extent to which senior faculty take credit for the work of junior colleagues has long been a scandal. In other cases ostensibly objective scholars have been found so beholden to businesses that underwrite their work, and sometimes actually *write* their work, as to question its intellectual integrity. Even worse are the many cases in which physical and social scientists alike have manipulated or falsified data to achieve desired results. This is a bipartisan affair. Scientists at a Berkeley lab altered data to reinforce their case that electronic waves cause cancer. A physicist at MIT has accused colleagues there of manipulating data on behalf of an antimissile defense system. (His charges are being investigated.) During his time in the White House, Bill Clinton relied on a figure he got from a college professor who told him that eighty thousand lobbyists worked in Washington. This professor later admitted that amount came off the top of his head. (The real figure is perhaps 10 percent of his top-of-head one.) Then there was the case of Emory professor Michael Bellesiles, whose book *Arming America* caused a stir by challenging the notion that most early American settlers owned guns. *Arming America* won the Bancroft Prize as that year's best work of history. Its author turned out to be as rigorous a scholar as Rush Limbaugh. Much of his book was based on spurious documentation. (To their credit, Bellesiles's historian colleagues eventually investigated and discredited his work. He resigned from Emory.)

Post-truthfulness in the academy isn't just a matter of sloppy scholarship based on dubious data. Researchers in the social sciences have come under fire for deceiving subjects even when this wasn't really necessary. Even those who study deception routinely mislead those they study. Among the many research studies I reviewed on this topic, phrases such as these were common: "Ss [subjects] were given false feedback," "Subjects were led to believe," and "The explanation . . . was the beginning of a cover story designed so that the subject would not be aware that the emphasis of the experiment was on lying." When he studied lying among college students, Robert Feldman did not tell them that their honesty was being assessed in ten-minute exchanges, nor that these exchanges were being taped. "That is a lie of omission," the University of Massachusetts psychologist later conceded, "and there is an irony here, in that while studying lying, we ourselves were somewhat deceptive."

Imposeurs can be found on college campuses. As we've noted, any number of college professors have pretended to be Vietnam veterans. Others have padded their résumés, falsified their degrees, or altered key elements of their background. Following his appointment as poet laureate of California, Quincy Troupe, a faculty member at the University of California at San Diego, acknowledged that he hadn't actually received the undergraduate degree from Grambling College that was listed on his résumés. Yet Troupe was not fired by UCSD, and his resignation was only accepted by the university in response to a public uproar about this deception, and after the poet further revealed that he'd attended Grambling for less than a semester. (Troupe had already been relieved of his laureate duties by the California state senate.)

When confronted with evidence of ethical lapses by one of their own, members of the academy generally react like members of any other organization: they pooh-pooh the revelations, rationalize, cover up, circle the wagons, and rage at anyone who dares to question their integrity. It was only after the press outcry that Joseph Ellis was chastised by Mount Holyoke's president for fabricating his background, then suspended for a year. At first that president and Ellis's colleagues seemed to have trouble understanding what all the fuss was about, and why the press was blowing such a petty matter all out of proportion. Teaching is theater, observed Mount Holyoke's dean of faculty, and Joe Ellis was a great actor. Philosopher David Nyberg, an adjunct professor at the State University of New York at Buffalo, speculated that making up so much about himself might simply have been Ellis's way of engaging with his students. "I think possibly this story of his could be conceived of as a successful narrative means for conveying some truth about history," said Nyberg on NPR's *Talk of the Nation*. "Truth about self is not the same thing as truth about history, and if it's a means that works, he's been a good teacher." In his own defense of Ellis, author Edmund Morris suggested that by dramatizing his personal history the historian may simply have been doing his best to reach a generation of students "rendered comatose by MTV." This was insulting to members of that generation, not only to their integrity and intellectual aptitude but to their capacity to hear the truth, no matter how unexciting. As a recent history graduate of Vassar wrote the *New York Times* in response to Morris's disparaging observation, "Whatever my generation's failings might be, we are not so unteachable that only lies can catch our attention."

Despite their disdain for members of the press, academics might consider what they could learn from those who report the news. I have worked both in institutions of higher education and in newsrooms, and found myself held to higher standards of verification in the latter. (As we'll see in the next chapter, this hardly means that journalists are paragons of virtue, just relatively so in this case.)

Footnoting respectable sources and adhering to acceptable intellectual positions mattered more among academics. Reporters are also more likely to scrutinize the veracity of each other's work. Faculty members scrutinize each other's work too but focus more on methodology, whose work has been cited, and where authors have deviated from the academic norm. When they uncover fabricators and plagiarists in their ranks, members of the press investigate such transgressions, publicize the results, and fire the culprits. This rarely happens in the academy. Quite the contrary. Far from firing them, academics defend confabulators with "What is truth?" apologias and "larger truths" gambits.

Larger Truths

Late in his career, Edward Said, a Columbia University professor and onetime president of the Modern Language Association, was found to have embellished his own background to bring it more in line with the Palestinian struggle he championed. Said claimed to have spent his first twelve years in a Jerusalem home from which he and his family were expelled by Jews in late 1947, along with hundreds of thousands of other Palestinian refugees. A *Commentary* article based on three years of research by Israeli-American lawyer Justus Reid Weiner discovered that Said's wealthy parents never owned a home in Jerusalem. Although Said was born in that city, he'd actually been raised in Cairo. Nonetheless, Said's colleagues in and out of the academy defended his honesty. One, Hanan Ashrawi, said that all Said had done was "compress all his unique gifts in the form of a personal narrative as living testimony of the essence of his Palestinianhood." Ashrawi thought that questions raised about the accuracy of Said's narrative consisted of "vicious attacks of petty minds." Nor did Columbia University see any reason to question the veracity of their faculty member.

This episode followed an earlier one involving Nobel laureate Rigoberta Menchú. When ethnographer David Stoll discovered that Menchú had fabricated key elements of her autobiography (as she later admitted), sympathetic members of the academy rushed to her defense. Their response was revealing more for what it said about academic attitudes toward truthfulness than about the Guatemalan activist herself. Her defenders might have called Menchú's transgression an unfortunate blemish on an admirable record. That wasn't enough, however. Many said they considered Menchú's book true in spirit, if not in fact, and therefore honest. True or false, such faculty members thought, her fanciful autobiography improved our understanding of oppression. That being the case, who were we to call it dishonest? When it came to Menchú's book, perhaps literal truth mattered less than larger truth, its defenders argued, since it aroused greater sympathy for social change among readers. Some charged that saying the book's author had doctored her data was tantamount to denying that the terrible brutality she portrayed had ever occurred in Guatemala. David Stoll himself was reviled as a defender of white privilege and an apologist for tyrants. A University of Pittsburgh professor said that the questions Stoll raised about "verifiability" were less important than his position on the question of "armed struggle." So what if Stoll had proven that key elements of Menchú's autobiography didn't actually happen? To his detractors, this characterized a narrow, overly literal, mean-spirited frame of mind. As the chair of Wellesley's Spanish Department told a reporter, about requiring students to read Menchú's memoir, "Whether her book is true or not, I don't care."

Pomo Profs

This professor was not just being fey. There is a broader intellectual backdrop to such apparently flippant remarks. That backdrop is broadly called *postmodernism*. To devout postmodernists, there is no such thing as literal truth, only what society labels *truth*. That is why they call concepts of truth *social constructs*, ones that vary from society to society, group to group, and individual to individual. Just as those raised in Christian surroundings may believe it is true that Jesus is the son of God, those raised in Muslim societies may believe just as fervently that Muhammad was God's prophet on earth. To a postmodernist, such conflicting truths are little different than truths in conflict on political issues, and on whether whether Rigoberta Menchú was honest. Who's to say?

What's more, they point out, traditional notions of truth have been used to justify oppression. At an extreme, Nazi convictions of Aryan superiority were used to justify genocide. So were Marxist "scientific" certitudes about class struggle. On a smaller scale, Dick Cheney's truth that our energy problems could be significantly alleviated by drilling the Alaskan tundra also illustrates how variable and subjective concepts of truth can be. Those who point this out feel it is their duty to undermine, or "deconstruct," the very notion of objective truth as a prop for privilege. An anthology assigned to my son in college, provocatively titled *The Production of Reality*, gave a forum to those who take this position. As the authors of one its essays argued, "We believe that the idea that there is absolute objective truth is not only mistaken but socially and politically dangerous."

It is undeniable that terrible misdeeds have been perpetrated in the name of truth. It is also the case that what is considered true can vary from one context to another. But that doesn't mean abandoning this concept will produce greater social justice. If this sounds like a critique of left activism, that is only because such activism dominates the political atmosphere on so many campuses. I hardly believe conservatives are more honest as a group, on campus or off. Post-truthfulness is a bipartisan affair. Conservatives were outraged by Bill Clinton's petty lies. As for those told by Ronald Reagan, well, so what if the Gipper did rail against virtually nonexistent "welfare queens" and make up parts of his autobiography? Like defenders of Rigoberta Menchú, Reagan's admirers dismissed such concerns as nitpicking. From this perspective, factual truth must give way to "larger truths." In their own minds those searching for larger truths have not turned their backs on honesty. Rather, they're pursuing something bigger, a higher level of honesty, one that may be reached by telling lies.

Totalitarians of every stripe are very receptive to this notion. They agree that the concept of objective truth is too meager, too rigid, to accommodate the grandeur of their vision. "If relativism signifies contempt for fixed categories and men who claim to be the bearers of an objective, immortal truth," wrote Benito Mussolini in the early 1920s, "then there is nothing more relativistic than Fascist attitudes and activity." As we discovered with Fascist and Communist leaders alike, those who pursue their own brand of honesty this way can put the rest of us in terrible jeopardy. Mussolini's ethical counterparts in the Soviet Union considered immutable truth to be a tool of oppression. Lenin called it "a petit bourgeois prejudice." The Communists' thoroughly dishonest house organ was called *Pravda* ("Truth"). George Orwell warned of this danger in his novel *1984*, with its ironically named Ministry of Truth, and in his essay "Politics and the English Language," which argues that to oppress others one must first degrade words such as *truth* on behalf of some greater good.

The larger-truth gambit has been around for centuries in one form or another, and has enough appeal that it will probably be around for centuries to come. But ratifying this notion rather than redoubling our efforts to be fair and objective and to determine factual truth in matters of dispute opens the floodgates to arbitrary power contests. It's my narrative against your narrative and may the best narrator win. As Daniel Farber and Suzanna Sherry ask rhetorically in their book *Beyond All Reason*, if facts are social constructs and truth is only relative, what distinguishes the "narrative" of a Holocaust denier from that of a Holocaust survivor? After all, each has his or her own version of the truth. This is the type of ethical absurdity that can result from an excess of relativism.

There are not only Holocaust deniers but Holocaust pretenders. In one case, a book called *Fragments* recorded the experiences of a Jewish Holocaust survivor from Latvia named Binjamin Wilkomirski. Wilkomirski wrote in horrifying detail about his childhood in a concentration camp. *Fragments* won many awards and widespread acclaim. Then hard-to-verify elements of Wilkomirski's memoir came under scrutiny. In his book *A Life in Pieces*, Blake Eskin assembled compelling evidence that *Fragments* was largely apocryphal. A DNA test conducted by Zurich's district attorney confirmed that "Wilkomirski" was not even Jewish. The author of *Fragments* turned out to be a Swiss gentile named Bruno Doesseker. This hoax was an insult to genuine Holocaust survivors. Not everyone saw it that way, however. When Doesseker's ruse was revealed, some of those who had been involved with the impostor refused to condemn him, or any other Holocaust pretender (of whom there are several). One moderator of a Holocaust forum defended a fanciful account of another such poseur as "emotionally honest even if it was based on a lie."

The idea that lying can be a form of honesty is somewhere between jaded and totalitarian. It begs the more important question: Who distinguishes benign lies from toxic ones? To postmodernists, that's a no-brainer. They're available for hire and up to the job. I think this is what they imply when referring to the need for "careful reading" or "close analysis" of texts (by them, of course). Like the medieval clergy, those who can analyze texts control the ethical action.

Like the clergy too, they use moral agility to defend their own. When it turned out that Yale's Paul de Man had written for a pro-Nazi newspaper in his native Belgium, then lied about his background after coming to America, academic colleagues came up with some impressive rationales for de Man's dishonesty. Most were simply variations on What is truth, anyway? Others were more creative, arguing that the collaborationist articles de Man wrote in Nazi-occupied Brussels were actually clever deconstructions of fascism. Only a few of his colleagues conceded that this man was a bald-faced liar whose reputation had been disgraced, if not his very ideas.

De Man's ideas were instrumental in creating a post-truthful intellectual atmosphere. In retrospect they were remarkably self-serving. "Considerations of the actual and historical existence of writers are a waste of time," de Man wrote. And: "It is always possible to face up to any experience (to excuse any guilt), because the experience always exists simultaneously as fictional discourse and as empirical event and it is never possible to decide which one of the two possibilities is the right one. The indecision makes it possible to excuse the bleakest of crimes because, as a fiction, it escapes from the constraints of guilt and innocence." In plain English that means any experience (such as de Man's own) exists both as it actually happened and as a fictionalized version in our minds. Neither version is more valid than the other. Once fictionalized, personal histories are exempted from being judged right or wrong. Thus, if Paul de Man wished to reinvent himself as a tolerant ethical humanist and faithful family man rather than a scofflaw and bigamist who once proposed solving Europe's "Jewish problem" by creating a colony for Jews outside Europe, who was to say which version of himself was more valid? As David Lehman pointed out in *Signs of the Times*, his perceptive recounting of the de Man episode, such an approach could be used "to explain away inconvenient facts and turn an unfortunate truth on its head."

Heirs of Protagoras

When I attended college during the 1960s, existentialism was all the rage. Its core concept was that actions mattered more than convictions, and that *authenticity* was more important than literal honesty. This attitude segued easily into the postmodern notion that truth is a social construct, with a New Age codicil that useful myths are more meaningful than barren truths. Even as the need for transparency gained traction in business and government, on campus it became fashionable for obscurity, duplicity, and outright fabrication to be considered acceptable. In this intellectual climate, dissembling was not just condoned but virtually celebrated. Jeremy Campbell exaggerated only slightly when he observed that to a postmodernist, being overly concerned with telling the truth "is a sign of depleted resources, a psychological disorder, a character defect, a kind of linguistic anorexia. Without at least the capacity to lie, a person is not fully human and may even require professional help."

Over and over again I read pronouncements by those who imagine they're the first ones to question the notion of immutable truth. "Oh my God," they seem to say. "Insight! Insight! Truth is relative. It's personal. It's subjective. There's no universal truth, only what's true for you or me!" Well, yes. This revelation is as ancient as sophistry, as modern as Hobbesianism. Protagoras thought that anything "is to me such as it appears to me, and is to you such as it appears to you." Several centuries later, Hobbes held that "True or False are attributes of Speech, not of Things."

No matter how liberating, modern, or even postmodern it can feel to throw off the traces of truthfulness, this is simply part of an age-old effort to defend deception on philosophical grounds. In *The Liar's Tale*, Jeremy Campbell shows how many concerted efforts there have been over the millennia to debunk the concept of truth and rationalize the dissemination of falsehoods. During the later Middle Ages, for example, the search for literal truth gave way to a quest for higher meaning. Having concluded that they could not hope to understand what went on around them in any factual way, European Middle Agers turned instead to myths, parables, and allegories. The sacred was ascendant. Angels and miracles were more important than unattainable truths.

Several centuries later, many agree with this position completely. Others have gone further and observed that lies can portray truth better than truth itself. This point too is usually made in a spirit of "Look what I just discovered!" But it's an insight that has also been around for quite some time. A Dostoyevsky character observed that a bit of falsehood must be mixed into truth to make it plausible. Pablo Picasso later said, "Art is a lie that makes us realize truth." Or, as Mort Sahl used to say, his humor contained "all of the truth and some of the facts."

Like Mort Sahl, postmodernists see themselves as intellectual pranksters. Deception, they argue, can be a creative, playful act. If indigenous tribes can have tricksters, why not the academic tribe? One problem is that its members tend to be serious-minded, almost grim individuals. Their playfulness has a forced quality, rather like the cursing of Twain's wife (according to her husband, Mrs. Clemens got the lyrics right when she cursed but missed the melody). What we're left with is pranks without laughter; all trick, no treat.

Some relativists cite the pervasive deception in tribal cultures and tribe-unifying role of myths and legends to justify their own tolerant attitude toward dishonesty. But what works for small groups of isolated people who have a long history behind them and a future ahead does not travel well to lonely crowds whose trust must be based on truthfulness. Within a community, legends and myths contribute to cohesion. In the absence of communal ties, they can have the opposite effect: contributing to a context in which prevarication is facilitated and trust degraded because nobody's sure what's mythical and what isn't. This is tribalism without the tribe.

No matter how valid intellectually, the difficulty of identifying what is objectively true does not give us license to say as if true what we know to be false. Unfortunately, one conclusion leads too easily to the other. Once we decide that truth is a social construct, it follows easily that lying may not be so bad after all. If there's no such thing as truth, what constitutes a lie? And if we can't say what lying is, who's to say it's wrong? That thought process leads to related questions. If we can't distinguish truth from lies, isn't honesty overrated? Possibly. But what of deliberate falsehoods propagated consciously with intent to deceive? It's quite a stretch to say these aren't lies. Yet those who condone dishonesty in the name of larger truths essentially say just that.

The arguable intellectual point that truth is relative leads naturally to the harder-to-defend conclusion that lies are relative too. As sociologist J. A. Barnes suggests in *A Pack of Lies*, what others call lies a postmodernist might call "meaningful data in their own right." There are those who don't shy away from that position. A biographer of Liberace thought the pianist's blatant lying under oath in court (denying having engaged in homosexual activity) might signify a broader truth about the danger of openness in this area. According to one reviewer, this biography was at its best when explaining of Liberace's perjury, "a lie like that was a curious, backhanded way of telling some larger truth." This is how the distinction between honesty and dishonesty grows vague along with inhibitions about being deceptive. If lies are simply "meaningful data," if they can express "larger truths," who's to say they're wrong? If that's the case, why be honest? Why not be dishonest? What's the difference?

No matter how modern the garb, debunking truthfulness as a social construct is simply the latest version of Pontius Pilate's mocking question: "What is truth?" Asking what constitutes truth is an appropriate topic for intellectual inquiry, but it doesn't follow that the difficulty of identifying what is objectively true gives us license to tell each other lies. As Sissela Bok emphasized in *Lying*, when considering this topic, we must distinguish between the epistemological and the ethical. Pilate's question is better suited to philosophers and psychologists than to parents and politicians. "What is truth?" is related to, but not the same as, the more germane everyday question "Are you telling me the truth?" Even the most ardent relativist would not take kindly to being lied to by a significant other. If told "I wasn't telling the truth when I said I'd been faithful to you," would our playful postmodernist respond, "Well, what is truth, anyway?"

Interesting intellectual paradoxes provide shaky ethical guidelines. In everyday life, credibility trumps relativism. A professor who assigned Rigoberta Menchú's autobiography was dismayed to find that once her students realized this author's memoir was partly fiction, "it tended to discredit her." I would hope so. So would most people. From the perspective of this postmodern professor, however, these students had yet to learn their lessons about the relativity of accuracy and the "danger" of objective truth.

In its less zany forms, postmodernism is a useful intellectual exercise, a valuable counterweight to rigid moralism. But, as F. G. Bailey points out, rigidly relativistic ethical concepts lose utility upon "reentry" into the utilitarian world of reality testing. It is one thing to say that value judgments are social constructs, quite another to say blue is red when you know it's blue. One is a matter of perception, the other a matter of deception.

After a reporter asked the University of Chicago's Stanley Fish if 9/11 signified the end of postmodern relativism, the aging enfant terrible of this school of thought remarked, "It seemed bizarre that events so serious would be linked causally with a rarefied form of academic talk." Forsaking moral absolutes did not mean one couldn't act against evil on the basis of available information, Fish contended. He was right to challenge the simplistic notion that relativism precludes action against wrongdoers. But Fish and his crowd can't get off the hook so easily by claiming that their views are mere academic chitchat. Postmodern attitudes toward "truth" have leaped the walls of the academy and become a key source of our eroding commitment to truth telling.

Applied Postmodernism

Postmodernism has lost its cutting edge. This school of thought is no longer an intellectual tsunami crashing on academic shores. But the overall idea that truth is chimerical has seeped out from classrooms and faculty lounges. Ideas about truthfulness-as-social-construct have found forums to reach those who may not even have heard the term *postmodern*. In the comic strip *Funky Winkerbean*, for example, a group of murder suspects are assumed to be telling the truth about their innocence after they pass a lie-detector test. When challenged on this point, a police sergeant observes, "Well, who's to say what the exact nature of truth really is? And how do we know what's true for me is true for you as well?"

Even if such postmodern perspectives raise important philosophical questions about the nature of truth, what's relevant primarily to intellectual discourse doesn't always travel well into daily life. Unfortunately, that's exactly where it's gone. After actress Ann Heche broke up with comedienne Ellen DeGeneres and wrote a book about their relationship, DeGeneres said she didn't plan to read the book and didn't care what her ex-partner said. "Her truth is her truth," the comedienne explained. Accused Beltway sniper John Allen Muhammad defended himself in court by challenging the very notion of truth when it came to testimony. Did "the truth, the whole truth, and nothing but the truth" have any meaning at all? Muhammad asked.

In the past, academic intellectual fads were limited to a small cadre of professors and students. Today, most Americans have attended college or at least taken a course there. Better-looking professors show up regularly on television to make their various cases. Popular books and articles by faculty members have more readers than ever. Many of these missives endorse postmodern relativism. As a result, the value system of the academy has crept into more nooks and crannies of everyday life than ever before. One pollster asked a sample of Christian Americans whether they agreed with this statement: "There is no such thing as absolute truth; two people could define truth in totally conflicting ways but both still could be correct." Thirty-three percent agreed strongly with that statement, 40 percent somewhat; 10 percent disagreed somewhat, and 15 percent disagreed strongly.

Postmodern attitudes toward truth have also entered the courtroom. As we've seen, even in traditional approaches to the law, objective truth is an ambiguous concept, but at least one that's paid lip service. Now the concept of truth-seeking itself has been challenged by some legal scholars. With what would they like it to be replaced? "Storytelling." "Narratives." Once released from the constraints of proving accuracy of testimony, such legal scholars argue, trial participants would be free to recount their own versions of the truth. This grows out of the political position that socially constructed versions of "objective truth" invariably favor the powerful and should be replaced with narratives and stories. All of us, and the oppressed in particular, could then tell our tale, state our case, without getting bogged down in nitpicking about mere facts. This position is part of a broader emphasis on "narrative truth" that extends far beyond academic walls.

Ten

Narrative Truths, and Lies

There is a narrative truth in life that seems quite removed from logic,
science, and empirical demonstration. It is the truth of a "good story."
—DON MCADAMS

Sometimes life isn't as neat as the narratives we build.
—KATHERINE RAMSLAND

After resigning as secretary of labor to join the Brandeis University faculty, Robert Reich wrote a memoir called *Locked in
the Cabinet*. Reviews of Reich's lively look back at his four years in
Bill Clinton's cabinet were generally positive. Reviewers especially
liked the many vigorous exchanges Reich reported in which he
went mano a mano, barb to barb with Republican antagonists, usually coming out ahead. A few weeks after this book was published,
an enterprising *Slate* reporter named Jonathan Rauch examined
some of its content more closely. By comparing actual transcripts
and videotapes of public events with the way Reich described
them, Rauch determined that many of his accounts were at best
embellished, at worst cut from whole cloth. C-Span videotape
showed that a congressional hearing Reich depicted as raucous was
in fact sedate. It included none of the vitriolic debates recalled by

the author. A tedious exchange of policy views at another taped congressional hearing had been recast by Reich as a fiery show-down between a cruel committee chair and a valiant labor secretary holding firm in the witness seat. An all-male lunch meeting that he remembered as filled with calumny and cigar smoke turned out to be a low-key breakfast in a no-smoking room with lots of women present. Other reporters found apocrypha of their own in Reich's memoir. The general conclusion was that his memoir had more to do with mythmaking than reality. Robert Reich had cooked his book.

The author had no choice but to admit that there were frequent gaps between what had actually happened and the way he portrayed it. His explanation? He was not dishonest, Reich insisted. Quite the contrary: "I was absolutely true to my memory." Without admitting any wrongdoing, Reich revised the disputed material in subsequent editions. "Memory is fallible," he explained in a foreword. What the former labor secretary did not explain was why he hadn't checked the public record when writing his book, as reporters did after it was published. The best excuse Reich could offer was that *Locked in the Cabinet* was not meant to be journalism. It was a memoir. If not *the* truth, it was *his* truth.

Robert Reich was hardly alone in improving his life's record. Far from it. What he was engaged in is increasingly common among contemporary writers of nonfiction: sweetening their material—or even making it up—for the sake of a better narrative.

So what? some ask. Lighten up, they say. To them there's simply no issue of consequence here. Some writers feel they can be truthful only when they dispense with the need to be factual. "Absolute occurrence is irrelevant," wrote Tim O'Brien. "A thing may happen and be a total lie; another thing may not happen and be truer than the truth." Fair enough—for fiction (which O'Brien primarily writes). But this conviction has not limited itself to the world of fiction. Even when writing nonfiction, some believe, if readers can be engaged better with fantasy than fact, more's the better.

Narrative Truths

John Berendt's *Midnight in the Garden of Good and Evil, the* "nonfiction" best-seller of its era, was highly fictionalized. Berendt himself admitted this (after others pointed out his many departures from the factual record). One could argue that the author's imaginative recounting of a crime committed in Savannah, Georgia, was merely creative license. That's certainly how he saw it. After whistles were blown on the many liberties he took with facts, Berendt said he saw no harm in "rounding the corners to make a better narrative." While admitting that he'd embellished some elements of his book and made up others, Berendt got a bit testy with those who questioned the propriety of calling his book nonfiction. "It was entertainment, it was show biz," he told the *New York Times*. Berendt hastened to add that his book was 99 percent accurate. This was not a bad percentage, he thought. Anyway, Berendt added, "the truth that I was telling was the actual story, and I do not think that I distorted the truth by cutting these corners."

The borders between fiction and nonfiction have grown increasingly vague. This is far better known to those who publish books than to those who buy them. I once heard a literary agent say she put novels and memoirs in the same category. Her real preference was for works of "narrative nonfiction." When used this way, the term "narrative" refers to a vague not-quite-true, not-quite-false genre of writing. In book publishing, it's generally accepted that works of narrative nonfiction such as *Midnight in the Garden of Good and Evil* will include as many fictional elements as are necessary to sustain reader interest. From that perspective, larger truths and narrative drive can best be achieved by relinquishing an outdated obsession with accuracy. This isn't easy. "The Puritan concept lingers," explained Tristine Rainer in *Your Life as Story*, a popular primer on memoir writing, "echoing in our heads, warning us to demarcate fact from fiction. . . . Just as there are fundamentalists who still do not accept the theory of evolution and consider it dangerous, there are many people who still insist that autobiographic writing has to be verifiable fact . . . [But] New Autobiography, having moved into the literary arena of poetry and fiction, is now concerned with the larger truths of myth and story, which permit, and sometimes require, imaginative reshaping."

New Autobiography has many practitioners:

- While signing copies of *Angela's Ashes* in his hometown of Limerick, Ireland, Frank McCourt was approached by a boyhood friend who wondered why McCourt wrote that he had a sister when he didn't. "This was true," McCourt responded. "Somehow or other I invented a sister for him who had none."

- In his memoir *Widower's House*, John Bayley featured two women—an old family friend named Margot, "dark, ample and dynamic," and a young graduate student named Mella, "fair and slight"—who shared Bayley's grief and bed after the death of his wife, Iris Murdoch. Bayley subsequently admitted that both women were figments of his imagination. "I had no lovers," he told a *Sunday Times* reporter. "Just daydreams."

- University of Montana faculty member Judy Blunt wrote a memoir called *Breaking Clean* which got rave reviews and a Whiting Award for promising new authors. Blunt's book portrayed her early life on a ranch in Montana, tending to her husband, his father, and ranch hands. She yearned to write and bought herself a typewriter. But, in a dramatic scene noted by many reviewers, her husband's father—who was angry because she was late serving lunch to the hay crew—took a sledgehammer to Blunt's typewriter and "killed it." After this episode was mentioned in a news article, the author's former father-in-law said it never happened. Blunt then admitted that the real story was considerably less dramatic. What was the real story? "I don't want to go into it," she told a reporter.

This is the post-truth credo: creative manipulation and invention of facts can take us beyond the realm of mere accuracy into one of narrative truth. Embellished information can be true in spirit—truer than truth. Edmund Morris called *Dutch,* his biography of Ronald Reagan with its fictional narrator and fanciful events, "an advance in biographical honesty." The book's publisher said Morris's imagined episodes in the life of his subject "merely tell the truth in ways altogether new." This is intellectually fashionable doublethink. It leads to a kind of looking-glass morality in which clunky accuracy is considered a lower grade of truthfulness than lyrical apocrypha. From this Joseph Campbellian perspective, myths and legends can portray deeper truths than mere facts. It puts a New Age gloss on the old Bolshevik conviction that information can be altered for a greater good, and that rigid notions of accuracy belong in history's dustbin along with bustles, button-hooks, and bourgeois notions of morality. For those not in the know, however, it means they routinely read fictionalized text that is mislabeled "nonfiction."

Apparently this is true of writing by Vivian Gornick. Gornick's memoir, *Fierce Attachments,* is considered a classic. When it was published in 1987, the *New York Times* called *Fierce Attachments* a "fine and unflinchingly honest book." Gornick subsequently published a well-regarded guide to writing personal narratives. That was why, when the memoirist spoke at Goucher College a decade and a half after *Fierce Attachments* was published, listeners were startled to hear her admit that she'd invented parts of it. Not only that, Gornick added, some articles she'd written for the *Village Voice* included composite characters. Gornick seemed surprised by the incredulity that greeted these admissions, not only among members of her audience but among those who read news accounts of this talk or heard it discussed by book critic Maureen Corrigan on NPR's *Fresh Air*. Corrigan, who teaches literature at Georgetown University, noted how much she liked Vivian Gornick's writing. The professor routinely assigned the author's books to her students. That was why she'd been so startled to hear her admission of literary legerdemain. Corrigan said she still considered Gornick a fine writer, and would continue to read her books, but now with her guard up.

Gornick fired back. Memoirs were a form of literature, she said, and therefore exempt from journalistic conventions of accuracy. The problem didn't lie with her; it lay with ill-informed readers who couldn't grasp this fact. "Memoir writing," Gornick lamented, "is a genre still in need of an informed readership." The problem, in other words, lay with ignorant readers, not deceptive writers. Needless to say, Maureen Corrigan didn't agree. As she observed, "It adds insult to injury to be told by the autobiographer in question that in accepting the conventional autobiographical contract that the writer is indeed trying to write the truth, you as the reader are a dope."

New Journalists

Readers in ancient Greece had no expectation that writing of any kind would be factually accurate. Herodotus freely incorporated legends, hearsay, and imaginative reconstructions into his histories. Thucydides' more factual accounts of historical events included words he put in subjects' mouths. Centuries later, Daniel Defoe's famous "journal" of a plague year proved to a product of his imagination. Defoe, who was four years old at the time of the plague he wrote about, cobbled his book together from stories he'd heard, family lore, extensive reading, and inventive re-creation.

When reading the works of such protohistorians, readers took for granted that much was a product of the writer's imagination. Boundaries between fiction and nonfiction were vague to nonexistent. More recently, however, a clear distinction has been made between texts that are considered factually accurate and ones that aren't. When reading material labeled nonfiction, contemporary readers assume that it's factual insofar as the author could ascertain facts. Journalists in particular consider this a hard-won victory over the flamboyant subjectivity of newspapers in the past. Others mourn the development. Bruce Chatwin, whose travel books (*In Patagonia, The Songlines*) were quite imaginative, thought the distinction between fiction and nonfiction was "extremely arbitrary, and invented by publishers." Hunter Thompson concurred. " 'Fiction' and 'nonfiction' are nineteenth-century terms," said the gonzo journalist.

Thompson was part of a new school (actually a reversion to an old school) called "New Journalism." In theory, New Journalists such as him combined novelistic writing techniques with rigorous reporting to produce vivid works of nonfiction. Their debt to novel writing presumably was limited to plot devices such as scene setting, character development, and foreshadowing. As we were to discover, there was far more to the story.

The modern precedent for this approach can be found among midcentury *New Yorker* journalists such as Joseph Mitchell, Lillian

Ross, A. J. Leibling, and John Hersey, who wrote with fictionlike flair. Because their employer had such an impeccable reputation for verifying facts, this new writing method was taken as just that: a method, a style, not a challenge to veracity itself.

The *New Yorker*'s four-part excerpt of Truman Capote's *In Cold Blood* in 1965 was a watershed event in the history of so-called literary journalism. At the time it was serialized, then published as a book, Capote's depiction of a gruesome Kansas murder and its aftermath was lionized for combining novelistic panache with meticulous reporting. For decades to come, *In Cold Blood* set the standard for well-reported works of nonfiction written with dramatic flair. Even though it was filled with re-creations of scenes he hadn't witnessed, Capote called his book "immaculately factual." When researching *About Town*, however, his definitive history of the *New Yorker*, Ben Yagoda examined edited galley proofs of Capote's book. There he found repeated notations by *New Yorker* editor William Shawn questioning scenes that Capote had re-created. "How know? d[iscuss] w/author," Shawn wrote continually in the margins. Nonetheless, Capote's work ran largely as submitted. It turned out that the *New Yorker*'s editor was right to question his methodology. Since Capote died in 1984, a long list of *In Cold Blood*'s embellished elements, including an altogether apocryphal ending, has been compiled.

Capote wasn't the only *New Yorker* writer whose reporting was more imaginative than immaculate. One profile Joseph Mitchell wrote about a ninety-three-year-old man, complete with an artist's sketch of its subject, turned out to be based on several men. For his reports from Spain, *New Yorker* correspondent Alastair Reid cobbled characters together from bits and pieces of actual human beings he'd met, put words in their mouths, created events that happened to them, then sent the results to William Shawn as journalism. When this came to light, Shawn could not decide whether to defend Reid (which he did) or his magazine's commitment to accuracy (which he also did). The *New York Times* had no such ambivalence. In an editorial, they took the *New Yorker* to task for publishing the reports. "Quotes that weren't ever spoken, scenes that never existed, experiences that no one ever had—all are said to be permissible in journalism, provided they're composed by honest reporters to illustrate a deeper truth." Eventually, of course, the *Times* itself would have its own problems along that line.

The full flowering of novelized nonfiction took place in the mid-to-late 1960s, when New Journalists were in their heyday. Tom Wolfe, Gail Sheehy, Nik Cohn, and many lesser lights employed dramatic story lines, vivid characterization, and re-created dialogue to produce fly-on-the-wall reportage. New Journalism offered readers considerably less than met the eye, however. Sheehy published an electrifying article in *New York* magazine, later expanded into a book, about a prostitute named "Redpants" whom the writer ostensibly followed around the streets of Manhattan as she hustled customers at the Waldorf-Astoria and checked in with a pimp named "Sugarman." There were no such people. Unbeknownst to readers, Redpants and Sugarman were composites of prostitutes and pimps Sheehy said she'd interviewed. *New York* later ran another piece of Sheehy's about twenty-four hours in the life of a procurer named David. This article actually telescoped activities that took place over several days' time. Again, readers were left in the dark. While conceding that this might have been a mistake, *New York* editor Clay Felker denied that they were putting one over on readers. "We're just trying to put a greater degree of reality into it," Felker explained.

The king of New Journalism (and editor of an anthology on that subject) was, of course, Tom Wolfe. Among his colleagues,

Wolfe was far more respected as a writer than as a reporter. The multitude of inaccuracies in an article he wrote about the *New Yorker* were picked over ad nauseam. Less well known were similar problems in articles Wolfe wrote farther from the scrutiny of colleagues in New York. One of his early pieces profiled members of the "Pump House Gang," a group of scruffy teenage surfers who hung around an old pump house by a beach in La Jolla, California. Wolfe's memorable piece of writing portrayed them as an out-of-control group who lived communally, drank daily kegs of beer, mounted toga parties, and toured the countryside east of San Diego engaged in "destructos" (demolishing old barns). After this article was published, the surfers admitted they'd only torn down an occasional barn—at the request of their owners. They confessed to regularly putting on the man in a white suit, much as tribal members pull the legs of anthropologists who come to study them. One pump houser remembered Wolfe as "some weird old man hanging around who asked questions while we made up a lot of the answers." Other gang members told Jane Weisman Stein of the *San Diego Reader* that Wolfe's story reported events that never happened, in particular a toga party no one could remember. Although Wolfe said many of them lived in the garage where they did hang out a lot, most actually lived with their parents.

The epitome of New Journalism's slippery authenticity was Nik Cohn's 1976 *New York* cover story called "Tribal Rites of the New Saturday Night." This electrifying thirteen-page portrayal of disco dancers in Brooklyn included an assurance that "everything described in this article is factual and was either witnessed by me or told to me directly by the people involved." Cohn's article highlighted a charismatic dancer named "Vincent." John Travolta later played Vincent in an era-defining movie based on the article, *Saturday Night Fever*. That movie and the musical play it inspired made Nik Cohn a wealthy man. Two decades after he wrote his article, Cohn confessed that he'd made the whole thing up. There was no Vincent, just a guy he'd once glimpsed outside a Queens disco, and some blokes he knew back in Britain who provided the inspiration for his story's protagonist. Even the disclaimer (which Cohn says were words an editor put in his mouth) was jive. "There was no excuse for it," Cohn admitted in a commemorative essay written twenty years after his short story ran as an article. "At the time, if cornered, I would doubtless have produced some high-flown waffle about Alternative Realities, tried to argue that writing didn't have to be true to be, at some level, real. But of course, I would have been full of it. I knew the rules of magazine reporting, and I knew that I was breaking them. Bluntly put, I cheated."

Driven Narratives

The success of such literary inventions put pressure on all writers of nonfiction to follow suit. What's worse, their competition was not just the fictionalized work of colleagues such as Cohn but movies and television programs that put drama ahead of accuracy. Writers who tried to maintain standards of veracity were not playing on a level field with those who didn't. H. G. "Buzz" Bissinger, who was able to write the compelling book *Friday Night Lights* without resorting to invention, lamented to a *New York Times* reporter that "more and more, the public expects nonfiction books to be like this: to have that perfect, seamless storytelling quality. That's an impossibly high bar."

In Cold Blood set that bar. Truman Capote's approach to writing this book was imitated by many. Popular writers such as Joe McGinnis, Richard Ben Cramer, and Bob Woodward "got inside the head" of their subjects through re-creations that were no more verifiable than Capote's. Were they authentic? Only the authors knew for sure. Ultimately it came down to trusting their verisimilitude. Readers obviously did. They made best sellers of such authors' books. Colleagues were more dubious. In his review of Richard Ben Cramer's biography of Joe DiMaggio, Wilfrid Sheed said that the author's overly omniscient "you are there" style only served to remind readers that they, and the author, were *not* there, and didn't really know what was going on in the minds of those Ben Cramer portrayed. "By trying to go the truth one better," warned Sheed, "the famous 'New Journalism' continually undercuts it."

One might imagine that book editors would be staunch allies of those struggling to keep the "non" in nonfiction. Some are. Others aren't. Jug Burkett said that on two separate occasions he showed editors persuasive evidence that a book they were about to publish was based on apocryphal accounts of combat experience by phony veterans. Both books were published anyway, as "nonfiction." When significant questions were raised about the veracity of *Opening Skinner's Box*, Lauren Slater's book about famous psychological experiments, her publisher defended it as "first rate narrative." When Kate Millett took substantial liberties in writing about a 1965 murder in *The Basement*, such as putting feminist monologues in the mouth of the sixteen-year-old victim, the book's editor defended his author. "All she has done is take the facts and fill them out," he said, "—make them come alive by imagination. I think good nonfiction has always done that."

We've come a long way from the time when Frederick Exley called his 1968 classic *A Fans Notes* "a fictional memoir," because he'd altered some facts about his life. That gesture of literary integrity would seem absurd to practitioners of New Journalism's latest descendant: *creative nonfiction*. "Creative" needn't imply permission to make things up, but it's often taken that way. In her

Pulitzer Prize–winning *Pilgrim at Tinker's Creek*, Annie Dillard wrote a dramatic portrait of her tomcat, a fighter who jumped through Dillard's bedroom window in the middle of the night, reeking of piss and blood, landed on the author's bare body, then kneaded her chest with powerful paws, leaving Dillard's skin red with bloody paw prints. "I looked as though I had been painted with roses," she wrote. At a public program some years later, an audience member asked Dillard what had become of her tomcat. The author exchanged amused glances with some panel colleagues, then admitted with a giggle that she owned no tomcat and never had. One like it did belong to a friend. With this man's permission she'd borrowed the saga of his bloody-pawed cat and made it her own.

Like *Pilgrim at Tinker's Creek*, a remarkable number of noted works of nonfiction published over the past few decades apparently were novelized in whole or in part. They include *Sybil*, *Sleepers*, *Roots*, *The Amityville Horror*, *The Last Brother*, *Mutant Message Down Under*, and a host of lesser-known titles. Any number of manuscripts purchased as nonfiction by editors have had to be published as novels. When the author of the New Agey Indian fable *The Education of Little Tree* turned out to be a white supremacist and Ku Klux Klan member, his best seller was simply moved to bookstores' fiction sections, where it continued to sell well.

Such literary fabulists pass their inventions off as facts. Another group—Dave Eggers, Paul Theroux, Rick Moody—flaunt their confabulation and challenge readers to distinguish fact from fiction in their books. As Eggers writes in the preface to his memoir *A Heartbreaking Work of Staggering Genius*, "this is not, actually, a work of pure nonfiction. Many parts have been fictionalized in varying degrees, for various purposes." When it comes to daring readers to distinguish fact from fantasy, Lauren Slater is in a league of her own. In a memoir called *Lying*, Slater portrayed herself as an epileptic prone to frequent seizures and blackouts, and with a tendency to fantasize, or possibly not, since she lies a lot. In his introduction to *Lying*, a University of Southern California philosophy professor said the author led readers to "a new kind of Heideggerian truth, the truth of the liminal, the not-knowing, the truth of confusion, which, if we can only learn to tolerate, yields us greater wisdom in the long run than packaged and parceled facts." Slater herself made no such lofty claim. She did say that her mother— who variously claimed to be a Holocaust survivor, a hot-air balloonist, and friend of Golda Meir's—taught her that truth was malleable, and that what you wished you were was just as real as what you actually were.

"She was so full of denial," Slater wrote of her mother, that "she's not to be trusted. Then again, neither am I. And anyway, just because something has the feel of truth doesn't mean it fits the facts. Sometimes I don't even know why the facts should matter. I often disregard them, and even when I mean to get them right, I don't. I can't. Still, I like to write about me. Me! That's why I'm not a novelist."

Slater then invited readers to join her on a journey of uncertain veracity based on "emotional memory" more than "factual memory." Was she hospitalized after having seizures? Or does she actually suffer from Munchausen syndrome? Did she have an affair as a teenager with a prominent married writer? Did he pressure her to have anal sex? Only your memoirist knows for sure. And she's not telling. Even Slater's epilepsy may be real, may be a metaphor, some of each, or something else altogether. Who's to say? After all, wrote the author, "diagnosis itself is a narrative phenomenon."

When the manuscript of *Lying* was completed, Slater gave it to six strangers to read. All took her accounts of being epileptic literally. This discouraged the author. Slater thought it meant that nearly any reader of *Lying* who didn't know her personally would be likely to misinterpret what she'd written.

Although some may enjoy the parlor game of trying to decipher books like Slater's, such fusions of fact and fiction are usually more fun to write than to read. This is why there will continue to be a generous supply of "nonfiction" books that may or may not be based on fact. Those who mingle fact with fiction and call it creative nonfiction argue that they aren't writing news copy. Unfortunately, it's hard for those who are reporting news to resist picking up the beat. They'd like to be creative too.

Creative Journalism

In a newspaper's worst nightmare, twenty-seven-year-old Jayson Blair fabricated or plagiarized so much material in 673 articles he wrote for the *New York Times* over four years' time that his employer was forced to publish a fourteen-thousand-word review of Blair's transgressions. This front-page article portrayed in painful detail how many times Blair had reported apocrypha as "facts," pretended to be places where he wasn't, and borrowed material written by other reporters.

This problem was not the *Times*'s alone. During a period of heightened vigilance following Jayson Blair's dismissal, many other newspapers fired reporters who had fabricated or plagiarized material. The most egregious case involved Jack Kelley, a star foreign correspondent at *USA Today*. During two decades' time, Kelley's vivid reporting from hot spots such as Iraq, Bosnia, Chechnya, Israel, and Cuba earned him five Pulitzer Prize nominations. His gripping eyewitness account of a suicide bomber who blew up a Jerusalem pizza parlor nearly won that award. This story was one of many that *USA Today* subsequently determined was largely imaginary. (Kelley had described three decapitated heads of victims rolling around the street, their eyes still blinking, something that simply didn't happen.) The newspaper's investigation revealed that their reporter not only fabricated material in one story after another, but, once challenged, wrote scripts for friends to follow when pretending to have been his sources.

During agonized postmortems of such episodes, editors and colleagues tried to figure out how these transgressions could have happened. Were they due to a star system that favored charismatic go-getters like Kelley and Blair? A lack of oversight on the part of overworked editors? Or was it a craving for "wow" journalism on the part of editors who suppressed warnings from others and doubts of their own to get great copy?

What seldom showed up in public consideration but did among journalists themselves was the pressure they felt to make their reporting not only accurate but dramatic, and with coherent story lines. On these terms they were not just to report the news but tell a great yarn in the same amount of time that they used to spend just reporting the news. Reporters were supposed to be both Ed Murrow and Ernest Hemingway. Along the way, the reconstructed scene, the imagined conversation, the getting inside the head of your subject, migrated from the pages of books and magazines to those of daily newspapers. "The most ambitious feature stories are expected to emulate the best short stories," journalist Don McLeese warned in the *Austin American-Statesman* well before the Jayson Blair episode, "—with the same sharply etched characterization, psychological motivation, evocative description, narrative momentum and moral purpose. Journalists who have spent an hour or two with someone offer the illusion that they have peered through the depths of the subject's soul—and that the reader can as well." Something had to give. Too often it was accuracy.

Obviously this emulating of fiction needn't entail making up news copy out of whole cloth. Under pressure to dramatize their stories, however, some journalists decided that this was the best way to go. *Slate* once had to retract a column written by a freelancer describing how residents of the Florida Keys used hooks baited with apples to "fish" for rhesus monkeys. After being used for medical research, these monkeys were abandoned on an offshore island. A *Slate* editor later explained that although the freelance writer had indeed gone monkey fishing, his original account of this experience was rather flat. The editor urged him to incorporate more writerly detail in his story. The freelancer chose to do this by inventing details.

Slate is just one of dozens of publications that have had to retract spurious material in recent years. Even the *New Yorker*, where fact-checking is such a fetish, ran an "Editor's Note" informing readers that an article they'd published about a writer's experience working for a dot-com company had blended fiction with fact. In a humiliating note to its readers, the *New Republic* admitted that twenty-seven articles it had published by a young journalist named Stephen Glass included fabricated material. Apparently Glass's material was so compelling that not just the *New Republic* but several other magazines skimped on fact-checking before running embellished articles he'd written. Many such incidents were reported in the *New York Times*. Yet, well before they hired Jayson Blair, the *Times* itself had repeatedly run "Corrections" notices admitting that articles on their pages included invented facts, plagiarized material, or both. Other newspapers, including the *Sacramento Bee*, the *San Antonio Light*, the *Arizona Republic*, the *Baltimore Sun*, *USA Today*, and the *Washington Post* have also retracted dubious stories written by their reporters. In Owensboro, Kentucky, the *Inquirer Light* had to admit that a heartrending first-person account by one of its staff members about having AIDS was fanciful.

With its insatiable appetite for colorful copy and high-profile writers, the media are a primary enabler of post-truthfulness. Despite the repeated corrections they had had to run about Jayson Blair's reporting, the *New York Times* kept assigning bigger and bigger stories to the energetic young reporter. Even after colleagues questioned the reliability of Jack Kelley's reporting, editors at *USA Today* nominated his work for Pulitzer Prizes. The *Boston Globe* put columnist Patricia Smith up for a Pulitzer long after serious questions had been raised about her veracity. Another *Globe* columnist, Mike Barnicle, lost a court case for putting words in a subject's mouth. His employer subsequently gave Barnicle a raise and put his picture on the side of local buses. Smith and Barnicle were finally fired after their journalistic transgressions grew too egregious to be ignored. Soon after he left Boston, Barnicle surfaced as a frequent commentator on radio and television. Stephen Glass parlayed his notoriety into a lucrative contract for a novel about a reporter who makes things up. Jayson Blair got a six-figure advance for a book about his own experiences along that line. His publisher characterized Blair as a "compelling" and "honest" writer. When last heard from, Patricia Smith had signed her own six-figure book contract for a biography of Harriet Tubman. According to *Publishers Weekly*, Smith planned to "use creative nonfiction techniques to present Tubman as a human being as well as an icon."

Ripple Effects

So what? some ask. Wouldn't readers prefer a story made compelling through artifice to one that's tediously factual? Wouldn't you rather read a gripping embellished story than a boring accurate one? Where's the harm?

Here's the harm: when a piece of writing labeled "nonfiction" is made up, even in part, an implied contract between reader and writer has been broken. Their bond of trust begins to fray. "I felt let down," biographer James Tobin said after learning that Truman Capote had made up the ending of *In Cold Blood*. A price must be paid for literary fabulism. In the case of Edmund Morris, even though reviews of the second volume of his Theodore Roosevelt biography were generally positive, some wondered if he'd made up material in this book as he had in *Dutch*.*

Each such episode erodes the broader sense of credibility essential for a healthy literary climate. It isn't just the fabricators who pay the price; it's every writer who must work in their wake. Reviewers of memoirs routinely question how much of the book they're considering is true, how much false. Some of the exploits were so dramatic, noted a *New Yorker* critic of a memoirist's work, that it "makes you wonder whether the facts in this memoir have been enhanced."

Up to a point any writer has permission to polish. We hardly expect a memoirist's memory of dialogue, say, to be word-perfect. If he or she takes minor liberties with chronology, most readers will understand. Do they expect authors of nonfiction to know for a certainty what's true without a doubt? Obviously not. Those writers can only be expected to make a good-faith effort to verify what they're writing. But doing your best and getting an occasional fact wrong is not the same thing as deliberately inventing material without letting the reader know. Few enjoy reading a book that purports to be truthful, only to discover that it's semi-

---

*I have a dog in this fight, having shared my research on Ronald Reagan's college days with Morris, and being a footnote in his embellished biography of the fortieth president. Since Morris took liberties not only with text material but with sources he cited, is it clear to readers that I'm an actual person and not a figment of the author's imagination?

truthful at best. Reading and liking work that's labeled nonfiction, then discovering it was partly fiction, is like admiring someone you meet, then finding out she isn't altogether who she said she was. You may still admire that person, and that writer's work, but now—like Maureen Corrigan reading Vivian Gornick—with your guard up.

Taking creative liberties such as cobbling together composite characters or re-creating dialogue is not a problem so long as readers are clear on the terms. Some authors finesse this issue by admitting that they dropped some fiction into their nonfiction, but in advisories one would hardly be likely to notice. In an Author's Note at the end of *Midnight in the Garden of Good and Evil*, Berendt wrote that he'd taken "certain storytelling liberties," but said they had mostly to do with chronology. *Girl Rearing*, by Marcia Aldrich has a brief message in tiny type on the copyright page that says, "This memoir is centered in my life story, but it is not a literal account of my life. Some incidents and characters are invented, shuffled from life, and recombined. Many names have been changed." Yet Aldrich's book was sold as nonfiction. In his best seller *The Devil in the White City*, Erik Larson first assured readers that his depiction of a serial killer in late-nineteenth-century Chicago "is not a work of fiction," then in notes at the end said of the protagonist, "I re-create two of his killings" using "threads of known detail to weave a plausible account." So is *The Devil in the White City* nonfiction or fiction? In books such as this it's almost as if we need a third category: *faction*, say, *fact-based fiction*, or *fictionalized nonfiction*.

The real issue is truth in packaging. Book buyers have a right to know what they're buying. Even Tristine Rainer, who celebrates the mingling of fact and fancy, cautions that readers won't have a problem with such mingling "*as long as they understand what the writer is doing.*" Everyone knows that Philip Roth plays games by mingling facts with fiction. That's part of this author's appeal. But Roth's not trying to fool anyone. He has enough integrity to call his blends of fact and fancy *novels.* So why don't more writers follow Roth's lead and call their fusion works fiction? For two reasons (at least). One has to do with the marketplace: on average, works of nonfiction sell better than ones of fiction. The other is more intangible. Nonfiction writers who fictionalize, then wrap themselves in the mantle of "narrative truth" or "larger truth" or "emotional truth," get to have it both ways. They enjoy the freedom to make things up while retaining the credibility that comes from calling their work nonfiction.

Another reason for playing games with facts is simple laziness. Tearing down the wall between fiction and nonfiction doesn't just unleash creative juices, it allows writers to forgo fact-checking. It was easier for Robert Reich to rely on self-serving "memory truth" when writing his memoir than to try to verify what he recalled. One might argue that it takes more skill to write a compelling work of nonfiction that sticks to facts as best the author can ascertain them. I have always told students and colleagues who are tempted to invent quotes (or "pipe" them, as it's known in the trade) that they can't possibly improve on things people will tell them if they make the effort to seek them out and listen to their stories. That's what Nik Cohn discovered. After fabricating his disco-dancers article, a chastened Cohn compensated by becoming a dogged reporter. In the process he found himself talking to people on the streets of New York who were far more intriguing than any he'd ever conjured. As Cohn put it, "what they told me was so vastly more interesting, and, so much wilder and weirder and more heartbreaking than anything I might have invented, that I could do nothing but shut up and marvel."

The impact of fabrication by nonfiction writers such as the early Cohn is at least limited to the world of letters. Post-truthfulness in the visual media is something else altogether. Because they have so many opportunities to propagate and model their alt.ethics on a massive scale, those who appear before cameras have a much broader impact on our ethical climate. That is why it's so very important to understand the value system of those whom we see so often on screens large and small.

Eleven

Masked Media

Why can't life be more like the movies? Viewers asked,
and then answered that it could.

—NEAL GABLER

You must lie to make it in show business.

—SYLVESTER STALLONE

Jay Leno's autobiography includes a self-deprecating story about having exit music begin just after he started telling jokes on a TV talk show. Except that didn't happen to him. It did happen to a colleague named Jeff Altman. As Leno subsequently admitted, when Altman told him this story, he liked it so much that he paid his fellow comedian a thousand dollars for the right to claim it was his. The *Tonight Show* host seemed puzzled by all the raised eyebrows when this was made public. What was the problem? He'd bought Altman's story fair and square. That story belonged to him now. What was wrong with that?

Entertainers such as Leno don't necessarily lack ethics. They just have an alt.ethical system all their own, one in which certain kinds of deception are perfectly acceptable. If this system were limited to TV and movie studios, it would affect only those who work there.

That's hardly the case, however. Media celebrities have become such a constant, outsized presence in our lives that their values are being propagated in unprecedented ways. Just what are those values?

Hollywood Ethics

When Winona Ryder was charged with shoplifting, the actress's colleagues debated whether her decision to go to trial was a good career move. Might the ensuing publicity help revive her flagging career? The year before that, many in the movie industry could not understand why there was so much commotion over the fact that Sony had invented a phony film critic named "David Manning" to praise four of its films, and why two studio executives who were involved in this gambit got suspended for thirty days. "In the context of Hollywood . . . they didn't do anything [wrong]," observed Neal Gabler of the Lear Center for the Study of Entertainment. "They were just trying to publicize the picture."

Nowhere is honesty more flexible a concept than in Hollywood. There, a combustible mixture of ambitious, insecure people engage in the art of artifice to make movies. Within movie studios, the success of one's work is ultimately measured by the quality of its duplicity (in the artistic sense). Those involved in movie production have lots of license to manipulate reality. It's hard to relinquish that license once the cameras stop rolling. "Hello, he lied" is a jest former *New York Times* editor Lynda Obst said she heard in her first month at a Los Angeles movie studio (and later used as the title of a book). "People seemed to lie to each other as a matter of course," Obst observed of her new surroundings. "No big thing."

In most contexts it's assumed that honesty is at least the default setting. Recall the psychologists' term for this assumption: *truth bias*. In show business no such bias applies. There, lies are told to gain advantage, because you don't like somebody, or simply because you think you can get away with telling lies and find it more amusing than telling the truth. Like Lynda Obst, those who get involved with show business after working somewhere else find one of their biggest challenges is getting used to the ethical climate that now surrounds them. "Out here it's almost a joke how taken for granted lying is," a friend of mine marveled after he left Philadelphia to became a screenwriter in Los Angeles.

When it comes to moviemaking itself, "true story" is an ambiguous concept. From *The Alamo* to *JFK*, there is a long tradition of movies that claim to be historically authentic yet are anything but. Director John Ford liked to proclaim the authenticity of his films about the American West, most of which had only a passing relationship with historical accuracy. Too many moviemakers want to have it both ways: play fast and loose with facts, then claim they haven't.

Even though on-screen credits for the Coen brothers' Oscar-winning movie *Fargo* say it is "based on a true story," newspaper reporters could find no episode like it in the public record. When pressed about this discrepancy, the moviemakers finally admitted that their story had no basis in fact. Why did they say it did? "We felt the audience would have certain expectations if they were told it was a true story that would allow us to do things that we wouldn't be allowed to do if they thought it was fiction," explained Joel Coen. But he couldn't understand why anyone would get upset about this ruse. "We didn't break any laws or anything," said Coen.

Deception of all kinds goes way back in show business. Apocrypha has been part of the actor-fan relationship as long as these two have related. Ever since the early part of last century, when a Jewish girl from Cincinnati named Theodosia Goodman was introduced as the daughter of a French artist and Arab princess whose name—Theda Bara—was an anagram of "Arab Death," veracity has been a scarce commodity in Hollywood. Imaginative self-invention is so routine among actors that we simply take it for granted. Hollywood, after all, is the place where a garrulous depressive named Marion Morrison who avoided military service in World War II was so successfully re-created as a laconic war hero named John Wayne that, decades after his death, Wayne-Morrison remains the gold standard of stoic American manhood.

Though they can't keep up with politicians in this area, actors are not immune to phony-vet syndrome. Brian Dennehy was one of those caught in Jug Burkett's net. Dennehy, who was never in harm's way while serving as a marine from 1959 to 1963, told a *New York Times* reporter that he'd suffered shrapnel wounds in Vietnam. In a *Playboy* interview Dennehy compared the reality of combat as he'd experienced it with the way it's portrayed on screen. The actor's military records showed that he didn't serve in Vietnam, however, was never in combat, and received no Purple Heart. Dennehy did not respond to a letter from Burkett asking him to explain this discrepancy. The phony-vet investigator concluded that Dennehy's embellishment of his military record was simply a ploy to gain credibility for tough-guy roles.

Among actors, the embellished résumé is an art form. Those who don't gussy up their vita are considered unimaginative (to say nothing of naive). Sylvester Stallone once advised a group of drama students to get busy fabricating credentials for themselves. This was absolutely essential to make it in show business, he told them. Stallone's advice was unique only in its candor. Hollywood's alt.ethics are seldom promulgated this directly. They don't have to be. An aspiring actor once said that acting coaches may not advise students to pad their résumés, but they do urge them to "be creative." This approach is even urged on those who work backstage, where looks and age shouldn't matter, but do. Thirty-something screenwriter

Lori Gottlieb was advised by an agent of twenty-nine (or so he said) to avoid telling any studio executive that she'd watched *Happy Days* and *Three's Company* on a TV with an antenna rather than as reruns on Nick at Nite. The agent also suggested that on her résumé Gottlieb subtract two years from the four she had spent in graduate school. This approach was hardly an anomaly. Nor is it necessarily looked down upon. When a youthful thirty-year-old actress named Kimberlee Kramer passed herself off as eighteen to win an on-screen role in a youth-oriented television series and a job writing scripts for this show, the head of the screenwriting program at UCLA pooh-poohed any suggestion that she might have crossed an ethical line. "Come on," said Richard Walter, "I admire her pluck."

Hollywood is a place where one is free—encouraged even—to misrepresent one's name, age, size, origins, and sexual orientation. (Think Rock Hudson.) Up to a point this is understandable. Who could fault Muzyad Yakhoob for becoming Danny Thomas, or Albert Brooks for forgoing his actual surname of Einstein? But why did Warren Beaty change his name to Warren Beatty? And what made an aspiring actress named Lucille Ball think, for a time, that being Diane Belmont from Butte, Montana, was more glamorous than being Lucy Ball from Jamestown, New York? For the longest time I couldn't figure out how Lucille Ball was able to babysit my father in Jamestown, where both grew up, if she was a year younger than he. That mystery was solved when I read this explanation from Ball herself: "The secret of staying young is to live honestly, eat slowly, and lie about your age." When it comes to their age, show-business figures don't just enjoy the courtesy one- or two-year discounts that we take for granted. Some have rung up eye-popping deductions: minus eleven years for Zsa Zsa Gabor, nine for David Brenner, eight for Carol Lawrence, seven for Anka Radakovich, six for Robert Conrad and Mike Douglas, four for Groucho Marx and Marlo Thomas.

Deception has been the coin of entertainment's realm for as long as there have been those who entertain for a living. What's new is the ubiquity of show business, and our receptivity to its value system. Ethics in today's entertainment industry are probably no lower than in the one that served our grandparents, but their era wasn't nearly as fascinated by show-business personalities as ours is. Our grandparents were more connected to live human beings, less connected to ones on television. They didn't have cable channels covering lifestyles of the rich and famous in minute detail, or hundreds of fan magazines and supermarket tabloids, to say nothing of Web sites propagating information about celebrities that could be true or might be false or somewhere in between. There was also less leisure time to consume Hollywood's products. Vaudeville routines were an occasional diversion for our grandparents, not daily fare, as sitcoms are for us. Black-and-white television sets didn't beam post-truth values on hundreds of channels into every room of their homes. There was no such thing as "reality shows," with their ambiguous positioning between truth and fiction and their emphasis on duplicity. Television was not our forebears' babysitter, friend, and moral mentor.

From Beaver to Baghdad

The emergence of post-truthfulness is linked inextricably with the rise of television. Its viewers are inundated from earliest childhood with this medium's mistruths, half-truths, and outright deceptions. Television is their primary companion (in the sense that they spend more time in its company than they do with any live human being). That being the case, it is hard for TV watchers to avoid absorbing the values they see modeled there.

Older viewers grew up against a backdrop of televised McCarthy hearings, rigged quiz shows, Eisenhower confessing his administration's fib about U-2 flights, Vietnam and its many credibility gaps, the Watergate hearings, and Iran-Contra's many lies. The implications of the fact that postwar American children were raised in television's glow has been picked over ad nauseam, but seldom in terms of its effect on their ethical sensibility. Television, wrote Landon Y. Jones in *Great Expectations*, gave those who grew up before its screens their "first lessons in the little dishonesties of adult life. . . . They assumed that the commercials were less than truthful, that grown-ups lied, and made judgments accordingly."

One can hardly overemphasize the role mass media have played in promulgating post-truthful values. This doesn't simply involve watching televised liars and emulating their ways. Nor is it just the commercials, reality shows, docudramas, infotainments, and "fact-based" features alone that have had this impact. Because television inherently favors the dramatic over the factual, even nonfictional shows have adopted the conventions of fictional ones. For that we have no one to thank more than ABC's Roone Arledge. Arledge was the architect of melodramatized sports broadcasts and news shows. His genius lay in integrating fictional storytelling techniques with material that was supposedly factual. In time all of television followed Arledge's lead. Even public television succumbed to the temptation to improve on facts, as they did in *Liberators*, a PBS documentary about two all-black army units that supposedly helped liberate the Dachau and Buchenwald concentration camps. "We were nowhere near these camps when they were liberated," said a veteran of the 761st Tank Battalion, one of two units featured in this film. "I first went to Buchenwald in 1991 with PBS, not the 761st." A former army captain who commanded C Company, the other unit featured, said he and his men were sixty miles away from Dachau on the day they allegedly took part in its liberation. (The documentary was withdrawn.)

In their quest for colorful guests and strong story lines, commercial television programs have repeatedly been duped by talk show guests with phony credentials and compelling stories. ABC's *20/20* was taken in by a guest posing as "Buckwheat" from the *Our Gang* comedy series. (William "Billy" Thomas, the actual Buckwheat, had been dead for ten years at the time.) Actress Tani Freiwald portrayed a sexual surrogate for Geraldo Rivera and Sally Jessy Raphael, and a sex-loathing housewife for Oprah Winfrey. Master hoaxer Alan Abel, calling himself "Bruce Spencer," fooled Jenny Jones but wowed her talk show's audience with a fanciful story of how his wife Superglued his penis to his leg after she caught him in the arms of another woman. Fooled may be the wrong word, however. As a see-no-evil, hear-no-evil medium, television is not just susceptible to deception but downright collusive.

After one British program was fined and another canceled for using actors to portray "real" people (several of whom met for the first time a few hours before they appeared on camera as "friends and relatives"), a panel discussion of this problem was held at the Edinburgh International Television Festival. One producer who had been involved in that type of fakery said she'd been told by researchers throughout the media how much pressure they felt to book colorful guests with little regard for their authenticity. When these researchers warned producers that some such guests might not be on the up and up, they were told "I didn't hear that." A debate ensued about the propriety of misleading viewers this way. Some panel members thought the practice was reprehensible. Others considered it perfectly acceptable. One panelist, who was introduced as a "researcher for the *Jerry Springer* show," later revealed that she was actually an actress from Chicago.

Talk shows could not exist without amusing personal anecdotes told by guests. There are only so many good anecdotes to go around, however. Given this shortage, one alternative is to buy some, as Jay Leno did. Another is to make them up. That's why so many of the stories shared by talk show guests are more amusing than accurate. These include an outrageously funny and completely apocryphal story actress Fran Drescher told Jay Leno about badly cutting her finger, calling 911, then taking a shower and changing her clothes so that she'd look her best when the paramedics arrived.

Far more than the print media, television is morally neutral. This is especially true of programs aimed at the eye, as most are. Visuals are the essence of televised communication, and visuals have no ethics. Apparent coverage of actual events has routinely proved to be old tape or new reenactments. Early in the Iraq war, a Sky News reporter used stock footage of a missile being fired from a submarine to illustrate his "exclusive" coverage of bombardment by the British submarine HMS *Splendid.* During the invasion of Afghanistan, Geraldo Rivera pretended he was present at a firefight which was actually taking place far away. (When his ruse was revealed, Rivera was rebuked mildly by his employer, Fox News.) The visual flimflam common in this medium needn't even be that blatant. At the suggestion of a producer, ABC News correspondent Cokie Roberts once donned a warm coat to do a stand-up report before a picture of the Capitol inside a studio, to imply that she was outside braving the elements. ABC reprimanded Roberts and her producer for this minihoax, but only after the press got wind of it.

Televised images are concerned with the appearance of honesty more than honesty itself. With its emphasis on dramatic intensity, TV invariably gives the nod to feelings over facts. After Oliver North's eyes teared up as he defended his patriotic right to lie during televised hearings about the Iran-Contra scandal, Norman Lear observed that television "loves moist." North came across as an appealing patriot who was emotionally honest, even if he did tell lies. On the visual scale of values, that was honest enough.

Narratives, Story Lines, and Dramatic Arcs

These are clear examples of how television has provided a morally ambiguous model for its viewers. But there's an equally important, though less obvious, way in which the medium has encouraged post-truthfulness. This has to do with the intriguing amoral world that's beamed onto our monitors on a regular basis. Situation comedies could not exist without characters deceiving each other. Lying is a primary source of sitcom laughs. "I only lie to protect you," a husband tells his wife on one, "or when it's convenient." (Laugh track.) As Evelin Sullivan points out in *The Concise Book of Lying,* lies for laughs rarely put relationships at risk, because they're so entertaining, harmless, and lacking in repercussions. This is not true off camera. Off-camera lies are seldom amusing, and often harmful. And they *do* have repercussions.

A more subtle inducement to be post-truthful has to do with television's portrayal of life in neatly packaged segments that have coherent stories, dramatic arcs, and clear resolutions. With its emphasis on heroes and villains and compelling story lines, professional wrestling pioneered a televised world of colorfully staged narratives. Few took those melodramas seriously, of course. More problematic is a broader misconception that happy families like the Brady Bunch or groups of interesting *Friends* are life's norm. It's easy to feel lackluster compared to such dramatized characters with their intriguing lives. This creates impetus to give our own lives the narrative thrust, plot devices, and interesting subplots of those we watch on television. The more we electronically record (and edit) our lives' progression, the truer this becomes. If we wish our life's story were more like a good screenplay, suggesting that it is already is one way to make that happen. Manipulating reality isn't inherent in this concept, but it's certainly implied. When developing a good story line about who we are and where we've come from, the temptation is nearly irresistible to trim and shape our life's narrative just as a screenwriter would.

In an era of pervasive media, it's hard *not* to conceive of life as an ongoing drama with through lines and backstories and denouements. As consumers of a constant stream of well-shaped drama in every medium, we all feel pressure to make the stories of our lives go with the narrative flow. *Narrative* once was a word used primarily by fiction writers and playwrights. Now it's become commonplace not only for writers of all kinds but for politicians, professors, wrestlers, marketers—anyone who feels the need for a compelling story line. And who doesn't? We discuss the "master narratives" of football games; political campaigns, court cases, and our own lives. I've even seen divorce referred to as a "narrative rupture." The Middle East conflict is depicted as a struggle between competing narratives. So is the war on terrorism. In the aftermath of 9/11, Joan Didion noted how strong the narrative she called *America Fighting Back* had become. "Everything is working to make this narrative work at the moment," said the author. "If the time comes when the country becomes dissatisfied with it for one reason or another, as they have done in other wartime situations, then the narrative will have to be adjusted."

George W. Bush understood this perfectly. Wars need themes, he realized, such as Operation Iraqi Freedom. They need strong story lines. A valiant "coalition of the willing," say, frees an oppressed people from the yoke of their evil dictator who has stockpiled horrific weapons of mass destruction which he's about to unleash. During that war heroic soldiers liberate a wounded woman POW in a daring nighttime raid on the hospital where she's being tortured (having emptied her ammo clip before being captured). After a rousing battlefield triumph, the war's commander in chief dons a flight suit so he can fly out to sea in a fighter plane and join his troops on an aircraft carrier steaming home. In the story's denouement, this dashing young warrior chief gives a stirring victory speech. A banner behind him reads: MISSION ACCOMPLISHED.

The fact that this story bore only a passing relationship with reality was neither here nor there. Although the public had been told this aircraft carrier was too far offshore to be reached by helicopter, in fact the USS *Abraham Lincoln* was so close to San Diego that its navigators kept turning the vessel in circles so their commander in chief would have seawater as a backdrop, not Sea World. This illustrated how well a modern politician such as George W. Bush has grasped the need for visual hocus-pocus on behalf of strong narratives. Republicans understand this far better than Democrats. To sell Bush's Medicare prescription benefit they taped actors posing as interview subjects praising the plan, then sent these tapes to local television stations (many of whom ran them as "news"). When the president gave a televised speech at a St. Louis trucking factory, his aides taped over the words MADE IN CHINA on boxes beside Bush, then placed a printed graphic of boxes reading MADE IN U.S.A. behind him.

Bush's penchant for neatly scripted scenarios underlay his penchant for misleading the public. Especially when it came to Iraq, the forty-third president seems to have had a narrative in mind that he tried to implement, ignoring and squelching information that didn't fit the script. This practice left Bush open to being called a liar. But the president's deceptiveness apparently has had more to do with manipulating data than telling outright falsehoods. It is characteristic of those who see life in scriptlike terms to use information selectively on behalf of narratives written in advance. As *New York Times* publisher Arthur O. Sulzberger Jr. said after so many premises for invading Iraq were discredited, "I blame the administration for believing its own story line to such a point that they weren't prepared to question the authenticity of what they were told."

Bush is partial to the notion that facts were whatever you say they are, and that any position can be repositioned by changing its name. When the facts don't fit your position, in other words, change the facts. Call the estate tax a "death tax." Present relaxed environmental regulations as a Clean Air Act. Tout increased logging in national forests as a fire-prevention measure called the Healthy Forest Initiative. With his reliance on language games, George W. Bush has been our most postmodern president. Since his motives are pure, he sees no reason not to engage in such verbal three-card monte.

George W. Bush is also a quintessential baby boomer. Even though Bill Clinton is generally regarded as our boomer in chief, the man who followed him in the White House is far better qualified for this title. One commentator called Bush "the genial boomer personified, ever ready to flash a feeling instead of a fact." When pressed about not keeping his facts straight, Bush routinely falls back on assurances of his good intentions. A strong sense of being on the "good" side of any moral divide has freed him to engage in all manner of data manipulation about tax cuts, Medicare, and Iraq. When valid questions were raised about the accuracy of his premises, instead of admitting that he might have made a mistake, the president defended his own purity of heart and questioned the motives of his critics. Self-righteousness like that is characteristic of those who belong to the generation that never quite grew up.

Twelve

Peter Pan Morality

Of the ideas that bind the baby boom, none is stronger than the belief that this generation has a mission in life.

–LANDON Y. JONES

Every baby boomer adamantly refuses to grow up.

–JOE QUEENAN

Because of its size alone, the baby-boom generation has had a disproportionate impact on the lives of everyone. In *Great Expectations*, his seminal work on baby boomers, Landon Y. Jones portrays this as a tornado of a generation, reshaping the landscape wherever it touched down. Although it's risky to generalize about a group as large and diverse as the 75 million Americans born between 1946 and 1964, since that group is so influential, and now provides most of our leaders, it is important to assess their influence not only on our culture, our politics, and our economy, but on our values.

Origins

Baby boomers came of age during a period of great upheaval. Between war, protest, civil rights, drugs, rock festivals, and sexual revolutions, there was a sense that everything was in flux, including values. A strong feeling of being *unique* was inescapable for those who grew up against this backdrop. So was their sense of mission. They would change the world, or at least themselves, and never succumb to the moral exhaustion of those who had raised them.

One thing that boomers felt clearly distinguished them from their parents was emotional candor. Sharing what you felt took precedence over literal honesty. The truth in one's heart mattered more than that in one's mouth. Literal honesty was for chumps. Or one's parents. The many emotional deinhibitors popular at the time—drugs, therapy, be-ins, encounter groups—put honesty of feelings ahead of the kind that involved facts. Feeling good about yourself was considered more important than being factually truthful. And besides, who were we to judge someone else's character? Moral texts such as *I'm OK, You're OK* advised this generation to avoid being judgmental. Best sellers such as *How to Be Your Own Best Friend* put individualism over community. The many baby boomers who grew up in suburbs with little sense of community were especially receptive to this message. As a group, boomers became even more mobile than their parents, further facilitating post-truthfulness. So did the ambiguous morality they saw on television, with its love of moist-eyed emotional candor.

Even those who didn't buy into this credo were surrounded by a culture consumed with opening up emotionally. Being "real" was the imperative of the era. Along the way *authenticity* became more important than *honesty*. When he was nailed for writing a fanciful column about two cancer patients, the *Boston Globe*'s Mike Barnicle defended it *authentic* if not accurate. His colleague Patricia Smith, who was fired for fabricating material, rationalized this practice by saying, "The heart of my columns was honest and heartfelt."

Boomers like them grew up at a time when there was a widespread sense of casting off inhibitions, of replacing unattainable objectivity with honest subjectivity, of substituting genuine feelings for elusive truths. They had a strong conviction that they were getting out from under their parents' inflexible moral code and emotional uptightness. As in therapy, the ethic seemed to be that if you were honest about how you felt, and well-intentioned in your dealings with others, the accuracy of what you said was irrelevant. If you told a lie but your motives were impeccable and your feelings sincere, no harm done, and possibly even some good. *I'm a good person. My heart is pure. My intentions are honorable. What more do you want?* This was a countercultural update of the old Catholic doctrine of mental reservation: that the content of our hearts matters more than the words in our mouths. In *Bobos in Paradise,* social critic David Brooks observed that even though his generation-mates are offended by great wrongs such as racial discrimination, they are "relatively unmoved by lies or transgressions that don't seem to do anyone obvious harm. They prize good intentions and are willing to tolerate a lot from people whose hearts are in the right place."

Members of the generation that grew up in this moral climate became heralds of a broader if-it-feels-good-do-it sensibility. That sensibility has disappeared in its most ludicrous forms, but a residue remains among those who came of age during a time when the status of feeling-truth was ascendant, that of factual truth in decline. In the post-truth era they helped create, these feeling-truth advocates became more honest emotionally (or tried, anyway), less honest intellectually. With his glistening eyes, bit lip, and eerie empathy, Bill Clinton was a perfect representative of this era.

Like his successor in the White House, Clinton gave the impression of not having quite grown up. In both cases their moral outlook had a callow quality. Like adolescents everywhere, baby boomers are prone to perceive the world in clear moral scenarios. This became a generational motif. As Landon Jones writes, "It was the task of the baby boom to make, if not the perfect society, then the perfect person." Perfection is hard to attain, however. Being perfect is extremely demanding, especially when it comes to morality. Faced with the moral ambiguities everyone confronts with age, one can admit to being morally imperfect, or continue the quest for perfection. Many members of a generation determined not to grow up stayed on the hunt for perfection well into middle age. Clarity of vision made baby boomers susceptible to moral rigidity. This didn't leave much room for a nuanced view of the world. As George W. Bush himself put it, "I don't do nuance."

As a group, members of this generation were unusually determined to preserve their youthful ideals, or at least keep up that appearance. This resulted less in lasting idealism than in ongoing arrogance. Among boom babies such as Bush, the Clintons, and Al Gore, routine dissembling has gone hand in glove with generational self-righteousness. The sense that they march to an unusually moral drummer never disappears from the boomer self-perception, even after they engage in the trimming that we all engage in with age. "They had not been the first generation to sell out," wrote Joe Queenan in *Balsamic Dreams*, "but they were the first generation to sell out and then insist that they hadn't."

Looking-Glass Ethics

One of the most perceptive assessments of Bill and Hillary Clinton's casual ethics was written by a *Newsweek* columnist who flayed the two for their moral relativism. "They bent the rules," he charged. "They cut corners." This commentator thought that flabby, self-indulgent ethics characterized baby boomers in general. His name was Joe Klein. At the time he wrote his *j'accuse*, Klein's novel *Primary Colors* was about to be published under the pseudonym "Anonymous." For months this boomer-journalist vehemently denied being its author. "For God's sake," Klein said at one point, "definitely I didn't write it." The columnist admitted his ruse only after handwriting analysis of manuscript revisions left him no alternative. Klein later faxed a message to *Newsweek* colleagues saying he regretted the energy they'd spent defending him "against a vicious, witless, disproportionate assault." Bill and Hillary could not have said it better.

Boomers of every ideological stripe practice the politics of self-righteousness. This allows them to alter facts and let themselves off moral hooks with little sense of wrongdoing. We're not discussing scalawags like the septuagenarian Edwin Edwards, who once said his job as governor of Louisiana was to lie on a regular basis. Younger public figures apparently kid themselves as much as anyone about their moral fiber. When Republican South Carolina governor David Beasley was found to have invented a history of himself as a high school track star and descendant of *Mayflower* passengers, he admitted only to "some exaggeration and that's it. And I take it very seriously if anyone were to suggest that these off-the-cuff remarks in any way reflected negatively on my personal integrity and/or character."

Boomers such as Beasley have a curious ethical code. That code is: *Since I said it, it must be true. Lies are things other people tell.* You see the logic: *I'm an honest person. I said it. Therefore, what I said is the truth.* At an extreme, when caught telling lies, some boomers even argue that this puts them on a higher moral plane than those who lack that kind of imagination. Joseph Ellis may have had himself in mind when he wrote that Thomas Jefferson's remarkable capacity to engage in denial and deception was "possible only in the pure of heart." After the smorgasbord of lies he had told about himself was made public, Ellis insisted, "I am an honorable man."

David Brooks calls this type of convoluted morality "spiritual fudge." In *Bobos in Paradise*, Brooks noted the many moral contradictions of his fellow boomers, such as revering community while being relentlessly mobile, or seeking salvation while eschewing religion. "All these fudges and compromises mean you don't want to delve too deeply," he concluded. "You aim for decency but not saintliness, civility but not truth."

Boomer values are more moralistic than moral, more self-righteous than righteous. This took us a while to figure out because, at least according to them, baby boomers were so much more ethical than their parents or grandparents. But the moral arguments boomers used as a cudgel against previous generations proved a little weak when it came to consistency. What at first looked like fierce moral commitment proved to be a durable form of adolescent self-righteousness. Essayist Roger Rosenblatt has labeled this attitude "neopuritanism." Neopuritans are better at telling others how to behave than at behaving that way themselves. The preachy high-stakes gambler William Bennett typified boomer neopuritanism, as did Newt Gingrich, the philandering sexual scold, and Rush Limbaugh, the antidrug drug addict. During his decades as a successful football coach, George O'Leary's stock in trade was a fanatic insistence on honesty, integrity, and never, *ever* being a quitter. O'Leary, who quit football teams at two different colleges without ever getting on the field, later concocted a history for himself as a three-year letterman at the University of New Hampshire with a graduate degree in physical education.

This is a recurring syndrome among baby boomers. They seem to have trouble taking their own moral advice. Not practicing what you preach is hardly limited to boomers (recall the paean to honesty written by preboomer Martha Stewart), but it does seem especially prevalent among members of this generation. Boomers such as O'Leary, Klein, and Limbaugh have had plenty of company in the glass houses from which they threw stones. Self-confessed liar David Brock once wrote a book "exposing" Anita Hill's alleged falsehoods. (Brock later apologized to Hill for defaming her.) Former Clinton aide Lanny Davis, who wrote a book on the need for candor in politics, had himself run for Congress with campaign literature claiming incorrectly that he'd graduated cum laude from Yale's law school. Before being exposed as a fabricator, and plagiarist, *USA Today*'s Jack Kelley was given to statements like "God has called me to proclaim truth."

"I Was There"

As an intrepid foreign correspondent, Jack Kelley was known for seeking out the world's hottest spots to cover. Like so many in his generation, living on the edge seemed important to him. It could also have had something to do with being on the tail end of the baby boom. Before Kelley came of age the Vietnam War had ended and other upheavals had settled down. One price to be paid for being surrounded by so much drama while growing up is a sense of having missed out on key generational events—as most did. Rather than fret over not participating in the turbulence, some claimed to have done so anyway. When children, grandchildren, or their peers ask male boomers what they did during the Vietnam War, "Nothing" is a hard word to say. The temptation is strong to say, "Loads. Let me tell you about it. We shipped out from . . ."

As governor of Minnesota, Jesse Ventura missed few opportunities to mention his service as a navy SEAL. SEALs took part in some of the most dangerous missions in Vietnam. When he was a professional wrestler, ringside announcers would ballyhoo Jesse "the Body" Ventura as a genuine war hero. Although vague on the details, Minnesota's governor did confide that he'd "hunted man." Ventura liked to wear SEAL hats and T-shirts around the governor's mansion. This prompted a former SEAL officer and Vietnam veteran named Bill Salisbury to look into Ventura's military record. Salisbury discovered that under his real name (Jim Janos), Ventura had belonged to a navy underwater demolition unit based in California and the Philippines. He had been a frogman, not a SEAL. Ventura could have volunteered for the more hazardous SEAL duty, but didn't. Although he may have been in coastal waters off Vietnam, and might even have landed briefly, Ventura's former executive officer said their duties during the war were primarily "routine stuff." Along with 3 million other Americans, Ventura was awarded the Vietnam Service Medal. He did not receive a Combat Action Ribbon. Eventually Ventura himself admitted that "to the best of my knowledge I was never fired upon." Because he presented himself as a plainspoken, no-BS politician, Ventura's stretchers about his war experience were that much more damaging to his credibility. One could only wonder about the validity of his claim about later becoming an antiwar activist.

Not just the war but war protests and other generation-defining events attract boomer poseurs. Woodstock is one. If all of those who claim they attended this rock festival had actually been present, there would not have been room for them all in the whole of Yosemite, let alone on Max Yasgur's farm. Think of them as rock festival reenactors. Suffused with what she called "Woodstock envy," a boomer named Mollie Fermaglich took advantage of having a job far from where anyone knew her to become so well versed on this event that she could claim to have been in there. This successful ruse, wrote Fermlagich in a confessional essay, earned her new respect at work as "the cool girl in publicity who went to Woodstock."

Others, black and white alike, invented histories for themselves as civil rights activists fighting bigots below the Mason-Dixon line. Congressman John Lewis of Georgia—a genuine hero who suffered terrible beatings while crusading for civil rights in the Deep South—later said with a laugh that the number of people who told him they marched across the Selma bridge with him could fill all of America's football stadiums. Lewis knew every fellow marcher in Selma. Few who claimed to have been one actually were. A more pathetic case of this type involved U.S. district judge James Ware. Ware spent years spinning a fanciful tale about watching his thirteen-year-old brother get shot by white racists in 1963 in Birmingham, Alabama. A Birminghan teenager named Virgil Ware had in fact been murdered that year, but he was not related to the judge.

Even though they were not the first to claim they'd "been there," boomers made this a generational obsession. This was due in part to the emphasis they placed on acquiring *experiences*. If not the greatest generation, they were the most gratification-seeking. It's been said that "rock 'n' roll values" consist of freedom, lack of respect for authority, and a desire for instant gratification. This pretty well sums up the values of a generation that grew up to a four-four beat. The deferred gratification of their parents and grandparents was a source of disdain. There was nothing deferred about the gratifications sought by boomers. Even their style of imposeurship became an instantly gratifying counterpart to the Pop Tarts boomers grew up eating. *I want to be, therefore I am. I wish I'd been, therefore I was. I'd like to have taken part, so I did.* Instead of working to become the person you want to be, simply claim to be that person and skip the interim steps. With his love of military dress-up as president (in contrast to any actual war veteran who preceded him as president), one might speculate that George W. Bush has tried ex post facto to be the combat soldier he avoided becoming during the war in Vietnam.

A key factor motivating many actual Vietnam pretenders is a feeling of loss at not having taken part in this generation-defining event, combined with a lack of compunction about claiming they had. When unmasked, boomer-imposeurs usually admit only to exaggerating a little, or perhaps "misspeaking," and impugn the motives of their unmaskers. (Ventura called a reporter who pressed him about his military record a "puke.") When his many petty prevarications were brought to the public's attention, Al Gore seemed outraged that anyone would question his honesty. Gore blamed reporters with "a hair trigger on" for making such a big deal about all his little fabrications. Gore's opponent in the 2000 election became notorious for never admitting a mistake (culminating in a White House press conference where a reporter's question about mistakes he might have made as president left George W. Bush literally speechless). Apparently being a baby boomer means never having to say you were wrong.

The Boomer Code

Those with such a strong sense of generational uniqueness don't consider the old rules germane. By seeing themselves as "different," they run the risk of concluding that traditional standards of behavior don't apply to them. This includes ethical standards. That became apparent as boomers matured into yuppies, then New Economy savants. Beware of any approach with "New" in its heading (New Economy, New Journalism, etc.). Invariably their "newness" includes contempt for old standards of integrity. When throwing out conventional ways of doing business, why retain a conventional set of ethics? Those who put so much emphasis on thinking outside organizational boxes are susceptible to thinking outside ethical boxes. The innovative management style that Enron pioneered included moral innovations as well. (My favorite was a Hollywood set of an electronic "trading floor" that Enroners cobbled together to wow gape-mouthed reporters.) So did many high-tech ventures in the Silicon Valley with their buccaneer culture.

New Economy business practices were not all that different than those employed by Old Economy robber barons, only they were dressed in business casual. We'd been warned about this. In the mid-1980s, the head of an executive-recruitment firm noted that while selecting and training managers, he'd been impressed by the competence of baby boomers, but also by their amorality. They wanted what they wanted when they wanted it, and were willing to cut ethical corners to reach their goals. Two decades later this observation proved remarkably prescient as one New Economy firm after another crashed and burned because of the anything-goes business practices of its boomer-yuppie executives. ImClone founder Sam Waksal ended up in jail not just for insider trading but for lying to the government and avoiding payment of sales taxes. After his conviction, ImClone's contrite CEO said that believing he was an honorable executive doing important work had deluded him into thinking he could cut ethical corners.

Though Microsoft still stands, its founder, Bill Gates, is a classic boomer executive who doesn't just engage in corporate shenanigans but strenuously denies doing so, then gets furious at anyone who questions his methods. After Microsoft was convicted of breaking federal laws, Gates would admit only which the government had "legitimate concerns," based on "new rules" of its own creation. After thoroughly reviewing Microsoft's practices, journalists and judges alike concluded that Gates's company routinely used unscrupulous tactics to maintain a monopoly. The fact that Gates eventually reinvented himself as a benign philanthropist didn't negate his questionable business practices any more than it did those of John D. Rockefeller or Andrew Carnegie.

The case of Microsoft illustrates how not just individuals but organizations that see themselves as "different" can feel exempted from conventional standards of integrity. For those who work in such settings, having their own ethical code is part of what makes them feel distinctive. Like entertainers and politicians, they don't feel ethics-free, just ethics-unique. It's one more case of alt.ethics at work, in this case ones based on the boomerish assumption that because their integrity is a given, they needn't abide by moral standards that apply to lesser mortals. Whether or not generational icons like Bill Gates passed this attitude on to future generations, when it come to facilitating post-truthfulness they gave them something even better: technology so advanced that it simplified the work of making things up.

Thirteen

Deception.com

[The Internet] supports that mainstay of all villages, gossip. It constructs proliferating meeting places for the free and unstructured exchange of messages which bear a variety of claims, fancies, and suspicions, entertaining, superstitious, scandalous, or malign. The chances that many of these messages will be true are low, and the probability that the system itself will help anyone to pick out the true ones is even lower.

–BERNARD WILLIAMS

On the Internet, a new persona is just a click away.

–DAVID BROOKS

While fabricating and plagiarizing news stories for the *New York Times*, Jayson Blair had staunch allies. Those allies were technological aids: cell phones, laptops, e-mail, and search engines. When Blair filed phony copy with datelines from around the country, his editors had no way of knowing where their reporter actually was. The only way they could reach him was by cell phone or e-mail. Neither medium put Blair anyplace in particular. In fact, no matter where Jayson Blair said he was calling or e-mailing from, it usually was from his apartment in Brooklyn.

A child of his times, the twenty-seven-year-old reporter had a keen appreciation of how helpful technology can be in facilitating deception. To describe a place he hadn't visited, Blair accessed photo files created by news photographers who had actually been there. To do "reporting," he read other journalists' articles posted on the World Wide Web. When he didn't feel like writing at all, Blair hacked into stories filed by colleagues at other newspapers, then helped himself to their copy. The near-instantaneous, around-the-clock availability of news coverage on the Internet gave Jayson Blair a constant source of material to plagiarize. Any student of his generation who grew up cutting and pasting material from helpful Web sites knew that drill.

Techno-Aided Deception

Technology has done for Jayson Blair's generation what television did for his parents': aided and abetted a climate of deception. Lying in person takes a certain amount of creativity and moxie. Lying online, by fax, or by phone does not. One is a Rembrandt; the other, Paint by Numbers.

Modern technology greases the skids of post-truthfulness. Among other things, it is 100 percent nonjudgmental. Those who use exercise equipment that requires entering their height and weight realize in a jiffy that this impersonal trainer can't expose, judge, or disparage them. In the words of one happy StairMaster user who had just punched himself in as a six-footer weighing 190 pounds, "It doesn't know if you're lying."

Even when we're dealing with live human beings, technology makes it easier to dissemble. Research has confirmed that we lie far more often by phone than in person. Voice mail makes it easier yet to tell lies. It's much simpler to fib to a recorded voice than to a live one. One reason answering machines caught on so quickly was that they took the tension out of lying at both ends. At one end, recorded messages are as likely to be false as true ("I can't come to the phone right now"). In response, fibs are easier to record than to tell someone who might challenge them ("I have to work late"). For those who had to dissemble live, cassettes of recorded background noise could be purchased to lend credibility to dubious excuses. ("I can't hear you over all the typewriters!") More recently, software developed by a Romanian company can add background sounds to cell calls: of traffic, a thunderstorm, or a dentist's drill. Alternatively, one can activate the sound of another phone's ring, providing the perfect excuse for ending a conversation. Particular background sounds can even be programmed to kick in automatically when calls come from certain numbers.

The advent of computers added a whole new range of perfect excuses to our post-truthful arsenal: "Our computer's down," "My hard drive crashed," "I never got your e-mail." Electronic mail is a dissembling godsend. With e-mail we needn't worry about so much as a quiver in our voice or a tremor in our pinkie when telling a lie. It is a first-rate deception-enabler. That's one reason e-mail is so popular. A digitized lie doesn't feel as though it has the same gravity as one uttered in person or murmured over the phone.

So much of our contact with others now is by e-mail, phone, or instant messaging that the opportunities to deceive others have increased exponentially. (One phony-degree service offers a "verification" phone number to give potential employers.) So is our sense that we're being deceived. *If I'm more likely to put people on electronically, aren't they more likely to reciprocate? And if they do, how can I know?* A lot of cat-and-mousing goes on trying to answer that question: using e-mail receipts, say, or voice-stress analysis. Caller ID can at least determine what immobile phone we're being called from. But, as Jayson Blair discovered, cell phones are the perfect antidote. When talking to those who are using one, we can only take their word that they are where they say they are.

As college students quickly discovered, cell phones with text capability are the ideal medium for discreetly sharing test questions and answers. These same students have become expert at mining the Internet for help with their assignments, legitimate and illegitimate. When it comes to deceiving others, however, all of the communication hardware—cell phones, answering machines, tape recordings—is simply bridge technology that gets us used to the idea of electronically aided dissembling. It is in cyberspace that this type of deception has blossomed into a wondrous garden of unreliable information.

No One Knows You're a Dog

On the eve of the Iraq war, a twenty-eight-year-old resident of Baghdad posted daily Web log reports using the pseudonym Salam Pax (the Arab and Latin words for "peace"). Salam Pax said he was an architectural engineer. His droll observations about life in prewar Iraq had many eager readers. But was Salam Pax who he said he was? A man? Twenty-eight? Iraqi? An architect? In Baghdad? There was no way to know. For all any reader of his Web log knew, Mr. Salam was actually a topless dancer in Topeka, Kansas.

In the absence of face-to-face (f2f) contact, incentives to be honest dwindle. This process reaches its logical conclusion in cyberspace. There, the will to deceive is not only triggered but reinforced. Online, dishonesty is as much the norm as honesty. Those who converse electronically take dissembling for granted, particularly about each other's identity. Half of those who took part in a Georgia Institute of Technology survey of Web users said they had given false information about themselves online more than once. Research done at Georgia Tech, MIT, and elsewhere has confirmed how routine deception is among those who interact electronically. Based on her findings, MIT psychology professor Judith Donath has concluded that "people online lie about everything." In addition to switching genders, Internet users commonly alter their age, what they do for a living, and where they live. Such dissembling goes with the cyberspace territory that many now consider their primary address. At the same time, a certain level of candor is necessary for the intimacy so prized on Usenet groups Donath has studied. In these groups one gets a parfait of fact and fiction, never knowing which is which.

With so few incentives to be honest or sanctions against dishonesty, the cyberhood is essentially an ethics-free zone. It is the perfect hothouse in which to germinate seedlings of post-truthfulness. "Online, the whole idea of 'truth' is completely out the window," observed veteran *New York Times* technology reporter Michel Marriott. Marriott has found that using his real name, e-mail address, and phone number when visiting chat rooms is a real conversation stopper. That's not how it's done. In a world where few are whom they seem to be, revealing your actual identity can cause serious confusion. When he does this, Marriott feels like a nudist at a costume party. Some chatters doubt that the *Times* reporter is who he says he is. Marriott suggests they enter his name in search engines to confirm his identity. Even then there are skeptics. Marriott himself finds this kind of exchange disconcerting because his chat-room colleagues know who he is, but he's not sure who they are.

It is hard enough to assess another person's authenticity in the flesh. Accomplishing this task online is nearly impossible. There we not only have few cues to the credibility of what others are telling us, we have no way of knowing whether they even are who they say they are. Was that an old flame in high school who just e-mailed me or was it actually an old nemesis posing as an old flame to settle an old score? Did a sexually precocious fifteen-year-old reveal her erotic fantasies last night, or an eighty-year-old man with liver spots and a vivid imagination? For some, such questions are of more than hypothetical interest. Police officers around the country routinely pose as available teenage girls online, then arrest older men who respond, after these men arrive in a designated parking lot expecting to find a nubile young thing in a hot pink tube top only to be confronted by a burly man dressed in khaki with a gun on his hip.

It's increasingly common for English-speaking customer service representatives to be based all over the world, in India especially. Before being put to work these Apus and Meenas are given new names ("Hi. This is Tina. How may I help you?"), trained in Ameri-speak ("You're good to go!"), and given a crash course in cultural icons ("When I was at Wal-Mart the other day . . ."). Some even develop spurious bios in case anyone asks about their background ("Back when I was a student at Sinclair Community College . . ."). Most are discouraged from telling customers where they actually live and who they actually are.

The more time we spend online, the more our lives are lived among those whom we can't see and don't know, and who we suspect may not be who they say they are. In cyberspace, our name, our age, our gender, where we live, what we do for a living, are all up for grabs. Deception is so casual online that it can even happen with little intent to deceive. We discovered this early in the history of electronic chat when our son joined an online group of soccer buffs. Before long a fellow buff invited him to join her at a professional soccer game. Perhaps they could meet for a drink beforehand, she added. At the time our son was fifteen (a fact he'd neglected to mention).

"On the Internet, no one knows you're a dog," observes a keyboard-tapping canine in a *New Yorker* cartoon. Here there are sites for whatever turns you on, including one for shorter men seeking the company of taller women. But any such site is open to poseurs as well as partisans. How do the tall women who log on know that their suitors are actually short? Maybe some are seven-footers on a height holiday. Provocateurs known as *trolls* stir up trouble in news groups because they enjoy the ensuing mayhem. Others post apocrypha on message boards out of sheer perversity. Online support groups for those with specific maladies are routinely joined by participants who pretend to be fellow sufferers. Physician Marc Feldman, who has explored this phenomenon, calls it "Munchausen by Internet."

Without evidence to the contrary, we have to take someone's online word about who he or she is. We seldom have corroborating cues beyond an e-mail address. This leaves it in the hands of the other party to represent him- or herself honestly. At the same time there are compelling reasons of privacy and security not to do so. Deception is even encouraged online, as a safety measure, or simply because it's fun. Creating a spurious persona that no one can penetrate is considered high digital art. Doing this is part of the online entertainment: an electronic masked ball. As MIT sociologist Sherry Turkle has pointed out, cyberspace gives form to postmodern values of surface over depth, simulation over reality, and playfulness over seriousness. Turkle's colleague Judith Donath adds that even though deception has always been with us, the Internet makes it easier and more tempting. "There are some people who wouldn't have spent any of their life pretending were it not for the medium," says Donath. "It is a little unprecedented."

Once one enters a chat room and is figuratively asked "Who are you?" it's hard to resist the temptation to introduce the person one might like to be, or an altogether fantastical self. Different personae can be created for different settings. This is where older people present themselves as younger people, women as men, men as women, cops as predators, fat people as skinny people, shy people as bold people, chaste people as lusty people, poor people as rich people, and vice versa. At one time the most popular source of legal advice on the Internet was a fifteen-year-old high school student in California posing as a lawyer. In an article about this boy, author Michael Lewis (*Liar's Poker*) referred to sociological "role theory" that suggests we have as many identities as the masks we choose to wear. The Web rewards those willing to replace old masks with new ones. It is the culmination of the American dream to be in a perpetual state of reinvention. The result has been compared to traveling abroad, free to present yourself to others as you might like to be, with little risk of being found out.

Cybercitizens list the freedom to be someone they aren't—or several people they aren't—as a key appeal of this exciting new universe. At best it offers a safe opportunity to experiment with alternative selves, explore different parts of our identity, as teenagers do. In this sense cyberspace is like an extended adolescence for participants of all ages. "If our culture no longer offers an adolescent moratorium, virtual communities do," observes Sherry Turkle in *Life on the Screen*. "They offer permission to play, to try things out. This is part of what makes them attractive." Online romance can be very adolescent, in the best and worst senses of that word. Teenage relationships usually involve limited commitment, Turkle points out, as do those online. They offer casual intimacy, without entanglement, or the need for genuine candor.

Like teenagers, Netizens of all ages tend to be more open about feelings than facts. The two are related. Lying about who you are makes it easier to be honest about how you feel. This is the perfect forum for emotional candor. In person we're attuned to a cacophony of signals given off by others: their appearance, dress, facial expressions, body language, smell, even pheromones (hormonelike chemicals released by attraction to another person). These cues help us assess each other. They can also inhibit our interaction. Not so online. Protected by anonymity there, we're released from the shackles of discretion. Conversing with strangers online can be like opening up to someone you've just me on a plane, safe in the knowledge that you'll probably never see that person again. In the absence of in-person inhibitions, online relationships can deepen fast. But this sense of depth can be misleading. At the very least, prospective suitors put their best font forward. One of the first things the electronically matched ask when actually meeting is, "Okay, what did *you* lie about?" When those who have grown close online connect in person, they commonly discover that they don't have enough rapport to sustain a relationship.

In the cyberhood, inhibitions are reduced about the impact one's deception can have on others. Nor is there any profound sense of concern about being caught lying in, say, a chat room. If you are, simply exit. All it takes is the click of a mouse. This is a new development in the history of human relationships. So is the volume of dubious data to which we're subjected online.

The result is what librarian Anne P. Mintz calls an "age of misinformation." A book Mintz edited called *Web of Deception: Misinformation on the Internet* explores the extraordinary amount of apocrypha circulating online. What stood out to her was the breadth of Net deception: regarding commerce, medicine, charities, political news, and almost any other topic one might think of. Even though deception and gullibility have been around for several millennia, note Mintz and her colleague Barbara Quint, "the new technology just puts that deception and gullibility into overdrive."

The Tangled Web

Soon after the SARS virus showed up in headlines, "remedies" showed up on the Internet. This is part of a much longer huckster tradition but one given far broader, and faster, reach online. A review of medical Web sites found a plethora of misinformation, folk remedies, and modern-day snake oil being peddled by out-and-out charlatans. Even the veracity of those who are on the up and up can't always be counted on. A study of 60 Web sites hosted by hospitals, medical professionals, and health news services determined that forty-eight of them—80 percent—provided inaccurate or out-of-date information.

The World Wide Web is a mishmash of rumor passing as fact, press releases posted as news articles, deceptive advertising, malicious rumors, and outright scams. Because it was deliberately designed to be a decentralized medium (reflecting its origins as a tool for national defense that could survive the loss of any one part), the Internet combines information and misinformation indiscriminately without enough gatekeepers determining which is which. Its strength is speedy dissemination of vast amounts of information. Its weakness is providing cues about the reliability of that information. There is no *Wired* seal of approval that Web sites can post. As a result, accuracy is an altogether relative concept online. Here a Matt Drudge can become a star "journalist" by unrepentantly posting facts and rumors without distinguishing between the two. Spurious quotations from the mouths of a Caesar, a Twain, a Hitler—whoever isn't around to correct the record—routinely circulate online. More than once Andy Rooney has found outrageous statements put in his mouth on the Internet. A posted "speech" said to have been given by Kurt Vonnegut at MIT's graduation turned out to be an old *Chicago Tribune* column. At one time former White House press secretary Pierre Salinger endorsed a spurious allegation circulating on the Internet that alleged that TWA Flight 800 had been shot down by an American missile.

No rumor is too outrageous for the Internet, no paranoid delusion beyond its pale. The collapse of the World Trade Center towers provided a field day for wild allegations launched into cyberspace as facts. One e-mail that raced from computer to computer alleged that a friend of a friend had dated an Afghani who broke up with her just before the towers were attacked, then warned his former girlfriend not to take any commercial airliners on September 11. Phony photos were posted, including one supposedly taken by a tourist on the observation deck of the first tower, that allegedly showed an airplane about to fly into the second one. (In fact, this observation deck wasn't open at the time the towers were attacked.) Another portrayed a "devil's face" in the smoke of the destruction. Subsequent postings assured Netizens that ironing their mail would kill anthrax spores, that French astrologer Nostradamus predicted the towers' collapse in 1654, that a man trapped high in a collapsing tower rode falling debris to safety, and that four thousand Jews who worked at the World Trade Center stayed home on September 11 because they knew what was about to happen.

Barbara Mikkelson, who along with her husband, David, runs the hoax-exposing Web site snopes.com, has done yeoman work debunking such nonsense. Mikkelson thinks the many myths that cascaded onto computer screens in the aftermath of 9/11 were a way to deal with anxiety. "We reach out to other people to find that the feelings we are experiencing are not out of line," she told the *Washington Post*. "One of the ways we do that is through our wild stories. We are saying, 'We are concerned about it, and are you feeling the same concern I am?'"

Human beings have always used myths to counter anxiety, but the Internet expands exponentially our ability to disseminate fables and do so fast. Old urban legends have been given new life in this medium: alligators in sewers, rats in soda bottles, cat food mislabeled as tuna. Apparently it isn't the authenticity or even the usefulness of such legends that makes them memorable and believable so much as the amount of horror they evoke. One study of urban legends found that, in contrast to Oliver Wendell Holmes's famous dictum that truthfulness determines winners in the marketplace of ideas, emotional arousal is what lends credence to such legends. *Disgust* proved particularly potent in promoting the dissemination of reports that licking secretions on the skin of a certain kind of toad could get you high, say, or that Marilyn Manson threw some puppies into the audience at a concert, then said he would only start performing after they were killed. Rumors like these were the ones most likely to be passed along by e-mail or posted on Web sites. This is one more example of feeling-truth trumping fact-truth. "What we've been able to show is as long as something has emotion it doesn't need content," said Chip Heath, a professor of organization behavior at Stanford University who conducted this study with colleagues at Duke. The pieces of information that are most likely to survive in the marketplace of ideas, they concluded, "may not always be those that are most truthful."

Enhanced Reality

As if it weren't enough to not know what or whom we're dealing with online, software programs now converse with human users as if they too were *Homo sapiens*. Consider the implications. Is the person with whom you're e-chatting real or digital? This is just one of many questions raised by new virtual realities. As graphic images, still and streaming, are added to the conversational mix, further questions arise: Was that picture I just received actually of the person who posted it? What visual material that comes to me online has been altered digitally? Are "live" webcam images transmitted in real time or were they prerecorded?

Webcameras have created a brand-new, wide-open form of global telecasting unfettered by regulation or norms. "But such free-form evolution has come at a cost," points out urban planner Thomas Campanella. "It is difficult, if not impossible, to separate truth from fiction, to determine with certainty which webcameras are conveying accurate visual information, and which are frauds. . . . Doubt creeps in with every mouse-click, and, for me, seems to increase proportionally with distance. Have we really been afforded the power to watch African water buffaloes wallow in real time, as I am now doing while writing this in a Hong Kong office? Or were those animals pixelated a day or a month ago, and long vanished?"

Some consider this a nonissue. What difference does it make if we're watching the sun rise over the Kalahari or simply an old *National Geographic* recording being broadcast by a kid down the street? Do we really care if it's real or digitized? So what if we're conversing with a person or a program? "Does it matter whether a telerobotic site is real or not?" asks Ken Goldberg in his book *The Robot in the Garden*. "Perhaps not to the majority of casual net surfers, but to those who spend enough time to care, to patiently interact with a purported telerobotic site, discovering the site to be a forgery can be as traumatic as the discovery by a museum curator of a forgery among one of the Rembrandts in the museum's permanent collection."

This type of experience conditions cybercitizens to suspect that nothing is as it seems. The more people crowd the cyberhood, the more society in general will be populated by those who assume that authenticity is a chimera. Along the way we will lose confidence in our own eyes and ears. At the same time, increasing numbers of us will contribute to this atmosphere because, having grown accustomed to dissimulating in cyberspace, we may find it easier do so in genuine space as well.

Life in cyberspace provides a hazardous template for life in real time. Behavior which is functional online may be dysfunctional off. More than once a mild-mannered teenager has been arrested for harassing others via the Internet. In custody, they seemed genuinely surprised that anyone took their threatening behavior seriously. Didn't the authorities understand that they were just playing electronic games? Perhaps this had something to do with John Walker Lindh's having seemed so oblivious to the actual consequences of fighting with Taliban forces in Afghanistan. Before he became an Islamic jihadist, the teenage Lindh had posed as an African American during Web conversations back in California. After that he adopted the online moniker "Brother Mujahid." Perhaps Lindh didn't grasp that training with al-Qaeda and fighting with the Taliban had serious, real-time consequences.

Incidentally, Salam Pax is an actual person. While Peter Maass was reporting from Baghdad during the war in Iraq, friends in New York e-mailed him suggesting that he try to chase down the Iraqi blogger. At the time Maass had more important things to do. He thought about turning the task over to his interpreter, a smart and clever young Baghdadi, but let it pass. Only after he returned to New York did Maass realize that clues mentioned in Salam's Web log suggested that this interpreter himself was Salam Pax. Others confirmed his identity. Salam was then hired by an English newspaper to write a weekly column, and wrote a book for an American publisher called *Salam Pax: The Clandestine Diary of an Ordinary Iraqi*.

In time we will undoubtedly develop cues to help us assess honesty and authenticity online. But I doubt that we'll ever come up with cues comparable to those that work in the flesh, especially among people who know each other well. Even though we overestimate our ability to detect deceptive behavior in others, we're able to do so better offline than on. And the feeling that we do have this ability in the presence of another person at least gives us a sense of assurance that we're not routinely being taken to the ethical cleaners. Online there is no such sense at all. Nor is one assumed. This makes the medium feel like a slippery moral slope. At the same time a sense of community is one of the main virtues sought in cyberspace. Genuine community is hard to establish without trust, however. When it comes to verisimilitude, cyber-communities are virtually the opposite of traditional ones because they reduce rather than increase incentives to tell the truth. Those who gather electronically populate an environment that's inherently wary. We interact online with our guard up, and should. That attitude is becoming more prevalent offline as well. The result is an increasingly suspicious society.

III

Consequences
and Conclusions

Fourteen

The Suspicious Society

When regard for truth has broken down or even slightly weakened, all things will remain doubtful.

–SAINT AUGUSTINE

At the outset of this book we wondered whether more lies than ever are being told. In a sense, the answer to that question is beside the point. Because if we *feel* more lies are being told—and we obviously do—the effect is the same regardless of whether that feeling is valid: a rising level of wariness. In an era as lie-tolerant as ours, suspicion is inevitable. As bad as deception itself is the sense that we're being deceived so routinely. From potential mates to prospective employees or even our neighbors, we feel less and less sure whom exactly we're dealing with, or how much of what they tell us to believe.

Truth Bias to Lie Bias

In the suspicious society, "Google" has become a verb. Not only employers and journalists but suitors routinely Google each other by entering names in Internet search engines to find out what legal problems they might have had, how often they've been married, or if they're at all who they said they were. Background-checking services abound, available for hire to investigate suitors, babysitters, roommates, employees, and business associates.

Earlier we discussed the well-established psychological principle that most human beings operate on the basis of a "truth bias"— that they assume whatever someone tells them is more likely to be true than false. As deception of all kinds becomes commonplace, the truth bias could give way to a lie bias. In that condition we'll question the veracity of anything we're told. Some already do. Before learning that half the subjects they'd watched on videotapes were telling the truth, a group of police officers studied by Paul Ekman tended to think all of them were lying. Sustaining that level of suspicion is taxing. Research on mental processes confirms that it takes far less effort to believe than to disbelieve (which is a primary reason for the truth bias). Being on guard lest someone succeed in telling us a lie is emotionally, spiritually, and physically draining. Moreover, suspicion not only doesn't enhance our ability to detect lies, it can even make us worse natural lie detectors. What we're left with is weariness born of wariness.

As an experiment, Rhodes College psychology professor Chris Wetzel warned members of his class "Detecting Con Artists and Impostors" that he'd lie to them once per lecture. Any student who regurgitated one of his lies on an exam would be penalized. Within weeks Wetzel had to end the experiment. "It became too disruptive," he explained. "You almost have to become a paranoid to question everything and see what's going on, and most of us are not willing to pay that price. It would almost drive you nuts to be that vigilant for the truth."

On a small scale, this experiment replicated what is happening in society as a whole. Wetzel's experience suggested why, even though we're deceived so often, most of us aren't very good at detecting deceivers. We are predisposed to believe what others tell us. If we weren't, the stability of individuals and society alike would collapse. Giving others the benefit of the ethical doubt makes a civil society possible, even though this means overlooking occasions when we think we might have been deceived. The truth bias is also the basis for personal relationships of all kinds. To live on the basis of a lie bias, in a state of perpetual suspicion, would virtually eliminate any prospect of human intimacy.

When lying becomes too prevalent, and liars too skilled, even those who tell the truth are subject to the assumption that they aren't. An old joke: Two Russians meet at a railway station in Moscow. One asks the other where he's going. "To Minsk," the first man responds. "You are such a liar!" says the second. "You say you're going to Minsk because you want me to believe you're going to Pinsk. But I know for a fact that you are going to Minsk. So why are you lying to me?"

Not long after 9/11, an e-mail from Afghan American writer Mir Tamim Ansary raced around cyberspace. This eloquent appeal, in which Ansary pleaded with the U.S. government not to bomb a country that had little left worth bombing, was eventually expanded into a book (*West of Kabul, East of New York*). Before then, however, Ansary's plea had been forwarded to so many inboxes that lots of recipients assumed it was a hoax.

The real danger is not that we won't develop the necessary skepticism about lies and apocrypha but that, once we do, we will discount legitimate information. This is the inevitable impact of promiscuous lying. A man I know whom I'll call Tom lies on a regular basis. Tom's lies—about where he's been, what he's done, whom he knows—are so offhand that anyone who doesn't know him well assumes he's a credible human being. Only those who must work with Tom realize how routinely he deceives them on matters large and small. Tom's lies are so frequent that his co-workers doubt even his most casual remarks. If Tom says he's going to lunch, they wonder where he's really going. If he says he met with the bursar, colleagues wonder whom Tom actually met with. If he says he isn't feeling well, they figure Tom's trying to get out of doing something.

This replicates on a small scale what happens more broadly when totalitarian regimes try to brainwash their populace into be-lieving lies. Instead, recipients of these lies begin to question everything they're told. In time they come to assume that nothing their government tells them can be believed—even that which can be proven. Ultimately members of such societies don't lose just a capacity to assess the credibility of official pronouncements, they lose interest. This was the fate of those who suffered decades of op-pression by Joseph Stalin, Mao Zedong, and Saddam Hussein. "There always comes a point beyond which lying becomes coun-terproductive," concluded political philosopher Hannah Arendt. "This point is reached when the audience to which the lies are ad-dressed is forced to disregard altogether the distinguishing line be-tween truth and falsehood in order to be able to survive."

Just Checking

We haven't reached that point yet. We're still more determined to uncover lies than resigned to being duped. A staple article in su-permarket tabloids is "How to Tell if Someone Is Lying." A genre of popular books includes Stan Walters's *The Truth About Lying: How to Spot a Lie and Protect Yourself from Deception*, and *Never Be Lied To Again: How to Get the Truth in 5 Minutes or Less in Any Con-versation or Situation* by David Lieberman. Lieberman's book is filled with creepy tips on how to spot the many dissemblers its au-thor assumes we confront every day. "Using a blend of hypnosis and a system I have developed called Trance-Scripts," he writes, "you'll be able to give commands directly to people's unconscious minds— all in conversation and without their awareness. Through this process you can persuade others to tell the truth."

For the less literate, a multitude of gadgets promise to alert them when someone is lying. These gadgets go by names such as Truster, Handy Truster, and the Truth Phone. Most are based on the shaky premise that stress can be detected in a liar's voice, especially on the telephone. Alternatively, a software program purports to spot lies in e-mail. The more such devices are in use, the more suspicious we become—not just that we're being lied to but that our voices and even our e-mails are being scrutinized for falsehoods.

Lie-detecting devices are both a measure of how suspicious we've become and a source of suspicion themselves. Being on high alert doesn't help much in detecting lies, but does make us more wary of liars and truth tellers alike. Suspicion simply begets more suspicion, not enhanced detection of deception. In one of Bella DePaulo's studies, personnel officers who were warned that some subjects might try to deceive them in a simulated job interview were no better able to identify deceivers than those who weren't warned. The warned interviewers were less confident about their judgments, however, and more inclined to suspect every subject was being dishonest. Subjects in turn felt less comfortable being interviewed by wary interviewers. "Increased suspiciousness," concluded DePaulo, "in and of itself, served only to destroy the confidence of both perceiver and perceived in their own interpersonal skills, and to erode their trust in each other. The effects on the persons who were suspected of deceit are especially noteworthy, because those persons had no direct way of knowing that they were the objects of suspicion."

Pinocchio's Revenge

The question Bella DePaulo says she's asked most often is "Where's the nose?" What clues will reveal when someone is lying as surely as Pinocchio's lengthening nose? She responds that none are that foolproof. Her survey of 120 studies of human lie detection found that most showed subjects spotted lies at little better than a chance rate. What this means is that anyone we meet could lie to us at any time about anything at all and we would have no reliable way to expose his or her deceptions. DePaulo calls this "Pinocchio's Revenge." Geppetto's boy retaliated for the anguish of his big-nose lie detector by making it nearly impossible for the rest of us to detect lies.

Some beg to disagree. Those with a professional need to unmask liars typically have great confidence in their ability to spot cues of dishonesty. According to the owner of a California polygraph service, liars always look uncomfortable, don't rest their hands on the arms of a chair, twist their feet, fidget, twitch, and let their eyes rove. A Chicago company that trains interviewers advises them that liars are more likely to slouch, turn away, avoid eye contact, make erratic changes of posture, or engage in grooming gestures when answering key questions. Variations on this theme are commonplace among polygraph operators, customs inspectors, and police officers everywhere. Nearly all their assumptions are little better than folklore. Research on interrogators of many kinds has determined that while most have definite opinions about tip-offs that lies are being told, these opinions are usually wrong. Study after study has shown that rules of thumb even professional lie catchers use to flush their prey are, to say the least, unreliable. Shifty eyes, cleared throats, changes of posture, twisted feet, delay in answering, hand over mouth—none of these commonly used lie-detection cues has any proven validity. As we've already noted, the most popular cue of all—unsteady eye contact—is worse than useless as evidence that lies are being told.

Among the many subjects he's studied who have a professional interest in uncovering deception, Paul Ekman has found no correlation whatsoever between confidence in their ability to spot lies and an actual ability to do so. Even agents from the Drug Enforcement Administration, the Bureau of Alcohol, Tobacco, and Firearms, the FBI, and the CIA, as well as police officers, customs inspectors, military officers, forensic psychiatrists, trial lawyers, and courtroom judges, have performed little better than anyone else in studies of lie detection conducted by Ekman and others. A German psychologist who expected police officer subjects to be superior detectors of lies found that they identified truthful statements made on videotape at a rate somewhat better than chance (58 percent), but did far worse than chance when it came to spotting dishonest videotaped statements (31 percent). In both cases these officers had been quite confident of their ability to distinguish between liars and truth tellers.

Unwarranted faith in their ability to spot liars is a key reason that so many of those with a professional interest in doing this are so bad at it. Any success they enjoy in unmasking liars is usually in spite of their invalid detection strategies, not because of them. Those strategies may be more impediment than help. A study in Britain found that those who judge themselves more "intuitive" detect lies of others at a lower rate (59 percent) than those who consider themselves more cerebral (69 percent). The psychologist who conducted this study thought it suggested that intuitive people rely too heavily on invalid body cues than those who simply listen carefully to what they're being told.

This isn't to say that there are no successful intuitive human lie detectors or useful ways to spot liars. Ekman has found that U.S. Secret Service agents are better-than-average lie detectors, perhaps because they're so attuned to recognizing anomalous behavior. He has also found specific individuals who have a flair for spotting liars. (Ekman calls them his "Diogenes Sample.") Just as there are natural performers who lie well, the psychologist has concluded, there seem to be natural-born lie catchers. This ability is unrelated to age, gender, job experience, or any other discernible factor. Ekman's eleven-year-old daughter proved unusually adept at detecting lies, nearly as good as the best Secret Service agent. The ability to spot lies seems to be a gift, much like the ability to hit a baseball or paint a picture.

Nonetheless, over three decades' time Paul Ekman has identified what he considers reliable evidence that lies are being told: fleeting, involuntary facial movements at variance with words being spoken. These "micro-expressions" could be little more than a forced smile, knitted eyebrows, or wrinkled forehead. When making presentations Ekman sometimes shows slow-motion video of a momentary snarl on the face of cool Kato Kaelin testifying dishonestly at O. J. Simpson's trial about not having a book contract; the British spy Kim Philby smirking briefly while denying that he was engaged in espionage; or Margaret Thatcher's fluttering eyelids as the Tory prime minister said she hadn't authorized the sinking of an Argentine cruiser during the Falklands war, a cruiser that a British ship was about to torpedo. (Thatcher later admitted her deception.) Since micro-expressions such as these usually last for less than a second, they are discernible only in slow-motion video. Spotting them takes an hour of analysis for each minute of tape, on average. Such a complex, time-consuming approach is not practical for most professionals, let alone a wife wondering if her husband is actually working late as he says he is. Although Ekman offers workshops for professionals in everyday applications of micro-expression analysis, the usefulness of this method for the average person is nearly nil.

It has been established that some easily spotted cues are more indicative of deceptive behavior than others. They include an elevated blink rate, dilated pupils, higher voice pitch, and artificial smiling. Wiping your mouth with your hand, straightening your desk as you speak, and preening your hair may indicate lying—but only in certain women. Some liars get tongue-tied and stumble over their words, but so do some truth tellers. (This cue is a tip-off only if you know how articulate the speaker is ordinarily.) And, yes, your nose does get bigger when you lie. Researchers at Chicago's Smell and Taste Foundation and at the University of Illinois have found that nasal tissues become engorged with blood when we dissemble, making our noses swell. This is usually not visible to others, however, though it is felt by dissemblers, who may touch their nose in response.

In the end there is no surefire, clearly discernible tip-off to all lying in every person. Cues vary from person to person, and occasion to occasion. Small, everyday lies ("I've got a call on the other line") are nearly impossible to spot because they're told so routinely. Big ones with a lot of high-voltage emotional content are more likely to produce cues. Accomplished deceivers are very good at repressing lie cues, however, and mimicking someone who is telling the truth. This includes those subjected to vigorous lie detection.

Wired Up

As long as some human beings have told lies, others have yearned for a reliable way to detect them. The methods they've developed have usually employed state-of-the-art technology. At one time this meant the thumbscrew, the garrote, and the rack. These lie-detection methods were not 100 percent dependable, however, because those being interrogated by such means were likely to say anything, true or false, to relieve their pain. In ancient India suspected liars were forced to chew dry rice. The amount that stuck to the roof of their mouth was then measured as a gauge of their honesty (the more rice, the more honest). This is not as wacky as it sounds: a dry mouth can be symptomatic of anxiety (presumably about being caught telling a lie). That's why the Bedouin custom of having suspected liars lick a hot iron, on the theory that if their tongue stuck to the iron they were lying, also had a certain logic. An ability to touch hot irons without blistering—a medieval European means of identifying liars—was logic-free, however. So was dunking possible liars in water to see if they'd sink or float, a no-win situation if ever there was one (in dunking theory, liars' bodies floated, only to be hauled from the water and hung; truth tellers sank, and drowned).

Modern lie-detection tools haven't progressed all that far from chewing dry rice and licking hot irons. This includes the polygraph. Since it was invented in 1921, no one who has paid serious attention to the so-called lie detector takes it seriously as a dependable tool for spotting lies. Two comprehensive studies commissioned by the federal government concluded that this contraption was fundamentally unreliable. A historian of the polygraph, Geoffrey Bunn of Toronto's York University, calls it an "entertainment device." After much research, University of Minnesota psychologist David Lykken concluded that the polygraph's effectiveness in catching lies is little better than chance.

All lie detectors do is measure autonomic nervous arousal. But truth tellers can be nervous, and liars calm (accounting for lots of false positives and negatives in polygraph results). A former American policeman says he can teach subjects how to fool a polygraph. This takes about ten minutes. So why are lie detectors still used so extensively (a million times a year in the United States alone, by one estimate)? After reviewing hundreds of studies for the *New England Journal of Medicine*, Los Angeles physician Robert Steinbrook concluded that "the polygraph appeals to an often simplistic desire for certainty in the face of complexity, and a misplaced faith in the power of a machine."

There's more to the story, however. Even though polygraphs are unreliable tools for assessing lies told by job applicants or government leakers, in specific criminal cases they have sometimes proved effective. This has less to do with the machine itself than the way it's used. Clever polygraph operators can get anxious suspects to confess wrongdoing by making them afraid that their lies are about to be exposed. This process is sometimes enhanced by lying to subjects about how foolproof lie detectors are. One hapless suspect confessed to arson after police in Doylestown, Pennsylvania, put a kitchen colander on his head with battery jumper cables leading from the colander to a photocopier that churned out paper reading "HE'S LYING."

Despite being discredited by scientific research, voice-stress analyzers are still in common use as lie-detection tools. More recent methods employ infrared cameras that measure facial heat thought to be associated with lying, and software programs that accelerate analysis of microexpressions. Those working with different kinds of brain scanners say they can identify neural activity associated with lying. Perhaps this points the direction toward lie detectors of the future. For now, however, lie detection by brain scan is unwieldy, unproven, and prohibitively expensive.

With luck we will never develop a lie detector that is 100 percent dependable. Not that this will stop us from trying. In the suspicious society there will always be a market for tools that promise to reveal deception. The demand for them is more telling than the products themselves. Lie-detection devices are both a measure of how suspicious we've become, and a source of our atmosphere of wariness.

Lies and Consequences

When one or a handful of those in any profession are exposed as dishonest, all others in that profession get a black eye. In the wake of the Enron–Arthur Andersen debacle, perceived ethics of all accountants plummeted in public opinion polls. (Business executives didn't fare too well to start with.) The integrity of clergymen in general suffered as a result of the many Catholic priests who were exposed as pedophiles and prevaricators. This syndrome could have something to do with how badly psychologists as a group fare in surveys of perceived honesty. One such survey, using sixty undergraduates as subjects, found they ranked eighth out of twelve professions on the perceived-honesty scale, below teachers and doctors (but ahead of politicians, at least). B. L. Kintz, the psychologist who conducted this study, seemed nonplussed by its results. When it came to attitudes toward lying, Kintz observed, "for some reason they [the subjects] believe that psychologists are not too unfavorably inclined." Kintz wondered why this might be. Here's one possibility: academic psychologists routinely enlist students in studies under false pretenses. Kintz's report of his own study, "Eye Contact While Lying During an Interview," has this to say about its methodology (in which an unknowing student subject was paired with a knowing confederate): "After introducing the two students, the experimenter explained the nature of the experiment. This explanation, however, was the beginning of a cover story designed so that the subject would not be aware that the emphasis of the experiment was on lying." At best such subjects are later debriefed about having taken part in a psychological experiment based on false premises. Tens (if not hundreds) of thousands of deceived student-subjects like them leave college with a circumspect view of psychologists' ethics. And they tell their friends.

Deception of any kind can have unexpected consequences. Dissembling in one area ricochets into others. Scientists who fake findings don't just debase the currency of research in their own field but weaken confidence in physicians who base treatment decisions on that research. Similarly, physicians who deceive patients about their condition and are known to do so create problems for more candid colleagues, whose patients may wonder if they're being deceived too. After all the revelations about reporters making things up, the credibility of journalists in general was damaged. Two-thirds of those polled in a survey by the Media Studies Center thought journalists often or sometimes made things up, and three-quarters thought they often or sometimes plagiarized other people's work. When duped too often, readers wonder how to distinguish between fiction and nonfiction. Finally they stop trying, but do remain suspicious. This is the price every nonfiction writer pays for the few who make things up: a climate of wariness in which all must work. At least wariness is better than cynicism, though. What most horrified journalists about the Jayson Blair scandal was how few of the many subjects he misrepresented felt compelled to complain. Gerald Boyd, the *Times*'s managing editor during this episode, noted that he used to hear from readers if his newspaper got so much as a middle initial wrong. The fact that hardly any subject or reader bothered to question Blair's far more egregious errors told him something about the degraded credibility of journalists as a group.

In the backwash of writer-embellishers, those who try to maintain standards of veracity now feel the need to say: *This is true; I didn't make it up. Trust me. I'm not a fantasist. I do not invent facts and call them the truth.* In an age of digital enhancement, photographer Elliot Erwitt thought he had to assure those who bought a collection of his photos that all were printed as taken. In an age of creative nonfiction, I felt the need to assure readers of one of my own nonfiction books that "everyone written about in this book is 100 percent real. There are no fictional characters, or composites."

Deceivers and their apologists rarely consider the broad implications of dishonest behavior. It may be morally ambiguous to tell small, benign lies. This is the parking ticket of ethical crimes. Each such case is of little consequence in itself. When enough of us peddle fantasies as reality, however, society as a whole begins to lose its grounding in reality. Casual duplicity picks at the threads of our social fabric. The sum of lying, big and small, is a culture in which credibility is on the run.

Credibility Gaps

Those who lie and are known to have lied—even on minor matters, even without malicious intent—have trouble getting others to believe their true statements. A single lie unmasked undermines every honest statement. It's hard to have confidence in those who we know tell lies, even if we condone this practice in principle. Friedrich Nietzsche himself, the eloquent defender of artful liars, once commented to a friend, "Not that you lied to me, but that I no longer believe you, has shaken me."

Once revealed, lies cast a shadow far back into the past and forward into the future. We understand why someone might lie to us, but trust them less once they do. The key question becomes: So what else are you lying about? Bill Clinton's credibility never recovered fully from all his fibbing, about Monica Lewinsky in par-

ticular. This was not because we didn't understand, and even for-
give, Clinton's lies, but because they raised questions in our minds
about how many others he might have gotten away with.

Reporters dated the unraveling of Al Gore's 2000 campaign for
president to the false statement he made during a debate with
George W. Bush about accompanying the head of the Federal
Emergency Management Agency to a disaster site in Texas. Republicans pointed out to reporters that this was simply untrue (it
was an underling he'd been with). The press then resurrected
Gore's many other fibs and stretchers, leaving him open to the
charge of being a "serial fabricator." Gore protested that most of
these gaffes were petty, which was accurate, but also beside the
point.

In a sense there is no such thing as a petty lie. Any lie of any size
once revealed puts all other statements from the same source in
play as possible lies. The core consequence of casual lying is shattered credibility. Credibility is like pottery. Once broken it can be
glued back together, but is never quite as strong. A car dealer who
said he had disciplined and even fired employees for lying about
themselves added that he might retain one who'd had time to establish a solid track record. On the other hand, said the business
owner, "I think they'd be very hard to promote because you could
never totally trust them again."

Given the opportunity, those willing to make small things up
about themselves are likely to make up bigger things about other
topics. Oliver North didn't just lie about trading arms for hostages
during the Iran-Contra scandal but misrepresented his service
record. Mike Barnicle's columns in the *Boston Globe* that included
fabrications and plagiarisms followed lies he told about writing
speeches for Robert Kennedy and being a screenwriter on the
movie *The Candidate*. Before making up a *Washington Post* article

that won a Pulitzer Prize, Janet Cooke claimed falsely on her job application that she had a degree from Vassar. Analyst Jack Grubman, who manipulated accounts at Salomon Smith Barney, also said he had graduated from MIT when he hadn't. Henry Reid, who claimed unearned graduate and undergraduate degrees, later sold parts of donated cadavers when he became the director of UCLA's body donor program. Lyndon Johnson didn't just puff up his own military experience and that of his grandfather but lied when he said North Vietnam had attacked an American ship in the Gulf of Tonkin. Once it became clear how routinely he deceived others about matters large and small, LBJ's reputation was irreparably damaged.

When a person we thought was honest turns out to be dishonest, it doesn't shake just our confidence in that person but our confidence in general. If we discover that someone we trust has told us a lie, we're forced to reexamine everyone we trust. When institutions we thought were trustworthy—churches, accounting firms, research laboratories—turn out to be unworthy of trust, we wonder if any institutions can be trusted. After a country's leader, or a clergyman, or a college professor gets caught manipulating the truth, we question whether *anyone's* honesty can be counted on. This is the way in which post-truthful behavior by specific individuals picks away at our social contract as a whole.

Even the most ardent postmodern relativist wouldn't argue that truth telling has no place in human discourse. No society could function on that basis. Civilization would crumble if we assumed others were as likely to lie as to tell the truth. Our social contract cannot survive lying so routine that citizens consider it normal. One sign of a healthy democracy is its citizens' capacity for outrage when they are deceived. Since Watergate, and Enron, and the cover-up of child-abusing priests, too many of us have resigned ourselves to lying being the norm among public figures. In the process we have become enablers of the post-truth society.

Political columnist David Broder once observed that the post-Watergate climate of duplicity was a product of reporters and voters who accepted deception as a way of life. This cynicism is worse than outrage. Strachan Donnelly, president of the Hastings Center in Briarcliff Manor, New York, believes it has led to a vicious cycle. Politicians deceive, their constituents become cynical, expectations for political conduct decline, which in turn makes it easier for politicians to keep deceiving. "We're getting what we're asking for, in a way," concluded Connelly.

That is the social cost of constant deception: suspicion followed by resignation. It is not just society that pays for deceptive behavior, however. Individuals do as well. Lying seldom has a positive impact on either the lied to or the liar.

Fifteen

The Price of Prevarication

I do more harm to myself by lying than I do to the man about whom I lie.
—MICHEL DE MONTAIGNE

A lie will easily get you out of a scrape, and yet, strangely and beautifully, rapture possesses you when you have taken the scrape and left out the lie.
—C. F. MONTAGUE

Ronnie Cornwell was a charming swindler. Cornwell's son David—the author John Le Carré—never ceased to be amazed by how unfazed his father's victims were about being conned by him. To the contrary, many assured the author that even after they discovered Mr. Cornwell's ruses, even ones that cost them lots of money, they forgave this delightful man. A lawyer from Buffalo, whose firm spent untold hours assessing Ronnie Cornwell's bogus Canadian land scheme, later wrote Le Carré that he would not have missed such an exciting experience for the world. This adoration was not reciprocated. Le Carré's father had little regard for those he so easily fooled, including, his son concluded, himself.

No Respect

This syndrome is typical of those who are good at deceiving others. The price they pay lies in the realm of diminished regard for others and for themselves. "The great danger is to the deceiver, not the deceived," says psychologist Richard Farson. "The deceived can be debriefed, but the deceiver cannot, because the erosion of respect is so subtle."

It's hard to respect those who swallow our fibs. It's harder still not to resent them. Each successful deception reminds us of our capacity for duplicity. That's why lies told to boost self-esteem invariably have the opposite effect. One chronic liar said she hated to have other people say they liked her, because so many of the things they liked weren't genuine. Psychotherapist Brad Blanton has found that some form of deceit usually underlies the depression, stress, and anxiety that patients pay him to treat. The more we lie and feel we're being lied to (these two go hand in hand; those who lie a lot assume they're being lied to a lot), the more wary we become. Lyndon Johnson's paranoia was exacerbated by his own constant prevarication. A chronic liar himself, LBJ was convinced that others were constantly telling him lies. This is characteristic of dissemblers. Those who routinely deceive others feel sure that they are reciprocating (especially husbands who lie about their fidelity and have no doubt their wives are doing the same thing). This was the basis for George Bernard Shaw's case against telling lies: "If you do, you will find yourself unable to believe anything that is told to you."

Imposture imposes a particularly stiff psychic tax: feeling disassociated from who we really are, knowing we've put one over on others, praying we won't be exposed. A friend of mine hung up the hairpiece he'd worn for years because he'd grown so weary of wondering how many people noticed. Imposeurs are in the same boat. Every lie they tell, big or small, puts pressure on them to maintain the pose. "The strain of living a double life at work or home will eventually take its toll," says British psychologist Aldert Vrij, an expert on deception. "In all but the most extreme and compulsive people, prolonged lies cause debilitating stress. You constantly have to cover your steps and you must always be one step ahead of the game. You have to ask, is it worth the effort?"

For a lesbian friend of mine, it wasn't. This woman once described for me how traumatic it had been to spend years pretending she had a husband. During that period my friend felt unable to deal with the consequences of being honest about her sexual orientation. She also felt a need to protect the privacy of her partner and their three children. The subsequent deception put her constantly on guard lest anyone discover the truth. This caused constant tension. It also degraded her self-esteem. "Lying became a habit," she explained, "something that made me very unhappy because I thought I was a good person."

Liars must play a continual game of I've got a secret. Eternal vigilance is the price of duplicity. The lie-condoning Nietzsche himself conceded that "lying is very exhausting." One subject in a study of those who had deceived relationship partners told an interviewer how harrowing this activity had been. Keeping her partner in the dark involved "a lot of work," she said. "You always have to be on your toes and it is exhausting." Neurological research confirms this observation. Brain researchers armed with MRIs have found that subjects engaged in lying register a lot more neurological activity than those who are telling the truth.

At a minimum, sustaining deceit levies a stressful tax of constant alertness. As an ancient proverb puts it, Liars need good memories. Life-liars invariably discover that something so petty as claiming an unearned degree to win a job when young becomes like a garish tattoo acquired during adolescence: a burden carried around for the rest of one's life. The puffing that insecure people—even gifted ones—may have felt they needed to do to get ahead early on can't just be turned off once they've arrived. By then deception is a way of life. Plus, they're saddled with old lies they initially told to give themselves an edge and now can't disown. The most burdensome lies we tell are those that are never exposed. Ethicist Michael Josephson compares them to buried land mines. One never knows when they might explode.

That's why imposeurs whose lies are exposed typically feel relief as much as shame. Tension evaporates. The need for vigilance is over. After a whistleblower told the media how many lies were on Warren Cook's résumé, the Maine executive and political adviser said he'd like to thank the person who had finally broken his chains of deceptions. "I feel set free," agreed a Cleveland schoolteacher who was fired for claiming falsely that he had a Ph.D. "It has been a positive thing, a very cleansing thing."

Like an old-time movie set, chronic dissemblers are stuck over time with an elegant facade that has no interior. That's how they come to feel about themselves. John Wayne–Marion Morrison grew increasingly frustrated by trying to become his screen persona when he knew that identity was so artificial. The same thing may have been true of his friend Ronald Reagan. Edmund Morris justified creating a fictional interlocutor in his biography of Reagan by explaining that this charming fabulist felt he had no inner life worth sharing with others (such as his biographer).

"The liar," observed poet Adrienne Rich, "in her terror wants to fill up the void, with anything." Rich made this observation in an essay called "Women and Honor: Some Notes on Lying." Her essay is an unflinching, tough-minded assessment of the price we pay for lying. No one has faced the consequences of doing so more squarely. Though addressed to women, most of her insights apply equally well to men. The best of them stand alone:

> The liar has many friends, and leads an existence of great loneliness.

> She may say, I didn't want to cause pain. What she really did not want is to have to deal with the other's pain.

> The liar may resist confrontation, denying that she lied. Or she may use another language: forgetfulness, privacy, the protection of someone else. Or, she may bravely declare herself a coward. This allows her to go on lying, since that is what cowards do. She does not say, I was afraid, since this would open the question of other ways of handling her fear. It would open the question of what is actually feared.

> There is a danger run by all powerless people: that we forget we are lying, or that lying becomes a weapon we carry over into relationships with people who do not have power over us.

Feminists such as Rich, Harriet Lerner, and bell hooks have pointed out how much it costs women to rely on deception as a survival strategy. They question whether "telling it slant" is worth the price. Canadian linguist Gillian Michell pointed out that those who take Emily Dickinson's advice don't just deprive men of information they need to hear, but over time lose the capacity to tell it straight, even to those who have no power over them, even other women. "We tell it slant," concluded Michell, "at the cost of perpetuating the situation that makes it necessary."

Lieaholism

Attempting to make sense of the fact that so many policemen he studied began as occasional liars and ended up as chronic liars, criminologist Carl Klockars speculated that "the lie appears to have some intrinsically appealing and seductive properties to it, such that those whose job it is to develop the capacity to lie skill-fully on certain occasions become inclined to use that skill casually and irresponsibly on others." As with any other skill, once we de-velop expertise at deceiving others, we wouldn't want to do so only when absolutely necessary. Like Klockars's cops, anyone who proves good at it can become dependent on dishonesty as a way of life. Once acquired, the habit of telling lies is as hard to break as any other habit. "An accursed vice," Montaigne called it, adding, "Whence it happens that we find some otherwise excellent men subject to the fault and enslaved by it."

Lying is like smoking. Some smokers can enjoy the occasional cigarette at a party or cigar at a poker game. Others can't. It's just as hard for some to limit themselves to a single little lie or two, no matter how petty. They risk becoming "lieaholics." That term is not frivolous, or misapplied. According to James Patterson and Pe-ter Kim, among the two thousand Americans they surveyed for *The Day America Told the Truth*, "the way some people talk about trying to do without lies, you'd think that they were smokers trying to get through a day without a cigarette." Others have found the same thing, especially among members of professions that put a premium on dissembling. A used-car salesman wrote Sissela Bok that reading her book on lying had motivated him to at least cut back on his compulsive telling of lies, if not stop it altogether. Ac-cording to a character in the movie *sex, lies, and videotape*, "Lying is like alcoholism, one is always 'recovering.'" One of Alan Wolfe's subjects, in Greensboro, North Carolina, called herself a recover-

ing liar. Lieaholics routinely employ the nomenclature of sub-
stance abuse when discussing their compulsion to deceive others.
A Tucson caller to National Public Radio's *Talk of the Nation* referred to himself unequivocally as a lying addict. Like any addic-
tive behavior, the caller said, his habitual telling of lies had cost
him friendships and jobs. The Tucsonian thought that the only
way he might overcome his addiction was with an Alcoholics
Anonymous approach, one step at a time.

Lies acquire lives of their own, and resist being killed off. They
take on auxiliary lies as bodyguards. One must be mounted on another lest this house of cards topple. As with cockroaches, the discovery of a single lie suggests that many more are lurking about
undetected. By the estimate of one psychologist, each lie we tell
requires an average of five more to back it up. To Alexander Pope
this estimate was low. "He who tells a lie is not sensible how great
a task he undertakes," wrote Pope, "for he must be forced to invent
twenty more to maintain that one."

Serial liars pay a stiff price: losing contact with their ability to
be candid with others, and ultimately with themselves. This is the
tougher part of the equation: eliminating the lazy lie, the casual
lie, those that are self-serving and unnecessary. "Honesty is like a
fight you have to fight within yourself," said one recovering liar.
"You really have to work on it," added another, "and it's not an
easy thing to do."

Craving Truth

Fortunately, we have allies in that struggle, including inner
ones. Although I don't believe that we are hardwired neurologi-
cally to be either honest or dishonest, I do believe that the unconscious craves truthfulness. This is simply because it would like our
inner self to be congruent with our outer self. Even when our

mouth tells lies, our spirit wishes it wouldn't. Paradoxically, that spirit is on vivid display among those who defend most vehemently their right to be dishonest. No one is more passionately concerned about the truth than an evangelist defending dishonesty. Ludwig Wittgenstein, who considered lying a mere "language game," was obsessed with the issue of truth telling. Friedrich Nietzsche's debunking of the concept of truth grew out of his ardent commitment to truthfulness. Mark Twain's flip celebrations of lying camouflaged a fierce morality. All were consumed by this topic.

Writers are among the loudest champions of their right to lie, and not just in fiction. "It is not unnatural that the best writers are liars," said Hemingway. "A major part of their trade is to lie or invent and they will lie when they are drunk, or to themselves, or to strangers." Added John Le Carré: "I'm a liar . . . Born to lying, bred to it, trained to it by an industry that lies for a living, practiced in it as a novelist. As a maker of fictions, I invent versions of myself, never the real thing, if it exists." There is usually a defensive hubris in such declarations. Hemingway and his spiritual descendants remind us ad nauseam, *"I tell lies. I'm a liar."* Anyone who devotes so much effort to devising rationales for his lying must yearn for a life less encumbered by fantasy. After noting how much time and energy he'd spent creating a fictional persona for himself, Ingmar Bergman observed that "he who has lived a lie loves the truth." Certainly this was true of Saint Augustine, the reformed liar turned truth crusader. Rousseau spent his entire adult life filled with remorse for a mean lie he had told as a child. So did Wittgenstein.

Anthropologists routinely discover great concern about honesty among groups of people who engage in a lot of deception. British anthropologist Julian A. Pitt-Rivers, for example, called the residents of a village in Spain's Andalusia region where he did fieldwork "the most accomplished liars I have ever encountered." Their lives revolved around perfecting the deceptive arts, Pitt-Rivers found, and exposing others who were doing the same thing. At the same time these Spaniards were "profoundly concerned with the truth." This was not paradoxical. Their very fixation on lying made them obsessed with truth telling. Brits like himself, Pitt-Rivers found, who were considered incompetent, amateurish liars by the Andalusians, were nonetheless envied by them for their naïve, honest innocence.

This is a recurring pattern among evangelical liars. They are as preoccupied with this issue as Immanuel Kant himself. That helps explain why so many apologists for dishonesty are so fascinated by lying, defensive about their right to tell lies, insistent that lies can be truer than truth, and determined to convince the rest of us. If lying were as inconsequential as they would have us believe, why spend so much time obsessing about it? At the very least that's an indication of this subject's consequence. Let's go further, however. When it comes to those who are so fervent about persuading others that it's okay to be deceitful, one can only wonder if the people they're trying hardest to persuade are themselves.

Nowhere is the yearning for truthfulness on more vivid display than in Lauren Slater's memoir *Lying*. When she addresses this topic in principle, the author is a passionate advocate of creative dissembling. Slater's seventh chapter consists of a long memo to her book's editor defending her right to "ponder the blurry line between novels and memoirs." By admitting that she's "a slippery sort," Slater writes the editor, she's simply being honest. To come clean in her memoir, therefore, would be dishonest. A novelist friend said Slater should call her fictionalized work a novel. She disagreed, pointing out that "a lot, or at least some, or at least a few of the literal facts are accurate." Anyway, Slater adds, even those elements that weren't literally true were metaphorically true. "My memoir, please," she pleads with her editor. "Sell it as nonfiction, please."

When defending her right to dissemble, Slater is verbose, bombastic, and defensive. When wondering why she finds it so hard to be truthful, the author lowers her voice, becomes more reflective. These soft-spoken interludes are far more convincing than her shrill postmodernity. They are more insightful too. Slater is especially eloquent on the price paid by prevaricators. Like Adrienne Rich, she acknowledges the loneliness of the liar. "No one knows you," explains Slater. "When people are interested in you, you understand it's for false reasons, and you get depressed." After pretending to have a drinking problem at an AA meeting, Slater writes, "I told myself that the figurative truth means more than the literal truth, but I still felt bad. I felt like a liar."

Slater confesses to her therapist that she researched epilepsy in the library, then faked seizures to attract attention. "I think I fooled you," she tells him.

"That doesn't surprise me," he said. "Exaggeration, trickery, we know that's part of your personality profile. I suspected all along you were hamming things up a bit."

His demeanor disturbed me. He seemed utterly unfazed. "I lied," I said, my voice rising, a bit righteously I might add. "I lied and a lie is a sin and a sin is never small, because it's a form of separation from God."

In the end, *Lying* is a morality tale, one woman's painful attempt to come to terms with her inability to tell the truth. Its author comes across as most genuine, most yearning, and most believable when she steps down from her soapbox and says plaintively that she wishes she could be more honest, could speak "fact and truth together."

A post-ethics case can be made for speaking fact and truth together. There are compelling reasons to be honest based more on social and personal imperatives than ethics as such. Virtue may be its own reward, but there are many other, more tangible reasons for telling truth.

Sixteen

The Case for Honesty

What is there to tie to but truth? Nothing. If we do not adhere to that, we are
done for—not that I don't sympathize with those who say
the truth can't be known.

—MAXWELL PERKINS

Tolerating deception is fashionable. Advocating honesty is not.
Standing foursquare for truth telling seems quaint, anachronistic, naive. Let's do so anyway. Let's make the case for honesty. The
peculiar sound of that sentence (does honesty need to have a case
made for it?) suggests the precarious state of truthfulness during
our post-truth era. Odd as it may seem that honesty should have to
be defended, it must be—on pragmatic as much as on ethical
grounds.

Post-Ethics Honesty

The case for honesty being the best policy must hold more water than "because it's right." This calls for less concern about questions like What is truth? or Is lying always bad? and more about
ones such as What's the best way to ensure my credibility? How
can I sustain my self-regard? and, most important, How can we all
live together with some semblance of trust?

The less face-to-face involvement we have with each other, the greater is our need for honesty. As direct contact with others declines and technology serves as a go-between, society needs more emphasis on truth telling, not less. One could accept every postmodern point about the elusiveness of truth (and even add some), yet still conclude that the attempt to be truthful is not only noble but essential for human well-being. What's the alternative? If we reach the conclusion that honesty is unnecessary because unattainable, with what do we replace it? Like Winston Churchill's democracy, the pursuit of honesty may be quixotic, but it's better than any alternative.

Historically Western society has shifted back and forth between tolerance and intolerance of lying. Today it has shifted too far toward the former. We need to move the needle back, at least to the center. This is not a categorical imperative so much as a matter of balance. With so many voices weighing in on behalf of deception during the post-truth era, counterweights of honesty are more necessary than ever. At the very least we need to reestablish that truth telling is our default setting, that honesty is assumed behavior, if not guaranteed. Truthfulness should always be the default, lies told with the greatest reluctance. Fib, sure, but only when unavoidable. Some won't swallow so much as a Tylenol without first asking, Is this really necessary? Can I get along without it? The same criterion should be applied to lie telling. We need to be more *picky* when deciding which lies to tell. Sissela Bok thinks any lie should be given "negative weight" when deciding whether to tell it. Unlike truth telling, which almost never needs justification, lies should be told only when there's a compelling reason to do so. "Mild as this initial stipulation sounds," concludes Bok, "it would, if taken seriously, eliminate a great many lies told out of carelessness or habit or unexamined good intentions."

Post-ethics honesty is analogous to trying to eat more sensibly. We may do so for the most part, but perhaps not as regularly as we might wish and with occasional lapses into banana splits and crème brûlées. These lapses may leave our silhouette less svelte than we'd like, and our eating habits less healthy, but we keep trying, and hope to succeed more often than not. The odd lie no more makes one a chronic liar than diet lapses lead to obesity. They are just that: lapses. Nutritional backsliding leaves us feeling too heavy, just as occasional lying leaves us feeling too flaccid spiritually, but we muddle through and keep trying.

Concluding that an activity is wrong doesn't mean we won't engage in it. We are human. There are times when we just can't deal with the consequences of telling the truth. But does it follow that because everyone engages in an activity at times it must be okay? That conclusion opens an ethical can of worms. Should shoplifting be condoned because so many teenagers use it as a rite of passage? Should rolling through Stop signs be legalized because it's such a common practice? Should we eliminate speed limits because they're routinely exceeded?

Even if we accept lying as inevitable now and again, it needn't follow that society should develop a deception-condoning moral code. Recognizing that dishonesty happens is not the same thing as deciding it's acceptable. Concluding that lies can sometimes be hard to avoid is not synonymous with concluding that they're routinely unavoidable. My concern is less about lying per se than about casual lying, recreational lying, self-deluded lies, and lies of convenience that are told when truth telling would work better in the long run. Recall the many studies in which subjects lied so routinely that they weren't even conscious of doing so. Post-ethics honesty means being mindful when telling a lie, and striving to minimize those events. Once we eliminate offhand lies, unthink-

ing lies, lazy lies, and unnecessarily self-serving lies, the answer to
the question When should one lie? becomes Not very often.

It's hard to improve on H. L. Mencken's credo: "I believe it is
better to tell the truth than to lie." Note that this credo does not
say one should *never* lie; simply that it's better to tell the truth.
Isn't that what we all do? one might ask. As we've seen throughout
this book, not necessarily. That is why there is so much need to
reaffirm our commitment to honesty. This means continually reaf-
firming that lying is wrong, we know it's wrong, even though it is
sometimes a lesser evil. There's something to be said for a bit of in-
consistency on this issue. By that I mean making a clear commitment to truth telling without expecting everyone always to be
truthful. Establishing a moral standard does not assume that everyone will adhere to this standard in every instance, or that anyone
who doesn't should be severely punished. The essence of maturity
is to accept ambiguity, including moral ambiguity. That's not the
same thing as saying that because everyone lies, lying's okay.
Rather, it is saying that the fact that we all lie doesn't make it
right. There's a difference.

This is a judgmental position, to be sure. But perhaps we need
more judgment on this issue. One reason we've lost our way in the
ethical woods is that we've adopted such an accepting, nonjudgmental stance in which no one is held accountable for being dishonest, or for much of anything. Along the way we've become too
concerned with our emotional well-being, not enough with our
ethical well-being.

Some take the opposite tack. Lies are as common as the common cold, they argue, so we should simply learn to live with them
as we have learned to live with rhinoviruses. According to this
school of thought, anything that's such a routine part of social discourse can hardly be called wrong. Speaking for many, philosopher

David Nyberg has suggested that honesty is "morally overrated," and that deception is "an essential component of our ability to organize and shape the world." Since we can never be fully honest all the time, those like Nyberg believe, it's better to admit this, accept our tendency to deceive others, and stop being so concerned about this tendency. That way of thinking has led to the post-truth era. To many it improves on a time when lies were considered the devil's work. Having determined that truth is hard to distinguish from untruth, and that lies can be benign, they conclude that maybe it's not so bad to tell lies after all.

After we open the dikes of acceptable dishonesty, however, where do we close them? Once we say, "Lying's not that big a deal. Everyone does it. Some lies are okay," identifying criteria for acceptable lies becomes a daunting task.

The Well-Intentioned Liar

Most attempts to distinguish acceptable from unacceptable lies are based on intent. From this perspective, one's intentions when being dishonest are more important than the simple fact of having lied. Many lies are unavoidable. Others are benign. Some are even beneficial. We must make distinctions. That is the crux of this argument. It's a hard one to contest. Of course all lies are not equal. Turning down a party invitation because you are "previously engaged" when you aren't is an innocuous little fib. Saying "I played football in high school" when you didn't does no harm to the lie's recipient. But telling a sex partner "I've tested negative for HIV" when you've tested positive does lethal harm. Obviously some lies are worse than others. The problem comes when we try to pin down which is which, and how that can be determined. Honesty is easier to determine than intent. We're far better able to ascertain *when* a lie has been told than *why*. If psychology has taught us nothing else, it's how mixed motives can be. Few can be cleaved cleanly into categories such as "benevolent" and "malevolent."

One practical problem with those who advocate ethics based on intent, or situational factors, is that many such factors are at cross-purposes and, in any event, too complex for average minds (or even above average minds) to keep straight. A National Public Radio interviewer who listened to an "ethicist" ruminate for several minutes on the nuances of a moral dilemma finally asked for guidance that was "more intuitive." That's the virtue of *Honesty is the best policy.* This policy is easy to keep straight, even if it's not always easy to honor. Saying "One shouldn't lie" has greater clarity, utility, and moral force than saying "One shouldn't lie except when _____." The "except when" approach begs two important questions: (1) What are the whens? and (2) Who identifies them? The most important question in any attempt to judge lies by intentions is: Who decides? Who determines which lies are benign and which malignant? Gray areas abound. Consensus is nonexistent. (Recall the wide range of exemptions different religions have for lies told by the faithful.) There is no Truth Tribunal to whom one can appeal. Invariably it is the person doing the condoning who determines which lies pass muster, especially his or her own. Obviously, the simpler "don't lie" approach leaves one susceptible to being simplistic. But a bit of oversimplification is preferable to a slippery quest for acceptable lying guidelines which leave too many doors open for casual dishonesty under the heading of Good Intentions.

How do we assess intent? Know it even? And even when we can, how do we achieve consensus on which intentions are good, which not so good? Those who endorse greater tolerance of dishonesty often point out how many lies are told for the sake of the lied-to. "An embroidering of the truth . . . ," suggests private eye

Precious Ramotswe in *The No. 1 Ladies' Detective Agency*, "sometimes gingered people up a bit, and it was often for their own good." Undoubtedly there are times when that's true. It can also be a rationalization. When someone says of any act "This is for your own good," it's usually for his.

As Sissela Bok emphasizes in *Lying*, those who rationalize dishonesty usually do so from the perspective of the liar, not the lie's target. The case for lying is more often made by those who dispense lies than by those who consume them. A candid assessment would show how many lies ostensibly told for the sake of the lied-to are actually told for the sake of the liar. Public servants who claim they've dissembled in the national interest invariably turn out to have dissembled in their own interest.

As a check on the serene belief in the purity of one's motives when lying, Bok suggests putting those motives on the table for public scrutiny. Few of our reasons for being deceitful are as clear to others as they are to us. We rarely feel well served by being hoodwinked, no matter how well intended the hoodwinker may be. When wondering if a lie is justified, imagine that someone whom you're about to deceive will discover this fact. Will she take it as evidence of your concern for her? There are far fewer such occasions than one might imagine.

Few this side of Immanuel Kant would argue that pure honesty is either possible or desirable. (I doubt that Kant himself really believed this.) A life without deception of any kind is inconceivable, the stuff of a Jim Carrey comedy. Unfettered truthfulness—what psychiatrist Willard Gaylin calls "truth dumping"—can be every bit as cruel as habitual lying. "That's a hideous dress you're wearing" is a completely unnecessary comment. So is "I find you far too boring a person to want to join you for dinner" or "Have you ever thought about getting rid of that ridiculous hairpiece?"

Like most, when asked "How are you?" I reflexively answer "Fine." This is false at least as often as it's true, but in general is easier to say and more considerate of the person who asks. At times, however, "Fine" is so blatant a lie that I can't get this word out of my mouth. In such cases I say "So-so" or "Not so hot." By the stricken look on my questioner's face I can tell in an instant that this was the wrong answer. It's also a rather thoughtless response on my part, a serious breach of social protocol.

Few want complete honesty from others without exception. Truth is a two-party proposition: one to tell, one to hear. It's an article of faith among marriage counselors that those who suspect their spouse of being unfaithful don't necessarily want to have this hunch confirmed. On a smaller scale, I'm grateful when someone who doesn't like a meal I cooked chooses not to share that information with me. And—like those who ask me—when I ask others how they're doing, most of the time I'd rather just be told "Fine," even when that isn't true. Such white lies serve the purposes of producer and consumer alike. But the color coding of lies isn't always as clear to the receiver as it is to the deceiver. Your white lie may look beige to me, or even brown.

Lies are shortcuts. They simplify complex situations. When our kids ask us "Did you ever smoke marijuana?" it's far easier to respond "No" than "Yes, but . . ." At the very least we may feel we simply don't have time to tell the truth and deal with the consequences. Because clerks at megastores who give me too much change get befuddled (to say nothing of annoyed) when I try to give it back, I seldom do anymore. Even then I'm not sure that this bit of trivial dishonesty isn't for my own convenience. The money involved matters less than the time and effort it would take to be scrupulously honest. So chalk up time pressure as one more source of post-truthfulness, albeit one that's probably a rationalization as often as it is a rationale.

This isn't to say that little lies of convenience should never be told. But when telling them we should be clear about what we're up to, and who benefits: us, usually. Saying they're for someone else's sake too often compounds dishonesty with self-deception. Seemingly compassionate white lies are generally told out of an excess of niceness, to save time, or because of an unwillingness to deal with the consequences of honesty. Laziness is one motivation for being dishonest, including emotional laziness. "For peace of mind," says a character in Amy Hempel's novella *Tumble Home*, "I will lie about any thing at any time."

False distinctions abound in this area. One's choice is not necessarily between compassionate lies and cruel truths but between thoughtless lies and thoughtfully presented truths. This bears on the healing arts. Dissembling was once considered part and parcel of those arts. Unwarranted reassurance of patients even had a label among physicians: "benevolent deception." They believed that we heal better if protected from the truth. Some still believe that. This bit of folk wisdom may be nothing more, however. One physician suggested that deceptive doctors make poor diagnosticians because they're more focused on reassuring patients than on determing what's wrong with them. Recent studies have shown that patients who are suffering from serious illnesses do best when told the truth about their condition, even if they are in the late stages of a terminal illness. Anyone who has sat by the bed of a loved one who is dying and colluded in the deception that this person is getting better knows how devastating that experience can be. Facing this truth is far more demanding, and infinitely more compassionate.

Truth telling is high-maintenance. Becoming a consistent truth teller takes courage, determination, and will. That is what honesty is all about. It's also about compassion. Even the petty fibs of everyday discourse are not always as harmless as we like to imagine. Lies told to "protect somebody else's feelings" can be manipulative, even hostile. At the very least any lie—no matter how small—is a vote of no confidence in the person to whom it's told. Regardless of the intent with which they're told, all lies announce boldly—as Jack Nicholson's character does in *A Few Good Men*—"You can't handle the truth!" When we do tell someone the truth, we're suggesting that we think he or she *can* handle it. This includes our children.

Honest Parenting

Ambivalence about honesty is on vivid display when it comes to parenting. On the one hand, children are admonished never to tell lies. On the other hand, they're told to tell their aunt Helen how much they like the mittens she knit for them. Among the two thousand Americans surveyed for *The Day America Told the Truth*, 59 percent of those who had children said they lied to their kids on a regular basis. They do this primarily to protect the feelings of others ("Don't forget to tell Aunt Helen that you love the mittens"), ease fears ("A hurricane should be fun!"), protect their relationship with a spouse ("Daddy and I weren't arguing; we were just rehearsing a scene for my play"), and make life easier for themselves ("Our cable company doesn't carry *South Park*").

While condoning the occasional fib, child psychologist Michael Lewis warns that routine parental lying has more to do with parents' needs than their children's, and can corrode this relationship. One way parents establish who's got the power in that relationship is by telling their children casual, convenient, and self-serving lies while demanding scrupulous honesty in return.

Most parents warn their kids not to lie, especially to them. At the same time many give them a dishonest model to emulate: their own. If ever teaching is done by modeling it is here. A child who hears a healthy parent turn down an unwelcome social invitation because "I'm not feeling well" learns an important, unfortunate lesson.

The best way to raise a liar is to deceive others regularly in the presence of one's children. Better yet, lie to them. Parents usually rationalize lies they tell their kids by saying they're insignificant, and for the children's own good. More often, however, they're for the convenience of the parent. Lying also helps preserve the illusion of parental omnipotence. The danger is that deceiving our children can become a reflex, something we do without even thinking about it. Routine deception of one's kids is a risky business, even when the lies told are small and benign. Telling them the truth, no matter how demanding that can be, is a form of respect. In the short run it creates problems; in the long run it builds a strong foundation for a solid relationship.

Lies that are told routinely as a child-rearing tool plant bombs that may take years to explode. A middle-aged woman I know has an edgy relationship with a mother who deceived her continually as a child. She still remembers the time her mother took her to the hairdresser just to "get the ends trimmed" from her long hair, then had the hairdresser cut it short. When trying to get her daughter to try a new food, this woman's mother would remind her that she hadn't liked ice cream until she'd made her try it (an untrue story). These lies may have been petty, white, and well intentioned. But when the daughter grew up and realized how routinely her mother had deceived her as a child, she never knew what statements of her mother's to believe.

The Social Value of Honesty

For individuals and groups alike, honesty is a perpetual feedback loop. Truth tellers build societies whose members have confidence in each other's credibility. In his book *Trust,* Francis Fukuyama argues that only societies whose members enjoy a high level of this kind of confidence can reap the benefits of political stability and a robust economy. Economic prosperity is built on a foundation of trust. Where suspicion reigns, the cost of doing business goes up (because of extended negotiations, lengthy contracts, litigation, and lawyers' fees). Stock markets teeter-totter on a fulcrum of confidence. Investors and businesspeople alike take more necessary risks when their trust level is high than when it's low. Stockbrokers see the impact of corporate scandals in the wariness of investors. Renegades in their own profession have contributed to a risk-averse investment atmosphere. If the honesty of a broker's recommendation or a company's financial statements can't be trusted, why buy stocks? Investor wariness in turn contributes to economic sluggishness. The suspicious society imposes a tax not just on our spiritual and social well-being but on our economic prosperity as well.

One reason there is so much emphasis on *transparency* in contemporary life is because complex economies function so much better when participants are candid. This is especially true when things aren't going well. Deceitful behavior only postpones days of reckoning, and in the process distorts the economy as a whole. Everyone paid a price for the alt.ethics that subsidized fantasy profits reported during the New Economy bubble. Failure is a form of feedback, after all. When their failures are covered up and made to look like successes, organizations are deprived of feedback necessary to make corrections. Problems cannot be lied away forever. Once the reality organizational lies are hiding becomes apparent, corrections take that much longer to make. According to Federal Reserve Board chairman Alan Greenspan, the many CEOs who told their accountants *not* to improve financial statements, because they needed to know where problems lay, did better in the long run than those who manipulated their accounts. The dishonest recommendations some brokers made to clients (advising them to buy stocks they privately called "dogs") cost their brokerages huge fines and untold amounts of lost credibility. In the case of Arthur Andersen, helping Enron cook its books cost this accounting firm its very existence.

The more suspicious society grows, the more valuable honesty will become. Employees who work for organizations they perceive as being truthful enjoy higher morale than those who suspect their employer is deceiving them. Organizations perceived to be dishonest also have a higher turnover rate. Companies that are seen as honest are more likely to retain employees. Integrity has market value.

Positive Trends

All is not gloom and doom on the honesty front. There is enough lingering outrage about deception by public figures to suggest how many of us remain concerned about this issue. Our intense interest in the subject of lying overall indicates that honesty still matters to us. Journalists continue to do their bit to expose lies and keep this issue on the national agenda. Despite their own transgressions, if there is any hero in the struggle against dishonesty, it is the print media. Even as higher educators dither about their commitment to truth telling and religious leaders hide bad behavior by members of the clergy, newspapers continue to honor the principle of truth seeking and truth telling. It may take time, but the press does investigate and publicize ethical lapses by its reporters, then fires those found guilty. Newsrooms are one setting in which dissembling remains a dismissable offense.

Just as some aspects of contemporary life encourage deception, others promote honesty. They include the modern concepts of "full disclosure" in commercial transactions, "informed consent" among medical patients, and "discovery" in legal proceedings (whereby contending parties must share crucial evidence with each other). Watchdog Web sites such as FactCheck.org, organizations like the Center for Public Integrity, and sundry freelance investigators using potent investigation tools like the Freedom of Information Act ensure that deception will continue to be a risky activity.

In some ways dishonesty has become riskier than ever. Many enablers of post-truthfulness also contribute to its demise. This is especially true in cyberspace, where the same technology both corrodes and promotes honesty. Those who use cybertools to deceive others are always at risk of being exposed by others using the very same tools. Plagiarizers have easy pickings on the Internet, but plagiarist-catching software can quickly identify purloined material. Limbs grafted onto family trees are collapsing under the weight of genealogical documents posted on the Internet. Résumés are easier to embroider in the information age, but such embroideries are easier to discredit. The epidemic of résumé fabricators, phony veterans, and sundry imposeurs is actually an epidemic of investigation by those who mine the Internet for evidence with which to expose lies put in play long ago. Google could be the best friend truth discovery has ever had. There are others. DNA testing, for example, which is such a powerful source of irrefutable evidence in cases of crime and paternity, has become an important modern incentive to be truthful. Undoubtedly there are many more to come.

Honesty Redux

Lying has existed in every society for all of time and undoubtedly always will. The question then becomes whether a given society facilitates or discourages dishonesty. Certainly we need more truth telling throughout our own society. But even more than this we need a context that rewards honesty and penalizes dishonesty.

In any given group of people, probably 10 percent are ethical by nature (because they are empathetic, altruistic, and self-assured), and 10 percent have no ethical inclination at all (because they are narcissistic, pathological, or just plain lazy). The other 80 percent are swing voters who move back and forth, depending on circumstances. Encouraging more honesty in that group requires a context very different from the current one, one with more incentives to tell the truth and stiffer sanctions against deception. Too many elements of contemporary society unwittingly do just the opposite: they reward deception and penalize candor. Altering those elements will do more than any religious revival to restore integrity.

In terms of encouraging honesty we are probably doing better on the policy front than on the personal one. We all might work not only on being more honest but on encouraging others to tell us the truth by letting them know that this is what we want and that we are up to the task. A capacity to *hear* the truth is at least as demanding as a capacity to *tell* the truth. Both are acquired skills. That's the case wherever people gather. According to management sage Warren Bennis, creating and maintaining a culture of honesty in any organization "requires sustained attention and constant vigilance." The payoff comes in the form of human groups whose members trust each other. Their truthfulness in turn reinforces the bonds of those groups.

Every bit as important as raising ethical standards is making human links strong enough that those who enjoy them think twice before telling each other a lie. Nothing encourages truth telling more than feeling connected to others whom we saw yesterday and may see tomorrow. Because honesty is so important among those who interact on a regular basis, telling the truth is a way of affirming human ties. The more tied we feel to others, the less likely we are to deceive them. Just as lying degrades human connections, truthfulness invigorates them. In this sense honesty is a sign of aspiration, of hope, of faith in the prospect of human community.

Acknowledgments

I would like to acknowledge invaluable help from the following people in writing this book:

Members of the Western Behavioral Science Institute's International Leadership Forum, who contributed many a valuable insight in our online conference "The Post-Truth Era."

For early encouragement and helpful suggestions: Colleen Mohyde, Meena Nayak, Patrick O'Connor, Charles O'Leary, and Jane Tomlin.

Research assistance: Louisa Bradtmiller, Gay Courter, and the many helpful librarians at the Greene County Public Library and the Olive Kettering Library of Antioch College.

Reading and commenting on specific sections of the manuscript: Joe Downing, Nicholas Johnson, Landon Jones, Chuck Watts, and Mary Tom Watts.

Reading and commenting on the entire manuscript: Andrea Adkins, Wendy Hart Beckman, Mary Boone, Richard Farson, T. George Harris, Lou Heckler, Kathryn Olney, and Robert Ellis Smith.

Help above and beyond: my brother Gene Keyes, who caught one glitch after another in late-night reading sessions as the manuscript was about to be completed, and who continually sent me useful information; my former editor and friend Bill Phillips, who reviewed the proposal for this book, read parts of early manuscript drafts, then volunteered to read the entire manuscript at a crucial stage; and my wife, Muriel, who came to my rescue at key moments to review the manuscript's final draft, do research, nail down citations, and give me her usual excellent suggestions.

This book could not have been published without the support of my editors at St. Martin's Press: Alicia Brooks, who acquired the project; Tim Bent, who oversaw the manuscript in its early stages; and Julia Pastore, who did an astute job of manuscript editing, as did Ethan Friedman, whose capable hands then saw the book through to publication.

Ellis Levine and Adam Goldberger gave me invaluable suggestions with their thorough review of the book's manuscript.

Finally, my agent, Michelle Tessler, recognized the need for a book on this topic, and gave this one strong, helpful support from beginning to end.

I would also like to acknowledge my sons, David and Scott, for their overall support, especially in the design and maintenance of my Web site. Thanks, guys.

Recommended Reading

Books

Bailey, F. G. *The Prevalence of Deceit*. Ithaca, NY: Cornell University Press, 1991.

Barnes, J. A. *A Pack of Lies: Towards a Sociology of Lying*. Cambridge, England: Cambridge University Press, 1994.

Bok, Sissela. *Lying: Moral Choice in Public and Private Life*. New York: Pantheon, 1978; Vintage, 1979.

Cabot, Richard C. *Honesty*. New York: Macmillan, 1938.

Campbell, Jeremy. *The Liar's Tale: A History of Falsehood*. New York: Norton, 2001.

Ekman, Paul. *Telling Lies: Clues to Deceit in the Marketplace, Politics, and Marriage*. New York: Norton, 2001.

Ford, Charles V. *Lies! Lies! Lies! The Psychology of Deceit*. Washington, DC: American Psychiatric Press, 1996.

Kerr, Philip, ed. *The Penguin Book of Lies*. New York: Viking, 1990.

Scott, Gini Graham. *The Truth About Lying: Why We All Do It, How We Do It, and Can We Live Without It?* Petaluma, CA: Smart Publications, 1994.

Shapin, Steven. *A Social History of Truth: Civility and Science in Seventeenth-Century England*. Chicago: University of Chicago Press, 1994.

Sullivan, Evelin. *The Concise Book of Lying*. New York: Farrar, Straus and Giroux, 2001.

Williams, Bernard. *Truth and Truthfulness*. Princeton, NJ: Princeton University Press, 2002.

Essays

Allon, Dafna. "Reflections on the Art of Lying, *Commentary*, June 1986.

Augustine. "Lying." In *Treatises on Various Subjects*. Sister Mary Sarah Muldowney trans. Roy J. Deferrari ed. New York: Fathers of the Church, 1952.

Augustine. "Against Lying." In ibid. Trans. Harold B. Jaffee.

Bacon, Francis. "Of Truth." In *Essays, Advancement of Learning, New Atlantis, and Other Pieces*. Ed. Richard Foster Jones. Garden City, NY: Doubleday Doran, 1937.

Black, Max. "The Prevalence of Humbug." In *The Prevalance of Humbug and Other Essays*, 115–43. Ithaca, NY: Cornell University Press, 1983.

Boyers, Robert. "Observations on Lying and Liars." *Review of Existential Psychology and Psychiatry* 13 (1974): 150–68.

Brougham, T. Alan. "Some Notes on the Art of Lying." *New England Review*, 93–100, Spring 1994.

Frankfurt, Harry. "On Bullshit." *Raritan* 6 (1986): 81–100.

Minnich, Elizabeth Kamarck. "Why Not Lie?" *Soundings* 68 (1985): 493–509.

Montaigne, Michel de. "On Liars." In *Essays*. J. M. Cohen, trans. Baltimore: Penguin, 1958.

Rich, Adrienne. "Women and Honor: Some Notes on Lying." In *On Lies, Secrets, and Silence: Selected Prose 1966–1978*. New York: Norton, 1979.

Notes

1. Beyond Honesty

3 Boorstin: Daniel J. Boorstin, *The Image: A Guide to Pseudo-Events in America* (Harper Colophon, 1964), 226.

3–4 Feldman: personal communication. "Good Morning America," ABC, February 22, 1998; *Cleveland Plain Dealer*, July 19, 1998; Associated Press, December 16, 1999; *National Post* (Canada), June 12, 2002; *All Things Considered*, National Public Radio, June 13, 2002; *Los Angeles Times*, March 3, 2003; Robert S. Feldman, "Nonverbal Disclosure of Teacher Deception and Interpersonal Affect," *Journal of Educational Psychology* 68 (1976): 807–16; Robert S. Feldman, "Detection of Deception in Adults and Children via Facial Expressions," *Child Development* 50 (1979): 350–55; Robert S. Feldman, "Nonverbal Disclosure of Deception in Urban Koreans," *Journal of Cross-Cultural Psychology* 10 (1979): 73–83; Robert S. Feldman, Jason C. Tomasian, and Erik J. Coats, "Nonverbal Deception Abilities and Adolescents' Social Competence: Adolescents with Higher Social Skills Are Better Liars," *Journal of Nonverbal Behavior* 23 (1999): 237–49; Robert S. Feldman, James A. Forrest, and Benjamin R. Happ, "Self-Presentation and Verbal Deception: Do Self-Presenters Lie More?" *Basic and Applied Social Psychology* 24 (2002): 163–70; Robert S. Feldman and Robert J. Custrini, "Learning to Lie and Self-Deceive: Children's Nonverbal Communication of Deception," in *Self-Deception: An Adaptive Mechanism?* ed. Joan S. Lockard and Delroy L. Paulhus (Englewood Cliffs, NJ: Prentice-Hall, 1988), 40–53.

4 "I think most of us assume": *All Things Considered*, National Public Radio, June 13, 2002.

4–5 Rodriguez and Rygrave: Noelie Rodriguez and Alan Rygrave, "Telling Lies in

Everyday Life: Motivational and Organizational Consequences of Sequential Preferences," *Qualitative Sociology* 13 (1990): 199.

5 Wittgenstein: Ludwig Wittgenstein, *Culture and Value* (Chicago: University of Chicago Press, 1980), 37e.

6 Hodson: *Independent on Sunday* (London, England), July 13, 2003.

6 priest: *Washington Post*, August 17, 1998.

6 priest's colleague: Cox News Service, December 14, 2001.

6 Gallup: *Princeton Packet*, November 21, 1999; *USA Today*, July 5, 2001.

6 West European poll: Stephen Harding and David Phillips with Michael Fogarty, *Contrasting Values in Western Europe: Unity, Diversity, and Change* (London: Macmillan, 1986), 8–9, 19–20, 25, 139–40, 221.

6–7 Josephson: www.josephsoninstitute.org; *Los Angeles Times*, December 10, 1991; *Dallas Morning News*, October 19, 1998; *USA Weekend*, October 16–18, 1998; Associated Press, October 19, 1998; *CNN Today*, October 19, 1998; *Washington Times*, October 20, 1998; *Los Angeles Sentinel*, November 4, 1998; *Dayton Daily News*, October 17, 2000, October 23, 2002; *Los Angeles Times*, October 30, 2002; *Washington Post*, November 3, 2002; *Minneapolis Star Tribune*, February 1, 2003; Randy Fitzgerald, "The Real Truth About Lies," www.208.20.99.200/articles/realtruth.htm.

7 how often lie: M. Hirsh Goldberg, *The Book of Lies* (New York: Morrow, 1990), 6; *Time*, April 3, 1978; *San Diego Union-Tribune*, August 14, 1996; *San Francisco Chronicle*, July 30, 1993; *New York Times*, May 17, 1988; Barry R. Schlenker, ed., *The Self and Social Life* (New York: McGraw-Hill, 1985), 183.

7 DePaulo's group: Malcolm Ritter, *Los Angeles Times*, August 27, 1995; *New Scientist*, August 26, 1995; University of Virginia press release, May 22, 1996; *Richmond Times-Dispatch*, May 22, 1996; *Toronto Star*, July 29, 1996; *Cleveland Plain Dealer*, September 1, 1996; Bella M. DePaulo, Deborah A. Kashy, Susan E. Kirkendol, Melissa M. Wyer, and Jennifer A. Epstein, "Lying in Everyday Life," *Journal of Personality and Social Psychology* 70 (1996) 979–95; Deborah A. Kashy and Bella M. DePaulo, *Journal of Personality and Social Psychology* 70 (1996) 1037–51; Deborah A. Kashy and Bella M. DePaulo, "Who Lies?" *Journal of Personality and Social Psychology* 70 (1996): 1037–51; Bella M. DePaulo and Deborah A. Kashy, "Everyday Lies in Close and Casual Relationships," *Journal of Personality and Social Psychology* 74 (1998) 63–79.

7–8 about Bella DePaulo: *Psychology Today*, January 1986, December 1986; *Hartford Courant*, March 29, 1997; *Orlando Sentinel*, April 18, 1997; *Psychology Today*, May–June 1997; *CBS This Morning*, April 22, 1998; *Times* (London, England), May 24, 1998; *Cleveland Plain Dealer*, July 31, 1998; *Washington Post*,

August 17, 1998; *Gold Coast Bulletin* (Australia) July 9, 2001; Cox News Service, December 14, 2001.

8 eager to make good impression: Deborah A. Kashy and Bella M. DePaulo, "Who Lies?", *Journal of Personality and Social Psychology* 70 (1996): 1038, 1049–50.

8 lie more to those we like: Kathy L. Bell and Bella M. DePaulo, "Liking and Lying," *Basic and Applied Psychology* 18 (1996): 243–66; Bella M. DePaulo and Kathy L. Bell, "Truth and Investment. Lies Are Told to Those Who Care," *Journal of Personality and Social Psychology* 71 (1996): 703–16.

8 attractive people: Bella M. DePaulo, John Tang, and Julie I. Stone, "Physical Attractiveness and Skill at Detecting Deception," *Personality and Social Psychology Bulletin* 13 (1987): 177–87; Bella M. DePaulo with Susan E. Kirkendol, "The Motivational Impairment Effect in the Communication of Deception," in *Credibility Assessment*, ed. John C. Yuille (Dordrecht, Netherlands: Kluwer, 1988), 51–70.

8 dishonest at least once a day: *San Diego Union-Tribune*, August 14, 1996; D. Eric Anderson, Matthew E. Ansfield, and Bella M. DePaulo, "Love's Best Habit: Deception in the Context of Relationships," in *The Social Context of Nonverbal Behavior*, ed., Pierre Philippot, Robert S. Feldman, and Eric J. Coats (Cambridge: Cambridge University Press, 1999), 378.

8 she thought he was lying: *Rocky Mountain News*, February 3, 1998.

8 hardly any succeed: *Hartford Courant*, March 29, 1997.

8 footnote: publications on deception by Bella DePaulo and colleagues: Bella M. DePaulo and Robert Rosenthal, "Telling Lies," *Journal of Personality and Social Psychology* 37 (1979): 1713–22; Bella M. DePaulo, Miron Zuckerman, and Robert Rosenthal, "Humans as Lie Defectors," *Journal of Communication* 30 (1980): 129–39; Bella M. DePaulo, Miron Zuckerman, and Robert Rosenthal, "The Deceptions of Everyday Life," *Journal of Communication* 30 (1980): 216–18; Bella M. DePaulo with Audrey Jordan, "Age Changes in Deceiving and Detecting Deceit," *Development of Nonverbal Behavior in Children*, Robert S. Feldman, ed. (New York: Springer-Verlag, 1982), 151–80; Bella M. DePaulo, Robert Rosenthal, Judith Rosenkrantz, and Carolyn Rieder Green, "Actual and Perceived Cues to Deception: A Closer Look at Speech," *Basic and Applied Social Psychology* 3 (1982): 291–312; Bella M. DePaulo, Audrey Jordan, Audrey Irvine, and Patricia S. Laser, "Age Changes in the Detection of Deception," *Child Development* 53 (1982): 701–9; Bella M. DePaulo, Robert Rosenthal, Carolyn Rieder Green, and Judith Rosenkrantz, "Diagnosing Deceptive and Mixed Messages from Verbal and Nonverbal Cues," *Journal of Experimental Social Psychology* 18 (1982): 433–46; Bella M. DePaulo, Keith

Lanier, and Tracy Davis, *Journal of Personality and Social Psychology* 45 (1983): 1096–1103; Carol Toris and Bella M. DePaulo, "Effects of Actual Deception and Suspiciousness of Deception on Interpersonal Relations," *Journal of Personality and Social Psychology* 47 (1985): 1063–73; Bella M. DePaulo, Julie I. Stone, and G. Daniel Lassiter, "Telling Ingratiating Lies: Effects of Target Sex and Target Awareness on Verbal and Nonverbal Deceptive Success," *Journal of Personality and Social Psychology* 48 (1985): 1191–1203; Bella M. DePaulo with Julie I. Stone and G. Daniel Lassiter, "Deceiving and Detecting Deceit," *The Self and Social Life*, ed. Barry R. Schlenker (New York: McGraw-Hill, 1985), 323–70; Bella M. DePaulo and Roger L. Pfeifer, "On-the-Job Experience and Skill at Detecting Deception," *Journal of Applied Social Psychology* 16 (1986): 249–67; Bella M. DePaulo, John Tang, and Julie I. Stone, "Physical Attractiveness and Skill at Detecting Deception," *Personality and Social Psychology Bulletin* 13 (1987): 177–87; Bella M. DePaulo, Susan E. Kirkendol, John Tang, and Thomas P. O'Brien, "The Motivational Impairment Effect in the Communication of Deception: Replications and Extensions," *Journal of Nonverbal Behavior* 12 (1988): 177–202; Bella M. DePaulo and Susan E. Kirkendol, "The Motivational Impairment Effect in the Communication of Deception," in *Credibility Assessment,* ed. John C. Yuille (Dordrecht, Netherlands: Kluwer, 1988), 51–70; Bella M. DePaulo, "Nonverbal Aspects of Deception," *Journal of Nonverbal Behavior* 12 (1988): 153–61; Peter J. DePaulo and Bella M. DePaulo, "Can Deception by Salespersons and Customers Be Detected Through Nonverbal Behavioral Cues?" *Journal of Applied Social Psychology* 19 (1989): 1552–77; Bella M. DePaulo, Carol Steele LeMay, and Jennifer A. Epstein, "Effects of Importance of Success and Expectations for Success on Effectiveness at Deceiving," *Personality and Social Psychology Bulletin* 17 (1991): 14–24; Bella M. DePaulo, "Should We Bemoan or Applaud the Loss of Innocence?" *Contemporary Psychology* 37 (1992): 935; Bella M. DePaulo, "Negotiating the Thickets of Truth and Deceits in Politics and in Everyday Life," *The Long Term View* 1 (1992): 5–8; Bella M. DePaulo, "Nonverbal Behavior and Self-Presentation," *Psychological Bulletin* 111 (1992): 203–43; Bella M. DePaulo, Jennifer A. Epstein, and Melissa M. Wyer, "Sex Differences in Lying: How Women and Men Deal with the Dilemma of Deceit," in *Lying and Deception in Everyday Life,* ed. Michael Lewis and Carolyn Saarni (New York: Guilford, 1993), 126–47; Bella M. DePaulo, "Little Liars: What Lawyers Want to Know and what Psychologists Can Tell Them," *Applied Cognitive Psychology* 7 (1993): 360–61; David A. Kenny and Bella M. DePaulo, "Do People Know How Others View Them? An Empirical and Theoretical Account," *Psycholog-

ical Bulletin 114 (1993): 145–61; Bella M. DePaulo and John Tang, "Social Anxiety and Social Judgment: The Example of Detecting Deception," *Journal of Research in Personality* 28 (1994): 142–53; Bella M. DePaulo, "Spotting Human Lies: Can Humans Learn to Do Better?" *Current Directions in Psychological Science* 3 (1994): 83–86; Kathy L. Bell and Bella M. DePaulo, "Liking and Lying," *Basic and Applied Psychology* 18 (1996): 243–66; Bella M. DePaulo and Kathy L. Bell, "Truth and Investment: Lies Are Told to Those Who Care," *Journal of Personality and Social Psychology* 71 (1996): 703–16; Bella M. DePaulo, Deborah A. Kashy, Susan E. Kirkendol, Melissa M. Wyer, and Jennifer A. Epstein, "Lying in Everyday Life," *Journal of Personality and Social Psychology* 70 (1996): 979–95; Deborah A. Kashy and Bella M. DePaulo, "Who Lies?" *Journal of Personality and Social Psychology* 70 (1996): 1037–51; Bella M. DePaulo and Matthew E. Ansfield, "Detecting Deception from Nonverbal Cues: Pinocchio's Revenge," *Legal Medical Quarterly* 20 (1996): 5–19; Bella M. DePaulo, "Book Review: *By the Grace of Guile: The Role of Deception in Natural History and Human Affairs*," *Political Psychology* 17 (1996): 387–90; Bella M. DePaulo, Matthew E. Ansfield, and Kathy L. Bell, "Theories About Deception and Paradigms for Studying It: A Critical Appraisal of Buller and Burgoon's Interpersonal Deception Theory and Research," *Communication Theory* 6 (1996): 297–310; Bella M. DePaulo, "Truth and Distortion: Insights and Oversights About Deceit," *Contemporary Psychology* 42 (1997): 711–12; Bella M. DePaulo, Kelly Charlton, Harris Cooper, James J. Lindsay, and Laura Muhlenbruck, "The Accuracy-Confidence Correlation in the Detection of Deception," *Personality and Social Psychology Review* 1 (1997): 346–57; Bella M. DePaulo and Deborah A. Kashy, "Everyday Lies in Close and Casual Relationships," *Journal of Personality and Social Psychology* 74 (1998): 63–79; Julie D. Lane and Bella M. DePaulo, "Completing Coyne's Cycle: Dysphorics' Ability to Detect Deception," *Journal of Research in Personality* 33 (1999): 311–29; D. Eric Anderson, Bella M. DePaulo, Matthew E. Ansfield, Jennifer J. Tickle, and Emily Green, "Beliefs and Cues to Deception: Mindless Stereotypes or Untapped Wisdom?" *Journal of Nonverbal Behavior* 23 (1999): 67–89; D. Eric Anderson, Matthew E. Ansfield and Bella M. DePaulo, "Love's Best Habit: Deception in the context of Relationships," in *The Social Context of Nonverbal Behavior*, ed., Pierre Philipott, Robert S. Feldman, and Eric J. Coats (Cambridge: Cambridge University Press, 1999), 378.

8 "Lying is a routine event": *Chicago Tribune*, October 6, 1996.

9 Campbell: Jeremy Campbell, *The Liar's Tale: A History of Falsehood* (New York: Norton, 2001), 12.

9 Wilde: Oscar Wilde, "The Decay of Lying," in *The Complete Works of Oscar Wilde* (New York: Harper and Row, 1989), 970–92.

9 Nietzsche: Friedrich Nietzsche, *Philosophy and Truth: Selections from Nietzsche's Notebooks of the Early 1870s*, trans. and ed. Daniel Breazeale (Atlantic Highlands, NJ: Humanities Press, 1979), 96.

9 Hemingway: Jeffrey Meyers, *Hemingway: A Biography* (New York: Harper and Row, 1985), 237–41.

10 church membership: Martin E. Marty, *Time*, October 27, 1975.

11 Ford: *Hartford Courant*, March 29, 1997.

11 O'Hair and Cody: H. Dan O'Hair and Michael J. Cody, "Deception," *The Dark Side of Interpersonal Communication*, ed. William R. Cupach and Brian H. Spitzberg (Hillsdale, NJ: Erlbaum, 1994), 181–213.

11 Wiseman: *Nature* February 2, 1995.

11 Bradlee: *Washington Post*, November 17, 1991.

12 Bok: Sissela Bok, *Lying: Moral Choice in Public and Private Life* (New York: Vintage, 1999), xviii.

13 lie: *Oxford English Dictionary Online* (New York: Oxford, 2003).

13 Tesich: *Nation*, January 6, 1992.

14 Hart: *USA Today*, March 15, 1984; *Philadelphia Daily News*, March 16, 1984; *New York Times*, March 26, 1984; *Newsweek*, June 8, 1987.

14 Kerry: *Hardball*, MSNBC, November 5, 2003; NewsMax.com, November 12, 2003.

14 Lerner: Harriet Goldhor Lerner, *The Dance of Deception: Pretending and Truth-Telling in Women's Lives* (New York: HarperCollins, 1993), 118.

14 Armstrong: *New Statesman*, April 14, 2003.

14 Churchill: speech to Parliament, February 22, 1906, "Quotations from Sir Winston Churchill, 1874–1965," www.TheSpeechSite.com.

14 "someone for whom truth": Arnold Goldberg, "On Telling the Truth," in *Adolescent Psychiatry, vol. 2*, ed. Sherman C. Feinstein and Peter L. Giovacchini (New York: Basic Books, 1973), 104.

14–15 Trump: *Washington Post*, December 27, 1987; Daniel Roth, "The Trophy Life," *Fortune*, April 19, 2004.

15 Churchill: *Frontline*, August 2–15, 2003.

16 *New Yorker* cartoon: *New Yorker*, November 25, 2002.

17 magazine publisher: *MORE*, June 1975.

18 chief of staff: CNN, February 26, 2003; Associated Press, July 24, 2003.

18 Medicare actuary: *New York Times*, March 18, 2004.

2. A Brief History of Lying

19 Bok: Sissela Bok, *Lying: Moral Choice in Public and Private Life* (New York: Vintage, 1979), 19.

19 Piaget: Jean Piaget, *The Moral Judgment of the Child*, trans. Marjorie Gabain (New York: Free Press, 1932, 1965), 139.

19 Koko: Francine Patterson, "Linguistic Capabilities of a Lowland Gorilla," in *Sign Language and Language Acquisition in Man and Ape*, ed. Fred C.C. Peng (Boulder, CO: Westview Press, 1978), 196–97; Francine Patterson and Eugene Linden, *The Education of Koko* (New York: Holt, Rinehart and Winston, 1981), 181–83.

20 Patterson's colleagues: H. Lyn Miles, "How Can I Tell a Lie? Apes, Language, and the Problem of Deception," in *Deception: Perspectives on Human and Nonhuman Deceit*, ed. Robert W. Mitchell and Nicholas S. Thompson (Albany: State University of New York Press, 1986), 177–91; Charles F. Bond Jr. and Michael Robinson, "The Evolution of Deception," *Journal of Nonverbal Behavior* 12 (1988): 300; Sue Savage-Rumbaugh and Kelly McDonald, "Deception and Social Manipulation in Symbol-Using Apes," in *Machiavellian Intelligence*, ed. Richard W. Byrne and Andrew Whiten (Oxford: Clarendon, 1988), 224–37.

20 ability to speak and lie related: George Steiner, *After Babel* (New York: Oxford, 1975), 222–29; Robert Trivers, *Social Evolution* (Menlo Park, CA: Benjamin/Cummings, 1985), 416; Charles F. Bond Jr. and Michael Robinson, "The Evolution of Deception," *Journal of Nonverbal Behavior* 12 (1988): 295–307; J. A. Barnes, *A Pack of Lies: Towards a Sociology of Lying* (Cambridge: Cambridge University Press, 1994), 149–56; Perez Zagorin, "The Historical Significance of Lying and Dissimulation," *Social Research* 63 (1996): 863–912; Paul Quinnett, *Darwin's Bass* (Sandpoint, ID: Keokee, 1996), 168–70.

21 Popper: Paul Arthur Schilpp, *The Philosophy of Karl Popper* (LaSalle, IL: Open Court, 1974), 1112–13.

21–22 Darwin: Campbell, *The Liar's Tale*, 25–26.

22 Buddha: Talk, Religion, Buddhism newsgroup, October 28, 2002, www.accesstoinsight.org/lib/bps/mis/waytoend.html.

22 Darwin: Charles Darwin, *The Descent of Man* (Chicago: Rand, McNally, 1874), 106, 111–16, 120–21, 126–27.

23 "There cannot be fidelity": Darwin, *The Descent of Man*, 114.

23 Moroccan term: Richard Firth Green, *A Crisis of Truth: Literature and Law in Ricardian England* (Philadelphia: University of Pennsylvania Press, 1999), 34, citing Lawrence Rosen.

23 German: Ernest Gellner, *Plough, Sword, and Book: The Structure of Human His-*

tory (Chicago: University of Chicago Press, 1988), 54; *The New English-German Dictionary* (New York: HarperCollins, 1999).

23 English speakers: Xavier Leon-Dufour, *Dictionary of the New Testament* (San Francisco: Harper and Row, 1980), 412; Green, *A Crisis of Truth*, 1–31; Bernard Williams, *Truth and Truthfulness* (Princeton, NJ: Princeton University Press, 2002).93–94, 290; William Empson, *The Structure of Complex Words* (Totowa, NJ: Rowan and Littlefield, 1977), 185–201.

23 *trouthe*: Green, *A Crisis of Truth*, 8–9, 15; *Oxford English Dictionary Online*.

24 " 'Truth' in Tivland": Paul Bohannan, *Justice and Judgment Among the Tiv* (London: Oxford University Press, 1957), 51.

24 Albert: Ethel M. Albert, "Culture Patterning of Speech Behavior in Burundi," in *Directions in Psycholinguistics: The Ethnography of Communication*, ed. John J. Gumperz and Dell Hymes (New York: Holt, Rinehart and Winston, 1972), 87, 100–101; Ethel M. Albert, "The Classification of Values: A Method and Illustration," *American Anthropologist* 58 (1956): 234.

24 "When I read": Frank A. Salamone, "The Methodological Significance of the Lying Informant," *Anthropological Quarterly* 50 (1977): 117.

25 insiders vs. outsiders: Eve E. Sweetser, "The Definition of *Lie*," in *Cultural Models in Language and Thought*, ed. Dorothy Holland and Naomi Quinn (Cambridge: Cambridge University Press, 1987), 43–66, 61; Bok, *Lying*, 145–47, 150–51; Sullivan, *The Concise Book of Lying*, 125.

25 Williams: Williams, *Truth and Truthfulness*, 121–22.

25 Bantu parents: Aalasdair MacIntyre, *After Virtue: A Study in Moral Virtue* (South Bend, IN: Notre Dame, 1989), 180.

25 Hingley: Ronald Hingley, *The Russian Mind* (New York: Scribner's, 1977), 104–7.

25 Muslim Lebanese: Michael Gilsenan, "Lying, Honor, and Contradiction," in *Transaction and Meaning: Directions in the Anthropology of Exchange and Symbolic Behavior*, ed. Bruce Kapferer (Philadelphia: Institute for the Study of Human Issues, 1976), 192–93.

25 Afghans: Khaled Hosseini, *The Kite Runner* (New York: Riverhead, 2003), 11.

25 Greek term: Ernestine Friedl, *Vasilika: A Village in Modern Greece* (New York: Holt, Rinehart and Winston, 1962), 80.

25–26 Samoans, Mead: Derek Freeman, *The Fateful Hoaxing of Margaret Mead: A Historical Analysis of Her Samoan Research* (Boulder, CO: Westview Press, 1999), 140.

26 Anderson, Saami: personal communication; Myrdene Anderson, "Cultural Concatenation of Deceit and Secrecy," in Mitchell and Thompson, *Deception*,

343; Myrdene Anderson, "Reindeer and Magic Numbers: The Making and Maintenance of the Saami Stereotype," *Ethnos* 56 (1991): 208.

27 Russians: Hingley, *The Russian Mind*, 90–99.

27 Incas: Barnes, *A Pack of Lies*, 142.

27 Spencer: Herbert Spencer, *The Principles of Ethics*, vol. 1 (New York: Appleton, 1897), 406–7.

27 Greek gods: Spencer, *Principles of Ethics*, 403; P. Walcot, "Odysseus and the Art of Lying," *Ancient Society* 8 (1977): 1–19; Steiner, *After Babel*, 219–20; Campbell, *The Liar's Tale*, 45–47, 147; Williams, *Truth and Truthfulness*, 73, 277.

28 Athena to Odysseus: *The Odyssey of Homer* (New York: Modern Library, 1950), 204.

28 Plato: Plato, *The Republic and Other Works*, B. Jowett, trans. (Garden City, NY: Doubleday Dolphin, 1960), 75; Plato, *Republic*, Robin Waterfield, trans. (New York: Oxford, 1988), 118.

28 Cicero: *De Officiis* (On Duties), Walter Miller, trans. (New York: Macmillan, 1913), 321–35.

28 Buddhists: Bok, *Lying*, 47–48; "About Buddhism," Nan Tien Temple, www.nantien.ozemail.com.au.

28 Hindu: Wendy Doniger trans., with Brian K. Smith, *The Laws of Manu* (London: Penguin, 1991), 164.

29 Muhammad, Muslims: Shahid Athar, "Reflections of an American Muslim," www.islam-usa.com; "Lying in Islam," Abudullah Al Araby, *Islam Review*, www.islamreview.com/articles/lying.shtml; Neil Ozman, soc.culture newsgroup, www.answering-islam.org/index/L/lying.html.

29 Talmud: Louis Jacobs, *Jewish Values* (London: Valentine, Mitchell, 1960), 151–53.

29 Both testaments: Spencer, *Principles of Ethics*, 402–3; Abraham-Sarah: Gen. 12:11–13; Richard Freund, "Lying and Deception in the Biblical and Post-Biblical Judaic Tradition," *Scandinavian Journal of the Old Testament* 5 (1991): 50, 58; Jacob: Gen. 27:19; Freund, 58–59; Egyptian midwives: Exod. 1:17–20; Devlin Donaldson and Steve Wamberg, *Pinocchio Nation: Embracing Truth in a Culture of Lies* (Colorado Springs, CO: Pinon Press, 2001), 23; Solomon: Hugo Grotius "The Character of Falsehood," in Philip Kerr, ed., *The Penguin Book of Lies* (New York: Viking, 1990), 113.

29 Sullivan: Sullivan, *The Concise Book of Lying*, 12.

30 Moses: Lev. 19:11; Sullivan, *The Concise Book of Lying*, 12.

30 New Testament: Sullivan, *The Concise Book of Lying*, 12–3.

30 Satan, no need for oaths: *John* 8:44; Dietrich Bonhoeffer, *Ethics*, (New York: Macmillan, 1949, 1965), 369; Aldous Huxley, "The Devils of Loudon," Jonathan Swift, "The Art of Political Lying," Cardinal Newman, "What the Catechism Says About Lying," in Kerr, *The Penguin Book of Lies*, 113, 151, 245; Bok, *Lying*, 7; Sullivan, *The Concise Book of Lying*, 23, 26–7, 46.

30 Augustine, "Against Lying," in Augustine, *Treatises on Various Subjects*, trans., Harold B. Jaffee, ed., Roy J. Deferrari, (New York: Fathers of the Church, 1952), 171; Zagorin, *Social Research* 63 (1996): 863–912; Saint Augustine, "A Letter to Consentius," in Kerr, *The Penguin Book of Lies*, 37. *Various Subjects* (New York: Fathers of the Church, 1952), 171; Zagorin, *Social Research* 63 (1996): 869–72; Augustine, "A Letter to Consentius," in Kerr, *The Penguin Book of Lies*, 37.

31 Koran verse: 3: 27, in Perez Zagorin, *Ways of Lying: Dissimulation, Persecution, and Conformity in Early Modern Europe* (Cambridge, MA: Harvard University Press, 1990), 4.

31 Koranic commentator: Zagorin, *Social Research* 63 (1996); 867–68, citing *Encyclopedia of Islam*.

31 mental reservation: Ibid., 869, 873, 889, 900–901, 904–5; Cabot, *Honesty*, 206–15; Blaise Pascal in Kerr, *The Penguin Book of Lies*, 117–21; Bok, *Lying*, 37–38; F. G. Bailey, *The Prevalence of Deceit* (Ithaca, NY: Cornell University Press, 1991), 2.

31 upright Protestants: Cabot, *Honesty*, 212; Zagorin, *Social Research* 63 (1996): 889.

32 U.S. oaths: 5 U.S. Code 3331 in Zagorin, *Social Research* 63 (1996): 904.

32 Wesley: John Wesley, in Kerr, *The Penguin Book of Lies*, 176; Bok, *Lying*, 34.

32 rise of science: Hannah Arendt, *Between Past and Future* (New York: Viking, 1968), 202; C. P. Snow in Cynthia Crossen, *Tainted Truth: The Manipulation of Fact in America* (Simon and Schuster, 1996), 160.

32 Weber: Max Weber, *The Protestant Ethic and the Rise of Capitalism* (New York: Scribner's, 1930, 1950).

32 Huguenots, Quakers: Ibid., 282–83.

32 Franklin: Ibid., 52, 282.

32 Kant: Immanuel Kant, *Critique of Practical Reason*, trans. and ed. Lewis White Beck (Chicago: University of Chicago Press, 1949), 347.

33 Simmel: *The Sociology of Georg Simmel*, Kurt H. Wolff, trans. and ed. (Glencoe, IL: Free Press, 1950), 313.

33 "Christian gentlemen": Steven Shapin, *A Social History of Truth: Civility and*

Science in Seventeenth-Century England (Chicago: University of Chicago Press, 1994), 81–3; Campbell, *The Liar's Tale*, 115, 119; Sullivan, *The Concise Book of Lying*, 122.

34 Wright: Robert Wright, *The Moral Animal: Evolutionary Psychology and Everyday Life* (New York: Pantheon, 1994; Vintage, 1994), 219.

3. The Honesty Connection

35 Wolfe: Alan Wolfe, *Moral Freedom: The Impossible Idea That Defines the Way We Live Now* (New York: Norton, 2001), 130.

35 Browne: Kerr, *The Penguin Book of Lies*, 458.

35 Ambéli, du Boulay: Juliet du Boulay, *Portrait of a Greek Mountain Village* (Oxford: Clarendon Press, 1974), 78, 191–92, 199–200.

36 One woman: Oprah.com Message Boards, January 5, 2002.

36 Burundi man: Ethel M. Albert, in Gumperz and Hynes, *Directions in Psycholinguistics*, 98.

37 du Boulay: du Boulay, *Portrait of a Greek Mountain Village*, 78.

37 DePaulo: Bella M. DePaulo and Deborah A. Kashy, "Everyday Lies in Close and Casual Relationships," *Journal of Personality and Social Psychology* 74 (1998): 75.

38 Wolfe: *Moral Freedom*, 103–5.

39 "Everyone knows the rule": Ethel Albert, in Gumperz and Hynes, *Directions in Psycholinguistics*, 91.

41 "antisocial personality": Remi J. Cadoret, "Epidemiology of Antisocial Personality," in *Unmasking the Psychopath: Antisocial Personality and Related Syndromes*, ed. William H. Reid et. al (New York: Norton, 1986), 29.

41 Ekman: Paul Ekman, *Telling Lies: Clues to Deceit in the Marketplace, Politics, and Marriage* (New York: Norton, 2001), 71.

41 Jackson: Jennifer Jackson, "Telling the Truth," *Journal of Medical Ethics* 17 (1991): 7–8.

42 Cooley: Charles Horton Cooley, *Human Nature and the Social Order* (New York: Scribner's, 1902), 358.

43 DePaulo: *Los Angeles Times*, August 27, 1995.

43 Wolfe: Wolfe, *Moral Freedom*, 104–5.

43 Ekman: Ekman, *Telling Lies*, 339–42.

44–45 "make a good impression": Deborah A. Kashy and Bella M. DePaulo, "Who Lies?" *Journal of Personality and Social Psychology* 70 (1996): 1038, 1048–50.

45 KGB agent: *Dayton Daily News*, October 4, 1998.

46 studies consistently find: *New York Times*, September 17, 1991; *Washington Times*, September 22, 1998; Caroline F. Keating and Karen R. Heltman, "Dominance and Deception in Children and Adults: Are Leaders the Best Misleaders?" *Personality and Social Psychology Bulletin* 20(1994): 312, 320; Bella M. DePaulo, "Spotting Human Lies: Can Humans Learn to do Better?" *Current Directions in Psychological Science* 3 (1994): 85.

46 those lied to by Clinton: *Newsweek*, September 14, 1998.

46 Schuller: *New York Times*, September 11, 1998.

4. Whistler's Druthers

47 Atlas: *New York Times Book Review*, April 26, 1981.

47 Whistler: Hesketh Pearson, *The Man Whistler* (New York: Harper and Brothers, 1952), 1.

47 Vespucci: Richard Shenkman, *Legends, Lies, and Cherished Myths of American History* (New York: Perennial, 1989), 5–6; Goldberg, *The Book of Lies*, 45–46.

47–48 Columbus: Dan Carlinsky, "Christopher Confusion," *Modern Maturity*, February–March 1992; Paul F. Boller Jr., *Not So! Popular Myths About America from Columbus to Clinton* (New York: Oxford University Press, 1995), 3–6; Bill Bryson, *Made in America* (New York: Avon, 1996), 60–61.

48 Washington, Weems: Bryson, *Made in America*, 61; Boller, *Not So!* 29–32; James W. Loewen, *Lies Across America* (New York: New Press, 1995), 362–66; Goldberg, *The Book of Lies*, 74–76.

48 Boorstin: Daniel J. Boorstin, *The Americans: The National Experience* (New York: Random House, 1965), 289–90.

49 Crockett: Boorstin, *The Americans*, 293–95; *New York Times*, March 22, 1986, November 23, 1998; Paul Andrew Hutton, "Davy Crockett—He Was Hardly King of the Wild Frontier," *TV Guide*, February 4, 1989.

49 memorable quotations: Ralph Keyes, *"Nice Guys Finish Seventh": False Phrases, Spurious Sayings, and Familiar Misquotations* (New York: HarperCollins, 1992), 56–71.

49 Pocahontas: Charles C. Bombaugh, *Facts and Fancies for the Curious* (Philadelphia: Lippincott, 1905), 390–91; *Dayton Daily News*, May 13, 2003; *Christian Science Monitor*, November 18, 2003.

49 Revere, Ross: Shenkman, *Legends, Lies, and Cherished Myths of American History*, 146–47; Richard Shenkman, *"I Love Paul Revere Whether He Rode or Not"* (New York: HarperCollins, 1991); *People*, January 12, 1987.

49 OK Corral: *New York Times*, October 31, 1981; *Philadelphia Inquirer*, January 24, 1986.

50 Earp: John Mack Faragher, "The Tale of Wyatt Earp," in *Past Imperfect: History According to the Movies*, ed. Mark C. Carnes, Ted Mico, John Miller-Monzon, and David Rubel (New York: Holt, 1995), 154–61.

50 western lawmen: Joseph W. Snell, "Kansas Cow-Town Life Was in Part a Comedy of Errors," *Smithsonian*, February 1980.

50 Underground Railroad: Larry Gara, *The Liberty Line: The Legend of the Underground Railroad* (Lexington, KY: University Press of Kentucky, 1996).

50–51 Sojourner Truth: Nell Irvin Painter, *Sojourner Truth: A Life, a Symbol* (New York: Norton, 1996), 98, 121–31, 141; Nell Irvin Painter, "Claiming Lives Lost," in *Flat-Footed Truths*, ed. Patricia Bell-Scott (New York: Holt, 1998), 99, 108, 120.

51 "what we need her to have said," Painter in Bell-Scott, *Flat-Footed Truths*, 120.

51 Boorstin: *The Americans*, 308–9.

51 Thoreau: Leon Edel, *Henry D. Thoreau* (Minneapolis: University of Minnesota Press, 1970), 9–10; Leon Edel, "The Mystery of Walden Pond," in *The Stuff of Sleep and Dreams* (New York: Harper and Row, 1982), 47–65; Robert D. Richardson Jr., *Henry Thoreau: A Life of the Mind* (Berkeley: University of California Press, 1986), 153; Carol Bly, *Beyond the Writer's Workshop: New Ways to Write Creative Nonfiction* (New York: Anchor Vintage, 2000), 262.

51 "bivouacked": Frank B. Sanborn, *Henry David Thoreau* (New York: Chelsea House, 1882, 1980), 212.

52 "Marilynizing": *Newsweek*, August 12, 2002.

52 Stewart: Martha Stewart, "On Honesty," *Martha Stewart Living*, June 1992.

53 Stewart's friend: Jerry Oppenheimer, *Martha Stewart—Just Desserts: The Unauthorized Biography* (New York: Morrow, 1997), 114.

53 Stewart's ex-husband, aunt: Christopher Byron, *Martha, Inc.: The Incredible Story of Martha Stewart Living Omnimedia* (New York: Wiley, 2002), 324.

53 McFadden: Cyra McFadden, *Rain or Shine* (New York: Knopf, 1986), 12.

54 Einstein: *New York Times Magazine*, February 18, 1979; *U.S. News & World Report*, December 9, 2002.

54 Hammer: Edward Jay Epstein, *Dossier: The Secret History of Armand Hammer* (New York: Random House, 1996); *New York Times*, October 14, 1996.

54 Greenfield: Meg Greenfield, *Washington* (New York: Public Affairs/Perseus, 2001), 65–66.

55 "It was a hot summer day": Richard Pollak, *The Creation of Dr. B* (New York: Simon and Schuster, 1997), 93.

55 Bettelheim: Pollak, *The Creation of Dr. B*, 14–17, 55, 57, 61, 80, 82, 91–93, 110–11, 126, 372.

55 "In a profession full of fakeness": Barbara Johnson, in David Lehman, *Signs of the Times: Deconstruction and the Fall of Paul de Man* (New York: Poseidon, 1991), 143, 233.

55–56 de Man: *New York Times*, December 1, 1987; James Atlas, "The Case of Paul de Man," *New York Times Magazine*, August 28, 1988; Lehman, *Signs of the Times*, 133, 143–44, 160, 164, 179–81, 187, 190, 198–203, 206–7, 233.

56 Lehman: Lehman, *Signs of the Times*, 207.

57 Tiffany's: Nelson W. Aldrich Jr., *Old Money: The Mythology of Wealth in America* (New York: Vintage, 1989), 58.

58 DNA testing: *New Yorker*, March 26, 2001; *Charlotte News-Observer*, June 25, 2001; *Dayton Daily News*, February 6, 2003, August 16, 2003.

58 Gordon: Mary Gordon, *The Shadow Man: A Daughter's Search for Her Father* (New York: Random House, 1996).

58 Rovere: Richard Rovere, *Arrivals and Departures: A Journalist's Memoirs* (New York: Macmillan, 1976), 243–65.

58 Blaise: Clark Blaise, *I Had a Father: A Post-Modern Autobiography* (Reading, MA: Addison-Wesley, 1993), 111, 139.

58–59 Wolff: Geoffrey Wolff, *The Duke of Deception: Memories of My Father* (Random House, 1979; Berkley, 1980), 71.

5. Great Pretenders

60 Gary: Romain Gary, *Life and Death of Émile Ajar* (New York: Harper and Row, 1979), 249.

60 Hellman: Lillian Hellman, *The Little Foxes* (New York: Random House, 1939), 25.

60–61 one survey of a large sample of Americans: James Patterson and Peter Kim, *The Day America Told the Truth: What People Really Believe About Everything That Really Matters* (New York: Prentice-Hall, 1991), 55.

61 Kopple: *People*, February 15, 1993, March 8, 1993.

61 Ellison: *New York Times*, February 28, 1988, in Mike Wilson, *The Difference Between God and Larry Ellison: (God Doesn't Think He's Larry Ellison): Inside Oracle Corporation* (New York: Morrow, 1997), 32.

61 wedding announcement: *New York*, June 30, 1980.

62 DeWolf: *San Diego Union*, April 13, 1975.

62 a group of job seekers: Ralph Keyes, *The Height of Your Life* (Boston: Little, Brown, 1980), 16.

62 a group of women: Ibid., 16.

62 casting director: Ibid., 233.

63 Werra: *Milwaukee Journal Sentinel*, September 21, 1995, February 8, 1996; *Sales & Marketing Management*, October 1996; *Adweek*, February 3, 1997, August 9, 1999, February 17, 2003; *Los Angeles Times*, July 18, 2000; *U.S. News & World Report*, November 13, 2000; *Philadelphia Daily News*, December 12, 2000; *Chicago Tribune*, August 27, 2001; *Business First*, September 28, 2001; *Network World*, October 8, 2001; *Wisconsin State Journal*, February 17, 2002; *Beloit Daily News*, March 7, 2002; *New Yorker*, November 4, 2002; *The Money Gang*, CNNFN, December 5, 2002.

63 as many as a quarter: *Boston Globe*, December 14, 1997.

63 Self: *Dallas Business Journal*, July 1, 2002.

63 Hogg: *Newsweek*, February 16, 2001.

63 Zarrella (Bausch & Lomb CEO): *Slate.com*, October 22, 2002; *Chicago Tribune*, October 27, 2002; *Dayton Daily News*, October 30, 2002; *New Yorker*, November 4, 2002.

63 Baldwin (USOC president): *Denver Post*, May 24, 2002; *New York Times*, June 16, 2002.

64 Papows (CEO of Lotus Development Corp): *Wall Street Journal*, April 29, 1999; *Computerworld*, January 10, 2000.

64 Mitchell (CEO of MCG Capital): *Moneyline*, CNN, November 1, 2002; *Washington Business Journal*, November 4, 2002.

64 Harris (Dartmouth AD): *New York Times*, June 12, 2002; *Richmond Times-Dispatch*, June 12, 2002.

64 DeLibero (head of Houston's Metropolitan Transit Authority): *Bergen* (NJ) *Record*, October 29, 2000; *Houston Chronicle*, October 31, 2000, November 1, 2000, November 4, 2000, November 7, 2000, November 8, 2000, December 19, 2003, April 21, 2004.

64 Burke-Tatum (head of Milwaukee's Social Development Commission): *Milwaukee Journal Sentinel*, February 6, 1996, February 8, 1996.

64 Troupe (poet laureate of California): *San Francisco Chronicle*, October 20, 2002; *New Yorker*, November 4, 2002; *Chronicle of Higher Education*, April 4, 2003.

64 Reid (director of UCLA's body donor program): *Los Angeles Times*, March 11, 2004.

64 Toronto reference-checking firm: Infocheck, Reuters, January 19, 2000; *Financial Times*, March 30, 2000.

64 Christian & Timbers: *Silicon Valley/San Jose Business Journal*, September 27, 2001.

64 Panzer (Wisconsin senate majority leader): *Wisconsin State Journal,* January 29, 2004; *West Bend* (WI) *Daily News,* February 24, 2004.

64 Musselman (Kentucky congressional candidate): *New York Times,* July 14, 1984.

64 Serbia (Connecticut controller candidate): *New York Times,* August 7, 1998.

65 Few (D.C. fire chief): *Washington Post,* May 29, 2002; *Firehouse.Com News,* May 29, 2002.

65 Lau, Brown (San Francisco police chief, mayor): *San Francisco Chronicle,* December 16, 2001, December 18, 2001.

65 UCLA, Yale: *Time,* February 5, 1979; *Esquire,* March 13, 1979.

65 Begelman: *Time,* February 5, 1979.

65 Cringely: *San Francisco Chronicle,* November 9, 1998, November 11, 1998; *New York Times,* November 16, 1998.

65 Lonchar (Veritas Software's CFO): *Slate.com,* October 22, 2002; *New Yorker,* November 4, 2002; *The Money Gang,* CNNFN, December 5, 2002.

65 Baughman (San Jose school superintendent): *San Francisco Chronicle,* May 25, 1993, November 20, 1993, December 16, 2001.

65 GAO study of bogus degrees: Associated Press, May 11, 2004; *Washington Post,* May 12, 2004.

66 Humana: *Philadelphia Inquirer,* February 11, 1988; *Washington Post,* July 12, 1994.

66 Veterans Administration doctors: *Washington Post,* July 12, 1994.

66 by one estimate: *New York Times,* December 7, 1984, December 12, 1985, June 19, 1988; *Wall Street Journal,* April 2, 1986.

66 Gulf War doctor: *ABC World News Tonight,* March 12, 1991, March 13, 1991.

66 Kovacs: *Dayton Daily News,* April 27, 1992.

66 Twedell: *Philadelphia Inquirer,* December 8, 1981.

66 Urich: *TV Guide,* October 14, 1978.

66 Tom O'Leary: Gary Smith, "Lying in Wait," *Sports Illustrated,* April 8, 2002.

67 George O'Leary: Ibid.

67 DeLibero: *Bergen (NJ) Record,* October 29, 2000; *Houston Chronicle,* October 31, 2000, November 1, 2000, November 4, 2000, November 7, 2000, November 8, 2000.

67 ValuJet mechanic: *Columbus* (OH) *Dispatch,* May 12, 1997.

67 Utah engineer: *Chattanooga* (TN) *Times,* July 14, 1998; *Cleveland Plain Dealer,* July 19, 1998.

67 Barnes: *New York Times,* May 3, 1981; *Los Angeles Times,* May 31, 1981; *USA Today,* April 18, 1996; *Los Angeles Times,* April 23, 1996.

68 Clifton: *Tampa Tribune,* March 9, 1992; United Press International, May 13,

1992; Associated Press, May 14, 1992; *St. Petersburg Times*, May 19, 1992; Associated Press, June 16, 1992.

68 Reagan, Korda: Michael Korda, *Another Life: A Memoir of Other People* (New York: Random House, 1999), 471.

69 concentration camps: Haynes Johnson, *Sleepwalking Through History* (New York: Norton 1991), 45; *Charlotte Observer*, June 28, 2001.

69 colluded with publicists: Johnson, *Sleepwalking Through History*, 46.

69 Reagan's autobiography: Ronald Reagan, *Where's the Rest of Me?* (New York: Duell, Sloan and Pearce, 1965), 27–30.

69 "You believed it" Lou Cannon, *President Reagan: The Role of a Lifetime* (New York: Simon and Schuster, 1991), 39.

69 O'Brien: *Chicago Tribune*, October 21, 1994, June 27, 1995, July 4, 1995, July 25, 1995, September 4, 1995.

69 Reynolds: *Current Biography*, 1973; *Sporting News*, September 23, 1978; Bernhardt J. Hurwood, *Burt Reynolds* (New York: Quick Fox, 1979), 19; Sylvia Safran Resnick, *Burt Reynolds: An Unauthorized Biography* (New York: St. Martin's, 1983), 11; *New York Times*, March 22, 1983.

69 Jackson: Marshall Frady, *Jesse: The Life and Pilgrimage of Jesse Jackson* (New York: Random House, 1996), 228–31; *Time*, May 28, 2001.

69 Hellman: Samuel McCracken, "'Julia' and Other Fictions by Lillian Hellman," *Commentary*, June 1984; Carl Rollyson, *Lillian Hellman: Her Legend and Her Legacy* (New York: St. Martin's, 1988), 513–16.

69–70 van der Post: J.D.F. Jones, *Storyteller: The Many Lives of Laurens van der Post* (London: John Murray, 2001), 360.

70 Lawrence: *Boston Globe*, December 14, 1997; *Newsweek*, December 15, 1997.

70 Polo: *Dayton Daily News*, February 23, 2000; Munchausen: *Dayton Daily News*, April 18, 1996; T. E. Lawrence: Denis Boak, *André Malraux* (Oxford: Clarendon, 1968), 3–4; Byrd: *Dayton Daily News*, May 10, 1996, *Newsweek*, May 20, 1996; *People*, June 3, 1996; Peary: *TV Guide*, December 10, 1983, *New York Times*, October 13, 1988; Picasso: John Richardson, *A Life of Picasso* (New York: Random House, 1991), reviewed in *People*, April 8, 1991; Andersen: Goldberg, *The Book of Lies*, 26, *Publishers Weekly*, April 9, 2001; Gibran: *Publishers Weekly*, November 9, 1998; Malraux: Boak, *André Malraux*, 1–11, 16–19; Gary: *Time-Life Book of Hoaxes and Deceptions* (Alexandria, VA: Time-Life Books, 1991), 31; Hemingway: Meyers, *Hemingway*, 237–41; O'Brian: *Smithsonian*, December 2003; West: Colin Jarman, ed., *Guinness Book of Poisonous Quotes* (New York: McGraw-Hill / Contemporary, 1993), 82.

70–71 Dylan: Anthony Scaduto, *Dylan: An Intimate Biography* (New York:

Signet, 1973), 9–11, 14, 20, 26; Anthony Scaduto, "Won't You Listen to the Lambs, Bob Dylan," *New York Times Magazine*, November 28, 1971; *Time*, November 14, 1969; *Newsweek*, November 4, 1963.

70–71 Waits: *Newsweek*, June 14, 1976; *Time*, November 28, 1977; *Fresh Air*, National Public Radio, May 21, 2002.

71 Ellison: Wilson, *The Difference Between God and Larry Ellison*, 20–21.

71 Steinem: Sydney Ladensohn Stern, *Gloria Steinem: Her Passions, Politics, and Mystique* (New York: Birch Lane, 1997), 227–29, 448.

71 Kiley: *People*, October 1, 1984, December 24–31, 1984.

71 athlete wannabes: Richard C. Crepeau, *Orlando Sentinel*, May 24, 1992.

71–72 Boston Police Department employee: Diane K. Shah, "Those Extraordinary Impostors," *Cosmopolitan*, June, 1979.

72 British "veterans": *Guardian* (London, England), August 21, 2001.

72 Graham:www.senate.gov/pagelayout/senators/one_item_and_teasers/graham;www.awolbush.com/whoserved.

72 Papows: *Wall Street Journal*, April 29, 1999.

72 Odysseus: P. Walcot, "Odysseus and the Art of Lying," *Ancient Society* 8 (1977): 11.

72 Civil War veterans: William Marvel, *Blue Gray*, February 1991, 32–33; discussed in B. G. Burkett and Glenna Whitley, *Stolen Valor* (Dallas: Verity Press, 1998), 166.

72 Mix: *Architectural Digest*, April 1994.

72 Faulkner: Stephen B. Oates, *William Faulkner: The Man and the Artist* (New York: Harper and Row, 1987), 23–24, 40.

72–73 McCarthy: Arthur Herman, *Joseph McCarthy: Reexamining the Life and Legacy of America's Most Hated Senator* (New York: Free Press, 2000), 30.

73 Cooley: *New York Times*, December 12, 1996; Burkett and Whitley, *Stolen Valor*, 172, 303.

73 Robertson: *New York Times*, October 10, 1987; *Washington Post Magazine*, December 27, 1987.

73 Tully: *San Diego Union*, December 27, 1985; *Newsweek*, January 13, 1986.

73–74 Dux: *Los Angeles Times*, May 1, 1988; Burkett and Whitley, *Stolen Valor*, 411–5.

74 Harkin: Burkett and Whitley, *Stolen Valor*, 182.

74 Dennehy: Ibid., 568; International Movie Database, www.imdb.com/name/nm0001133/bio.

74 Johnson: *New York Times*, March 18, 1999; Burkett and Whitley, *Stolen Valor*, 164, 182–83.

74 Burkett: *New York Times*, May 18, 1996; *Dayton Daily News*, November 12, 2000; Newhouse News Service, June 22, 2001; Burkett and Whitley, *Stolen Valor*, 173.

74 Boorda: *New York Times*, May 17, 1996; *Newsweek*, May 27, 1996.

75 Nolte: *Dayton Daily News*, January 2, 1993, March 25, 2003.

75 Dike: *Psychiatric News*, January 3, 2003; *Los Angeles Times*, March 3, 2003; *Sunday Times* (London, England), April 13, 2003; *Independent on Sunday* (London, England), July 13, 2003.

75 Ekman: *Telling Lies*, 297–98; *Fresh Air*, National Public Radio, May 22, 2003.

75–76 DePaulo: Peter J. DePaulo and Bella M. DePaulo, "Can Deception by Salespersons and Customers Be Detected Through Nonverbal Behavioral Cues?" *Journal of Applied Social Psychology* 19 (1989): 1552–77.

76 Nietzsche: Friedrich Nietzsche, *The Will to Power*, trans. Walter Kaufmann and R.J Hollingdale, ed. Walter Kaufmann (New York: Vintage, 1968), 505.

76 Keating: Gannett News Service, April 24, 1995; *Los Angeles Times*, May 15, 1995; *Buffalo News*, February 18, 1996; *Washington Times*, September 22, 1998; *Wisconsin State Journal*, February 14, 1999; Caroline F. Keating and Karen R. Heltman "Dominance and Deception in Children and Adults: Are Leaders the Best Misleaders?" *Personality and Social Psychology Bulletin* 20 (1994): 312–321.

76 "He was a very good communicator": *Network World*, January 27, 2003.

77 "Dr. Anthony Thomas": *Dayton Daily News*, March 12, 1993, March 22, 1993, March 27, 1993.

77 Werra: *The Money Gang*, CNNFN, December 5, 2002.

78 Berne: Suzanne Berne, *A Crime in the Neighborhood* (Chapel Hill, NC: Algonquin, 1997), 190–91.

78 Ross: Connie Bruck, *Master of the Game: Steve Ross and the Creation of Time Warner* (Simon and Schuster, 1994), 84.

78 Florio: *Fortune*, July 20, 1998.

78 Papows: *Wall Street Journal*, April 29, 1999.

79 Nancy Reagan: Sidney Schanberg, *Dayton Daily News*, April 10, 1991.

79 Sorensen: *Hartford Courant*, September 19, 1984, in Burkett and Whitley, *Stolen Valor*, 173.

79 Cook: *Bangor Daily News*, September 27, 2003, September 30, 2003; *Portland* (ME) *Press Herald*, October 5, 2003.

79 Dickey: Christopher Dickey, *Summer of Deliverance: A Memoir of Father and Son* (New York: Simon and Schuster, 1998), 30, 53–54, 88; *All Things Considered*, National Public Radio, August 25, 1998.

80 DePaulo: Bella M. DePaulo, Deborah A. Kashy, Susan E. Kirkendol, Melissa M. Wyer, and Jennifer A. Epstein, "Lying in Everyday Life," *Journal of Personality and Social Psychology* 70 (1996): 991.

80 Barnes: Barnes, *A Pack of Lies*, 93.

6. Why Lie?

81 Minnich: Elizabeth Kamarck Minnich, "Why Not Lie?" *Soundings* 68 (1985): 493.

81–82 Beschloss: Michael Beschloss, *Reaching for Glory: Lyndon Johnsons's Secret White House Tapes, 1964–1965* (New York: Simon and Schuster, 2001), 119–26; *Fresh Air*, National Public Radio, November 29, 2002.

82 "Bull" Johnson: Robert Caro, *The Path to Power* (New York: Vintage, 1990), 160.

82 Goodwin: David Broder, *Dayton Daily News*, September 23, 1992.

82 McClelland: *Philadelphia Inquirer*, April 10, 1983.

82–83 Grazer: *New Yorker*, October 15, 2001.

83 "the more concerned someone is": Deborah A. Kashy and Bella M. DePaulo, "Who Lies?" *Journal of Personality and Social Psychology* 70 (1996): 1038.

83 Steinem: Stern, *Gloria Steinem*, 233.

83 biographies of Hammer, Ross, and Ellison: Edward Jay Epstein, *Dossier: The Secret History of Armand Hammer* (New York: Random House, 1996); Connie Bruck, *Master of the Game: Steve Ross and the Creation of Time Warner* (New York: Simon and Schuster, 1994); Ellison: Wilson, *The Difference Between God and Larry Ellison (God Doesn't Think He's Larry Ellison): Inside Oracle Corporation* (New York: Morrow, 1997).

83 Ross: Bruck, *Master of the Game*, 85.

83–84 Autry: James Autry, *Life and Work: A Manager's Search for Meaning* (New York: Morrow, 1994), 21.

84 van der Post, Jones: Jones, *Storyteller*, 359.

85 Farson: personal communication.

85 Stewart: Byron, *Martha, Inc.*, 194.

86 Nixon: Anthony Summers, *The Arrogance of Power: The Secret World of Richard Nixon* (London: Victor Gollancz, 2000), 4.

86 Karlen: personal communication.

87 Popcorn: *Newsweek*, June 15, 1987.

87 Bacon: Francis Bacon, *Essays, Advancement of Learning, New Atlantis, and Other Pieces* (Garden City, NY: Doubleday Doran, 1937), 4.

87 Malraux: in Meyers, *Hemingway*, 238–39.

88 Montaigne: Michel de Montaigne, "On Liars," in trans., J. M. Cohen, *Essays* (Baltimore: Penguin, 1958), 31.

88 Klockars: Carl B. Klockars, "Blue Lies and Police Placebos: The Moralities of Police Lying," *American Behavioral Scientist* 27 (1984): 542–43.

89 Blair: *NewYork Observer*, May 21, 2003.

89 Ekman: Ekman, *Telling Lies*, 76–79; *Men's Health*, May 1996.

89 Burstein: Ben Burstein, "The Manipulative Personality," *Archives of General Psychiatry* 26 (1972): 319.

90 Minnich: *Soundings* 68 (1985): 497.

90 hooks: *All About Love: New Visions* (New York: HarperCollins, 2001), 35–6.

90–91 Ekman: Ekman, *Telling Lies*, 76.

91 "drug of choice": Ed Williams, *The Charlotte Observer*, June 24, 2001.

91 Blum: Richard H. Blum, *Deceivers and Deceived: Observations On Confidence Men and Their Victims, Informants and Their Quarry, Political and Industrial Spies and Ordinary Citizens* (Springfield, IL: Charles C. Thomas, 1972), 242.

92 Nietzsche: Nietzsche, *The Will to Power*, 505.

92 Irving: John Irving, *Cider House Rules* (New York: Modern Library, 1999), 87–8.

92 Spencer: Spencer, *The Principles of Ethics*, 407

93 Rich: Adrienne Rich, "Women and Honor: Some Notes on Lying," in *On Lies, Secrets, and Silence: Selected Prose 1966–1978* (New York: Norton, 1979), 191.

7. Sex, Lies, and Sex Roles

94 Gay: John Gay, *The Beggar's Opera* (1727); act 2, scene 13.

94 Garcia-Aguilera: Carolina Garcia-Aguilera, *Bloody Waters* (New York: Putnam's, 1996), 78.

94 Chaucer: Geoffrey Chaucer, "Prologe of the Wyf of Bathe," *Canterbury Tales* (New York: Henry Holt, 1928), 283.

94 Elizabethan poets: Shapin, *A Social History of Truth*, 89.

94 Earl of Essex: Ibid.; The Lied and Art Song Texts Page, www.recmusic.org/lieder/get_text.html?TextId=4662.

94 Hume: Barnes, *A Pack of Lies*, 7.

94–95 Conrad: Joseph Conrad, *Heart of Darkness*, in Campbell, *The Liar's Tale*, 218.

95 1970 psychologist: Robert L. Wolk and Arthur Henley, *The Right to Lie: A Psy-*

chological Guide to the Uses of Deceit in Everyday Life (New York: Wyden, 1970), 123.

95 classic study: Michael Lewis, Catherine Stanger, and Margaret W. Sullivan, "Deception in 3-Year-Olds," *Developmental Psychology* 25 (1989): 439–43.

95 study with added variables: Georgia N. Nigro and Andrea L. Snow, "Sex, Lies, and Smiling Faces: A Brief Report on Gender Differences in 3-Year-Olds' Deceptions," in *Cognitive and Social Factors in Early Deception*, ed. Stephen J. Ceci, Michelle DeSimone Leichtman, and Mary Elizabeth Putnick, (Hillsdale, NJ: Lawrence Erlbaum, 1992), 63–68.

95 the makers of this study: Ibid., 67.

96 late 1960s study: Blum, *Deceivers and Deceived*, 222–30, 235–37.

96 hooks: *All About Love*, 36.

96 lied to parents as teenagers: Blum, *Deceivers and Deceived*, 224.

96–97 Ontario study: Michael Ross and Diane Holmberg, "Recounting the Past: Gender Differences in the Recall of Events in the History of a Close Relationship," in *Self-Inference Processes: The Ontario Symposium*, vol. 6, ed. James M. Olson and Mark P. Zanna, (Hillsdale, NJ: Lawrence Erlbuam, 1990), 145–46.

97 Infocheck: *Toronto Sun*, December 4, 1998; *Calgary Herald*, December 7, 1998; *Gazette* (Montreal), January 9, 1999.

97 Feldman: *National Post*, June 12, 2002; Robert S. Feldman, James A. Forrest, and Benjamin R. Happ, "Self-Presentation and Verbal Deception: Do Self-Presenters Lie More?" *Basic and Applied Social Psychology* 24 (2002): 167, 169.

98 DePaulo: Bella M. DePaulo, Robert Rosenthal, Judith Rosenkrantz, and Carolyn Rieder Green, "Diagnosing Deceptive and Mixed Messages from Verbal and Nonverbal Cues," *Basic and Applied Social Psychology* 3 (1982): 309–10; Bella M. DePaulo, Julie I. Stone, and G. Daniel Lassiter, "Deceiving and Detecting Deceit," in *The Self and Social Life*, ed. Barry R. Schlenker (New York: McGraw-Hill, 1985), 342; Bella M. DePaulo, Jennifer A. Epstein, and Melissa M. Wyer, "Sex Differences in Lying: How Women and Men Deal with the Dilemma of Deceit," in *Lying and Deception in Everyday Life*, ed. Michael Lewis and Carolyn Saarni (New York: Guilford, 1993), 143.

98 "socioemotional specialists": Bella M. DePaulo, Deborah A. Kashy, Susan E. Kirkendol, Melissa M. Wyer, and Jennifer A. Epstein, *Journal of Personality and Social Psychology* 70 (1996): 980.

98 could not have been more wrong: Bella M. DePaulo, Julie I. Stone, and G. Daniel Lassiter, "Deceiving and Detecting Deceit," in Schlenker, *The Self and Social Life*, 342; Bella M. DePaulo, Jennifer A. Epstein, and Melissa M. Wyer,

"Sex Differences in Lying: How Women and Men Deal with the Dilemma of Deceit," in Lewis and Saarni, *Lying and Deception in Everyday Life*, 143.

98 men and women lie at same rate: Bella M. DePaulo, Jennifer A. Epstein, and Melissa M. Wyer, "Sex Differences in Lying: How Men and Women Deal with the Dilemma of Deceit," in Lewis and Saarni, *Lying and Deception in Everyday Life*, 128.

98 men "ham": Bella M. DePaulo, "Nonverbal Behavior and Self Presentation," *Psychological Bulletin* 111 (1992): 223.

98 women feign feelings: Ibid.; Bella M. DePaulo, Jennifer A. Epstein, and Melissa M. Wyer, "Sex Differences in Lying: How Women and Men Deal with the Dilemma of Deceit," in *Lying and Deception in Everyday Life*, Lewis and Saarni 141.

98 art students: Ibid., 126–47; Bella M. DePaulo, Deborah A. Kashy, Susan E. Kirkendol, Melissa M. Wyer, and Jennifer A. Epstein, "Lying in Everyday Life," *Journal of Personality and Social Psychology* 70 (1996): 981.

98 "other people's feelings": Bella M. DePaulo, Deborah A. Kashy, Susan E. Kirkendol, Melissa M. Wyer, and Jennifer A. Epstein, "Lying in Everyday Life," *Journal of Personality and Social Psychology* 70 (1996), 993.

98 "they thought that the women": Ibid., 990.

99 "at least some of the times": Bella M. DePaulo, Jennifer A. Epstein, and Melissa M. Wyer, "Sex Differences in Lying: How Women and Men Deal with the Dilemma of Deceit," in Lewis and Saarni, *Lying and Deception in Everyday Life*, 143.

99 DePaulo originally thought: Ibid.

99 spare other *women's* feelings: Bella M. DePaulo, Deborah A. Kashy, Susan E. Kirkendol, Melissa M. Wyer, and Jennifer A. Epstein, "Lying in Everyday Life," *Journal of Personality and Social Psychology* 70 (1996): 993.

99 what's more: Ibid., 990.

99 least stressed of all: Ibid.

99 women did report: Bella M. DePaulo, Jennifer A. Epstein, and Melissa M. Wyer, "Sex Differences in Lying: How Women and Men Deal with the Dilemma of Deceit," in Lewis and Saarni, *Lying and Deception in Everyday Life*, 132.

99 before assessing lying by gender: Bella M. DePaulo, Deborah A. Kashy, Susan E. Kirkendol, Melissa M. Wyer, and Jennifer A. Epstein, "Lying in Everyday Life," *Journal of Personality and Social Psychology* 70 (1996): 993.

100 Scott: Wolk and Henley, *The Right to Lie*, 133.

100 Dickinson: Emily Dickinson, *Poems* (New York: Knopf, 1993), 18.

100 Rich: Rich, *On Lies, Secrets, and Silence*, 188.

100 Ford: Newhouse News Service, June 22, 2001.

100 beauty contestants: Miss New Jersey: *Dayton Daily News*, September 2, 1991; Miss Mississippi: *Houston Chronicle*, September 10, 1992; *Sacramento Bee*, September 12, 1993; Miss Virginia: *Roanoke Times and World News*, June 27, 1996.

101 Baldwin: *Denver Post*, May 24, 2002; *New York Times*, June 16, 2002.

101 DeLibero: *Bergen* (NJ) *Record*, October 29, 2000; *Houston Chronicle*, October 31, 2000, November 1, 2000, November 7, 2000, November 8, 2000, December 19, 2003, April 21, 2004.

101 Guerrero: *New York Times*, October 12, 1992; *New Yorker*, May 12, 2003.

101 9/11 poseurs: Associated Press, September 17, 2001.

102 Weingarten: *Washington Post*, August 17, 1998.

102 Seinfeld: *New York Times*, August 16, 1998.

103 Shakespeare: Sonnet 138, *Shakespeare: The Complete Works* (New York: Harcourt, Brace and World, 1952), 1620–21.

103 Doniger: *Social Research* 63 (1996): 664.

103 Hubner: John Hubner, *Bottom Feeders: From Free Love to Hard Core—The Rise and Fall of Counterculture Heroes Jim and Artie Mitchell* (New York: Doubleday, 1993), 62.

103 dry observation: Edward O. Laumann, John H. Gagnon, Robert T. Michael, and Stuart Michaels, *The Social Organization of Sexuality: Sexual Practices in the United States* (Chicago: University of Chicago Press, 1994), 129; *Toronto Sun*, February 14, 1995.

104 Kinsey: James H. Jones, *Alfred C. Kinsey: A Public / Private Life* (New York: Norton, 1997), 522, 577–79, 589.

104 Hite: *Washington Post Magazine*, December 27, 1987.

104 Ford: *Washington Post*, August 17, 1998; Ford, *Lies! Lies! Lies!* 263.

104 One study of sexually active college students: Susan D. Cochran and Vickie M. Mays, "Sex, Lies, and HIV" *New England Journal of Medicine*, March 15, 1990, 774–75.

105 a similar study: David Knox, Caroline Schacht, Judy Holt, and Jack Turner, "Sexual Lies Among College Students," *College Student Journal* 27 (1993): 269–72.

105 number of sex partners: Laumann et al., *The Social Organization of Sexuality*, 184–85.

105–6 sex researchers: *New Scientist*, July 14, 2003; *Journal of Sex Research* 40 (2003): 27–35.

106 Bellow: *Social Research* 63 (1996): 670.

106–7 Maher: Bill Maher, *True Story* (New York: Random House, 1994), 76.

107 Blum: Blum, *Deceivers and Deceived*, 28–29.

107 analysis of blood samples: *Washington Post*, January 18, 1998; *New York Times*, February 22, 2000.

108 "Ever since I have started using": www.easydiploma.com, testimonial.

108 one study of couples in different relationship stages: Sandra Metts, "An Exploratory Investigation of Deception in Close Relationships," *Journal of Social and Personal Relationships* 6 (1989): 174.

108 another study: Jo Ann Burns and B. L. Kintz, "Eye Contact While Lying During an Interview," *Bulletin of the Psychonomic Society* 7 (1976): 87–89.

108 one study found that any alteration: Gerald R. Miller, Paul A. Mongeau, and Carra Sleight, "Fudging with Friends and Lying to Lovers: Deceptive Communication in Personal Relationship," *Journal of Social and Personal Relationships* 3 (1986): 495–512.

108–9 "relational intimates concentrate": Ibid., 504.

109 these researchers also discovered: Ibid.

109 a study of couples in different stages: Sandra Metts, "An Exploratory Investigation of Deception in Close Relationships," *Journal of Social and Personal Relationships* 6 (1989): 174, 177.

109 one wife found: *Redbook*, January 1993.

109 DePaulo has found we lie more to those we like: Kathy L. Bell and Bella M. DePaulo, "Liking and Lying," *Basic and Applied Psychology* 18 (1996): 243–66; Bella M. DePaulo and Kathy L. Bell, "Truth and Investment: Lies Are Told to Those Who Care," *Journal of Personality and Social Psychology* 71 (1996): 703–16.

110 Proust: Marcel Proust, *On Reading*, ed. and trans. Jean Autret and William Burford (New York: Macmillan, 1971), 53, 55; Alain de Botton, *How Proust Can Change Your Life* (London: Picador, 1997), 138–39.

8. Mentors and Role Models

113 Nixon: Nomination acceptance speech, Miami Beach, Florida, August 8, 1968.

114 Right and wrong: Eva S. Moskowitz, *In Therapy We Trust: America's Obsession with Self-Fulfillment* (Baltimore: Johns Hopkins University Press, 2001), 15.

114 Lying is considered symptomatic: Sullivan, *The Concise Book of Lying*, 151–57; Ford, *Lies! Lies! Lies!* 133–46, 243–44; W. Shibles, *Lying: A Critical Analysis* (Whitewater, WI: Language Press, 1985), 85; Luis R. Marcos, "Lying: A Particular Defense Met in Psychoanalytic Therapy," *American Journal of Psychoanalysis* 32 (1972): 195; Edward M. Weinshel, "Some Observations on Not Telling the Truth," *Monographs of the Journal of the American Psychoanalytic*

Association 27 (1979): 504; *New York Times*, May 17, 1988; *Los Angeles Times*, March 3, 2003.

114 Forrester: John Forrester, *Truth Games: Lies, Money, and Psychoanalysis* (Cambridge, MA: Harvard University Press, 1997), 70.

114–15 Ford: Ford, *Lies! Lies! Lies!* 241–42, 249.

115 Lacan: John Forrester, *Truth Games*, 4–5; Campbell, *The Liar's Tale*, 201.

115 To a therapist, lies can expose: Forrester, *Truth Games*, 67–109; Ford, *Lies! Lies! Lies!* 211, 237–38, 242–44, 249; Campbell, *The Liar's Tale*, 13, 108, 190, 196–200.

115–16 Goldberg: Arnold Goldberg, "On Telling the Truth," in *Adolescent Psychiatry*, vol. 2, ed. Sherman C. Feinstein and Peter L. Giovacchini (New York: Basic Books, 1973), 101, 104, 105.

116 "useful myths": *New York Times*, March 14, 1998; O, January 2002.

116 narrative therapy: *Newsweek*, April 17, 1995. See also Dan P. McAdams, *The Stories We Live By: Personal Myths and the Making of the Self* (New York: Morrow, 1993); Jill Freedman and Gene Combs, *Narrative Therapy: The Social Construction of Preferred Realities* (New York: Norton, 1996); Harlene Anderson, *Conversation, Language, and Possibilities: A Postmodern Approach to Therapy* (New York: Basic Books, 1997).

116 "as if" advocate: therapist Sylvia Mills, in Gini Graham Scott, *The Truth About Lying: Why We All Do It, How We Do It, and Can We Live Without It?* (Petaluma, CA: Smart Publications, 1994), 70–71.

116 Vaihinger: Hans Vaihinger, *The Philosophy of "As If,"* discussed in Pollak, *The Creation of Dr. B*, 15–16.

116 Bettelheim: Bruno Bettelheim, *Freud's Vienna and Other Essays*, 106–8, cited in Pollak, *The Creation of Dr. B*, 15.

117 Pollak: Pollak, *The Creation of Dr. B*, 16–17.

117 Freud to Stekel: Leslie H. Farber, "Lying on the Couch," *Review of Existential Psychology and Psychiatry* 13 (1974): 125.

118 Florida prosecutor: *Time*, September 16, 2002; *Dayton Daily News*, November 15, 2002.

118 *Black's Law Dictionary* (St. Paul, MN: West Group, 1999), 904.

119 Clinton: *New York Times*, September 29, 1998.

119 Barnes: Linda Barnes, *The Big Dig* (New York: St. Martin's, 2002), 30.

119–20 Kronman: *American Lawyer*, January–February 1996.

120 Brougham: Monroe H. Freedman, *Lawyers' Ethics in an Adversary System* (Indianapolis: Bobbs-Merrill, 1975), 9.

120 Supreme Court: Ibid., 4.

120–21 Buffington: Lamont E. Buffington, "From the Chair," www.michbar.or/neg/june97.

121 Bok: Bok, *Lying*, 170.

121–22 Frankel: Marvin E. Frankel, "The Search for Truth: An Umpireal View," *University of Pennsylvania Law Review* 123 (1975): 1032–34, 1036–39.

122 volunteering information: Davis, *Truth to Tell*, 89.

122 Harlan: Freedman, *Lawyers' Ethics in an Adversary System*, 3.

122–23 Spence: *Harper's*, July, 1997.

123 commentator: David Graham, *Toronto Star*, July 23, 2001.

124 Bailey, *The Prevalence of Deceit*, 125.

124 Biden: *New York Times*, September 22, 1987; *Newsweek*, September 28, 1987; *Washington Post Magazine*, December 27, 1987.

124 Issa: *San Francisco Chronicle*, May 29, 1998.

125 Harkin: David S. Broder, *Changing of the Guard* (New York: Simon and Schuster, 1980), 68; Burkett and Whitley, *Stolen Valor*, 182; *Pittsburgh Tribune-Review*, September 21, 2003.

125 Switzler: *New York Times*, June 7, 1986, June 17, 1986; Burkett and Whitley, *Stolen Valor*, 182.

125 Caputo: *New York Times*, February 18, 1982, February 23, 1982; *New York Post*, March 6, 1982; Phil Reisman, *Journal News* (White Plains, NY), June 28, 2001.

125 Gore: *New Orleans Times-Picayune*, November 16, 1997; *Time*, January 31, 2000, February 14, 2000, October 16, 2000; *New York Times*, October 6, 2000; *Dayton Daily News*, October 10, 2000; *Newsweek*, October 16, 2000.

125 Bill Clinton: *Seattle Times*, July 9, 1998; *Time*, August 31, 1998.

125–26 Hillary Clinton: *Chicago Tribune*, April 3, 1995; *Washington Times*, August 18, 1995; *Boston Herald*, August 27, 1995; *Roanoke* (VA) *Times and World News*, February 25, 1996; *Lewiston* (ME) *Morning Tribune*, January 20, 1996; *Dayton Daily News*, July 6, 2003.

126 Shultz: *Newsweek*, June 31, 1993.

126 Reagan: Anthony Marro, "When the Government Tells Lies," *Columbia Journalism Review*, March–April 1985.

126 "I told the American people": March 4, 1987, speech, the Reagan Information Page, www.presidentreagan.info/speeches/iran_contra.cfm.

126 Kerrey: *New Yorker*, March 5, 2001.

126 Theodore Roosevelt's daughter: Alice Roosevelt Longworth, *Almanac of TR*, www.theodore-roosevelt.com/alice.html.

126 "Rhetorical excesses": August 7, 2003, speech at New York University, www.algoredemocrats.com.

126–27 Gore's family: *New York Times*, October 6, 2000.

127 Truman: *Esquire*, August 1971.

127–28 Greenfield: Greenfield, *Washington*, 66–67.

128–29 Schwarzenegger: Wendy Leigh, *Arnold: An Unauthorized Biography* (Chicago: Congdon and Weed, 1990), 464–47, 61, 68, 102–3, 118–19, 143, 264; Nigel Andrews, *True Myths: The Life and Times of Arnold Schwarzenegger* (New York: Birch Lane, 1996), 16–18, 52–53, 180, 182, 234, 270; *Los Angeles Times*, September 22, 2003; *San Diego Union-Tribune*, September 29, 2003; *Parade*, October 5, 2003; *Chicago Reader*, September 19, 2003.

9. It's Academic

130 Hook: Leonard Roy Frank, ed., *Random House Webster's Quotationary* (New York: Random House, 1999), 881.

130 cheating on campuses: David Callahan, *The Cheating Culture* (Orlando, FL: Harcourt, 2004), 216–18, 229–32, 288.

131 MIT survey: *Dayton Daily News*, December 15, 1993.

131 Duke survey: *Tulsa World*, May 26, 2002, citing study by Donald McCabe, president of Center for Academic Integrity at Duke.

131 broader sampling of college students: *Personnel Journal*, October 1996, citing study by Reid Psychological Systems of Chicago.

131 two midwestern professors: *Chronicle of Higher Education*, February 1999; *American Prospect*, May–June 1999.

131 DePaulo's finding: Bella M. DePaulo, Deborah A. Kashy, Susan E. Kirkendol, Melissa M. Myer, and Jennifer A. Epstein, "Lying in Everyday Life," *Journal of Personality and Social Psychology* 70 (1996): 991, 993–94.

131 "intrigued by the fact": Ibid., 991, 993.

131 "Education gives some people": *Panama City* (FL) *News Herald* May 23, 1999.

131 liars less likely to refer to selves more likely to use passive voice: Bella M. DePaulo, Robert Rosenthal, Carolyn Rieder Green, and Judith Rosenkrantz "Diagnosing Deceptive and Mixed Messages from Verbal and Nonverbal Cues," *Journal of Experimental Social Psychology* 18 (1982): 435; Bella M. DePaulo with Julie I. Stone and G. Daniel Lassiter "Deceiving and Detecting Deceit," in *The Self and Social Life*, ed. Barry R. Schlenker (New York: McGraw-Hill, 1985), 338–39; Bella M. DePaulo, "Nonverbal Behavior and Self Presentation," *Psychological Bulletin* 111 (1992): 232.

132 Northern Arizona instructor: "Methods-L List Discussion of Lying with Research," www.geneseo.edu/~soc1212/ethics/lying-researchers.html.

132 Bailey: F. G. Bailey, *The Prevalence of Deceit*, xi.

133 researchers beholden to business: *Guardian* (London, England), February 7, 2002; *Austin Chronicle*, April 16, 2004.

133 Berkeley: William Safire, *Dayton Daily News*, July 30, 1999.

133 MIT: *New York Times*, January 2, 2003; *San Francisco Chronicle*, March 3, 2003; *Boston Globe*, April 30, 2004.

133 number of lobbyists cited by Clinton: *New York Times*, May 12, 1993.

133 Bellesiles: *Boston Globe*, January 29, 2002, February 8, 2002; *Morning Edition*, National Public Radio, March 4, 2002; *St. Petersburg Times*, April 6, 2002; George Will, *Newsweek*, May 20, 2002; www.instapundit.com, October 25, 2002.

134 "false feedback": Elliot Aronson and David R. Mettee. "Dishonest Behavior as a Function of Differential Levels of Induced Self-Esteem," *Journal of Personality and Social Psychology* 9 (1968): 121.

134 "led to believe": Gregory C. Elliott, "Some Effects of Deception and Level of Self-Monitoring on Planning and Reacting to a Self-Presentation," *Journal of Personality and Social Psychology* 37 (1979): 1282.

134 "The explanation": Jo Ann Burns and B. L. Kintz, *Bulletin of the Psychonomic Society* (1976): 87.

134 Feldman: *All Things Considered*, National Public Radio, June 13, 2002.

134 Troupe: *San Francisco Chronicle*, October 20, 2002; *New Yorker*, November 4, 2002; *Chronicle of Higher Education*, April 4, 2003.

135 Mount Holyoke's dean of faculty: *Time*, July 2, 2001.

135 response to Ellis: "Joe Ellis Quotes: By and About Joseph Ellis," www.viking-phoenix.com/public/rongstad/history/400historians/josephellis/ellis-quotes.htm; *Talk of the Nation*, National Public Radio, June 25, 2001.

135 Nyberg: *Talk of the Nation*, National Public Radio, June 25, 2001.

135 Morris: *New York Times*, June 22, 2001.

135 Vassar graduate: *New York Times*, June 23, 2001.

136 Said: Justus Reid Weiner, "'My Beautiful Old House' and Other Fabrications by Edward Said," *Commentary*, September, 1999, 23–31; *Guardian* (London, England), August 23, 1999; *New York*, September 27, 1999.

136 Ashrawi: Hanan Ashrawi, "The Sun and the Sieve: Edward Said and His Petty Slanderers," August 24, 1999, www.miftah.org.

137 Menchú, Stoll: Rigoberta Menchú, *I, Rigoberta Menchú: An Indian Woman in Guatemala* (London: Verso, 1984); *New York Times*, December 15, 1998; David Stoll, *Rigoberta Menchú and the Story of All Poor Guatemalans* (New York: Westview / Perseus, 1999); Arturo Arias, ed., *The Rigoberta Menchú Controversy* (Minneapolis: University of Minnesota Press, 2001).

137 "Many said": W. George Lovell and Christopher H. Lutz, "The Primacy of Larger Truths," in Arias, *The Rigoberta Menchú Controversy*, 171–95; Doris Summer, "Las Casas's Lies and Other Language Games," Ibid., 237–50; Elzbieta Sklodowska, "The Poetics of Remembering, the Politics of Forgetting," Ibid., 251–69; Daphne Patai, "Whose Truth? Iconicity and Accuracy in the World of Testimonial Literature," Ibid., 270–87.

137 University of Pittsburgh professor: John Beverly, "What Happens When the Subaltern Speaks," in Arias, *The Rigoberta Menchú Controversy*, 223–24.

137 chair of Wellesley's Spanish Department: Marjorie Agosin, in Daphne Patai, in Arias, *The Rigoberta Menchú Controversy*, 271.

138 the authors of one of its essays argued: George Lakoff and Mark Johnson, "Metaphors We Live By," in *The Production of Reality*, ed. Jodi O'Brien and Peter Kollock (Thousand Oaks, CA: Pine Forge Press, 2001), 134.

139 Reagan: Anthony Marro, "When the Government Tells Lies," *Columbia Journalism Review*, March–April 1985.

139 Mussolini: Campbell, *The Liar's Tale*, 287.

139 Lenin: Frank, *Random House Quotationary*, 885.

139 Orwell: George Orwell, "Politics and the English Language," in *The Orwell Reader: A Treasury of the Best of George Orwell Fiction, Essays, Reportage* (San Diego: Harcourt Brace Jovanovich, 1956), 355–66.

140 Farber and Sherry: Daniel A. Farber and Suzanna Sherry, *Beyond All Reason: The Radical Assault on Truth in American Law* (New York: Oxford University Press, 1997), 108–9.

140 Wilkomirski: Binjamin Wilkomirski, *Fragments: Memories of a Wartime Childhood* (New York: Schocken, 1996); *New York Times*, November 3, 1998.

140 Eskin: Blake Eskin, *A Life in Pieces: The Making and Unmaking of Binjamin Wilkomirski* (New York: Norton, 2001).

140 DNA test: Associated Press Worldstream, December 12, 2002.

140 "emotionally honest": Eskin, *A Life in Pieces*, 218.

141 "de Man's colleagues:" Lehman, *Signs of the Times*, 160, 201–2, 216.

141 "de Man wrote": Ibid., 137, 179, 209, 219.

141–42 de Man's background, proposal: Ibid., 181, 238, 270.

142 Lehman: Ibid., 242.

142 Campbell: Campbell, *The Liar's Tale*, 260.

142 Protagoras: Harvey Siegel, *Free Inquiry*, 18 (Fall 1998): 35.

143 Hobbes: Thomas Hobbes, *Leviathan* (New York: Dutton, 1950), 26.

143 Campbell: Campbell, *The Liar's Tale*, 136.

143 Dostoyevsky character: Iris Murdoch, *Metaphysics as a Guide to Morals* (London: Allen Lane 1993), 105.

143 Picasso: T. Alan Brougham, "Some Notes on the Art of Lying," *New England Review*, 93–100, Spring 1994.

143 Sahl: *People*, June 20, 1994.

144 Barnes: Barnes, *A Pack of Lies*, 60.

144–45 Liberace biography: Darden Asbury Pyron, *Liberace: An American Boy* (Chicago: University of Chicago Press, 2000), 230–34.

145 one reviewer: *New York Times*, July 27, 2000.

145 Bok: Bok, *Lying*, 9–14.

145 professor who assigned Menchú: in Daphne Patai, in Arias, *The Rigoberta Menchú Controversy*, 281.

146 Bailey: F. G. Bailey, *The Prevalence of Deceit*, 118, 120.

146 Fish: *New York Times*, October 15, 2001.

146–47 *Funky Winkerbean: Continental*, December 1998.

147 Heche: *Dayton Daily News*, September 18, 2001.

147 Muhammad: *New York Times*, October 21, 2003.

147 one pollster: Donaldson and Wamberg, *Pinocchio Nation*, 21.

148 some legal scholars: Farber and Sherry, *Beyond All Reason*, 34–51.

10. Narrative Truths, and Lies

149 McAdams: Don P. McAdams, *Personal Myths and the Making of the Self* (New York: Morrow, 1993), 28–29.

149 Ramsland: Katherine M. Ramsland, *Bliss: Writing to Find Your True Self* (Cincinnati: Walking Stick Press, 2000), 89.

149 Reich: Robert Reich, *Locked in the Cabinet* (New York: Knopf, 1997, Vintage, 1998); Slate.com, May 30, 1997, February 7, 1998; *Washington Post*, May 29, 1997, June 5, 1997; *Boston Globe*, June 1, 1997; *Sacramento Bee*, June 12, 1997; *Time*, June 30, 1997; Nicholas Lemann, *New Republic*, July 28, 1997; George Will, *Newsweek*, September 1, 1997.

150 "I was absolutely true": *Washington Post*, May 29, 1997.

150 "Memory is fallible": *New York Times*, February 24, 1998.

150 "the best excuse Reich could offer": *Morning Edition*, National Public Radio, June 10, 1997.

150 O'Brien: "How to Tell a True War Story," in Tim O'Brien, *The Things They Carried* (Boston: Houghton Mifflin, 1990), 89.

151 Berendt: *New York Times*, February 24, 1998.

152 Rainer: Tristine Rainer, *Your Life as Story: Writing the New Autobiography* (New York: Tarcher / Putnam, 1997), 34–6.

152 McCourt: *Newsweek*, August 25, 1997; *Scotsman* (Edinburgh), March 20, 2001.

152 Bayley: *Sunday Times* (London, England), March 18, 2001; *Daily Telegraph* (London, England), March 19, 2001; *Guardian* (London, England), March 19, 2001; *Scotsman* (Edinburgh), March 20, 2001, March 25, 2001; *Evening Standard* (London, England), March 21, 2001.

152–53 Blunt: Judy Blunt, *Breaking Clean* (New York: Knopf, 2002): *Newsday*, February 24, 2002; *Pittsburgh Post-Gazette*, April 21, 2002; Associated Press, May 12, 2002; *Halifax* (Nova Scotia) *Daily News*, May 14, 2002; *Regina* (SK), *Leader-Post*, May 18, 2002.

153 Morris: *New York Times*, October 2, 1999.

153 Morris's publisher: Edmund Morris, *Dutch: A Memoir of Ronald Reagan* (New York: Modern Library, 2000), xiii.

153–54 Gornick-Corrigan: Salon.com, August 1, 2003, August 12, 2003; *Fresh Air*, National Public Radio, August 5, 2003, August 14, 2003; *Newsday*, September 9, 2003.

154 ancient Greece: Kerr, *The Penguin Book of Lies*, 13; Barnes, *A Pack of Lies*, 49: Jay Parini, "Fact or Fiction: Writing Biographies Versus Writing Novels," Jay Parini, *Some Necessary Angels* (New York: Columbia University Press, 1997), 248; Ben Yagoda, "In Cold Facts, Some Books Falter," *New York Times*, March 15, 1998; Williams, *Truth and Truthfulness*, 155–61.

155 Defoe: Goldberg, *The Book of Lies*, 25–26; Kevin Kerrane and Ben Yagoda, *The Art of Fact: A Historical Anthology of Literary Journalism* (New York: Touchstone / Simon and Schuster, 1997), 23–24; Richard West, *Daniel Defoe: The Life and Strange, Surprising Adventures* (New York: Carroll and Graf 1998), 266–77.

155 Chatwin: Nicholas Shakespeare, *Bruce Chatwin: A Biography* (Nan Talese / Doubleday, 2000), in *Publishers Weekly*, December 20, 1999; *Time*, February 21, 2000.

155 Thompson: *Publishers Weekly*, January 13, 2003.

156 "immaculately factual": *New York Times Book Review*, January 27, 1980; George Plimpton, *Truman Capote* (New York: Nan Talese / Doubleday, 1999), 198.

156 Yagoda: Ben Yagoda, *About Town: The New Yorker and the World it Made* (New York: Scribner's), 347.

156 Shawn wrote: Ben Yagoda, *New York Times*, March 15, 1998.

156 long list: Gerald Clarke, *Capote: A Biography* (New York: Simon and Schuster, 1988), 358–59; Ben Yagoda, *New York Times*, March 15, 1998.

156 Mitchell: *Washington Post*, August 6, 1992; *New York Times*, August 12, 2002; Slate.com, July 12, 2003.

156 Reid: *New York Times*, June 19, 1984; Thomas Maier, *Newhouse: All the Glitter, Power, and Glory of America's Richest Media Empire and the Secretive Man Behind It* (New York: St. Martin's, 1994), 266–68; Yagoda, *About Town*, 400; Slate.com, July 12, 2003.

157 Shawn could not decide: Yagoda, *About Town*, 400; Slate.com, July 12, 2003.

157 *New York Times* editorial: *New York Times*, June 20, 1984.

157 Sheehy-Felker: *Wall Street Journal*, August 13, 1971.

157–58 Wolfe: Tom Wolfe, *The New Journalism* (New York: Harper and Row, 1973); Yagoda, *About Town*, 340; *Columbia Journalism Review*, Winter 1966; *New York Review of Books*, February 3, 1966; *San Diego Reader*, July 19, 1973.

158–59 Cohn: *New York*, June 7, 1976, December 8, 1997; *Times* (London, England), December 5, 1997; *New York Times*, June 8, 1997; *Greensboro* (NC) *News and Record*, November 14, 2002.

159 Bissinger: *New York Times*, February 24, 1998.

160 Sheed: *New York Times Book Review*, October 29, 2000.

160 Burkett: Burkett and Whitley, *Stolen Valor*, 414–15.

160 Slater: *Times* (London, England), April 2, 2004.

160 Millett: *New York Times Book Review*, January 27, 1980.

161 Dillard: Annie Dillard, *Pilgrim at Tinker's Creek* (New York: Bantam, 1975), 278; Mike Harden, *Columbus Dispatch*, January 15, 1996, personal communication.

161 novelized books: *Sybil*: *New York Times*, August 19, 1998, *Los Angeles Times*, August 27, 1998; *Sleepers*: *Newsweek*, August 11, 1997, *New York Times*, October 22, 1996; *Roots*: *Publishers Weekly*, October 6, 1997; *The Amityville Horror: Human Behavior*, June 1978, *Wall Street Journal*, November 15, 1978; *The Last Brother*: Ellen Goodman, *Dayton Daily News*, July 16, 1993, *San Francisco Chronicle*, July 20, 1993, July 26, 1993, *Newsweek*, August 2, 1993, *People*, August 9, 1993; *Mutant Message Down Under*: *Boston Globe*, September 26, 1994.

161 *The Education of Little Tree*: *New York Times*, October 4, 1991; *Newsweek*, October 14, 1991; *People*, October 28, 1991; *Independent* (London, England), March 21, 2001.

161 Theroux: *Esquire*, September 1996.

161 Moody: *Fresh Air*, National Public Radio, May 9, 2002; *Publishers Weekly*, June 10, 2002; *New York Times Book Review*, July 7, 2002.

161 Eggers: Dave Eggers, *A Heartbreaking Work of Staggering Genius* (New York: Simon and Schuster, 2000), ix, xxxix.

162–63 Slater: Lauren Slater, *Lying: A Metaphorical Memoir* (New York: Random House, 2000), x, 5, 145, 127, 220, 161–2.

163 Blair: *New York Times*, May 11, 2003.

163 other newspapers: *Washington Post*, March 15, 2004; *New York Times*, March 22, 2004.

163–64 Kelley: *American Journalism Review*, February–March, 2004; *USA Today*, January 13, 2004, March 19, 2004, April 22, 2004; *New York Times*, March 20, 2004, April 23, 2004; *Washington Post*, March 23, 2004.

164 McLeese: *Austin American-Statesman*, June 23, 1998.

165 *Slate* episode: *New York Times*, June 25, 2001; Slate.com, June 25, 2001, May 8, 2003.

165 *New Yorker* episode: *New Yorker*, November 27, 2000, December 11, 2000; *New York Observer*, December 11, 2000.

165 Glass: *New Republic*, June 29, 1998; *Time*, May 25, 1998; *Newsweek*, June 22, 1998; Buzz Bissinger, "Shattered Glass," *Vanity Fair*, September 1998; Samuel Hughes, "Through a Glass Darkly," *Pennsylvania Gazette*, November–December 1998.

165 *New York Times* correction notices: *New York Times*, February 19, 1982, February 22, 1998, October 21, 1998, February 21, 2002.

165 other newspapers: *Sacramento Bee*, November 22, 2000; *San Antonio Light: New York Times*, February 18, 1986; *Arizona Republic: Dayton Daily News*, August 22, 1999; *Baltimore Sun*, May 3, 2003; *Washington Post: Newsweek*, April 27, 1981.

165 *Owensboro Messenger-Inquirer: Dayton Daily News*, May 15, 1999.

166 Kelley nominated for Pulitzers: *Washington Post*, January 8, 2004; *USA Today*, March 21, 2004; *Editor & Publisher*, March 22, 2004.

166 Smith: *New York Times*, June 20, 1998; *Boston Globe*, June 21, 1998; *Chicago Tribune*, August 12, 1998; *Chicago*, September 1998; *Boston Magazine*, October 1998.

166 Barnicle: *Boston Herald*, June 21, 1998; *New York Times*, August 17, 1998; *Newsweek*, August 17, 1998, August 31, 1998; *Boston Magazine*, October, 1998; *New York Press*, March 24–30, 1999; *Brill's Content*, April 2000.

166 *Publishers Weekly: Publishers Weekly*, October 21, 2002.

167 Tobin: *Authors Guild Bulletin*, Fall 2000.

167 Morris reviews: *Time*, November 19, 2001; *Fort Worth Star-Telegram* review in *Dayton Daily News*, December 16, 2001.

167 footnotes about Morris's sources: *Washington Post*, October 3, 1999; *Publishers Weekly*, October 11, 1999; *Times*, November 19, 2001.

167 *New Yorker* critic: Laura Miller reviewing James Frey's *A Million Little Pieces* (Nan Talese Doubleday, 2003) in *New Yorker*, May 12, 2003.

168 Berendt: John Berendt, *Midnight in the Garden of Good and Evil*, 389; Aldrich: Marcia Aldrich, *Girl Rearing: Memoir of a Girlhood Gone Astray* (New York: Norton, 1998), 4; Larson: Erik Larson, *The Devil in the White City* (New York: Crown, 2003), xi, 395–96, 431.

168 Rainer, *Your Life as Story*, 35.

169 Cohn: *New York*, December 8, 1997.

11. Masked Media

171 Gabler: Neal Gabler, *Life the Movie: How Entertainment Conquered Reality* (New York: Knopf, 1998), 57.

171 Stallone: *Bergen* (NJ) *Record*, October 9, 1991.

171 Leno: Jay Leno, *Leading with My Chin* (New York: HarperCollins, 1996), 185–86; *Montreal Gazette*, December 7, 1996; John Leo, *U.S. News & World Report*, December 16, 1996, citing admission by Leno in *New York Post*; *Chicago Tribune*, January 1, 2002.

172 Ryder: *Dayton Daily News*, December 1, 2002.

172 Sony episode: *Los Angeles Times*, June 24, 2001.

172 Gabler: *Los Angeles Times*, June 24, 2001.

172 Obst: Lynda Obst, *Hello, He Lied: And Other Truths from the Hollywood Trenches* (New York: Broadway, 1996), 13.

173 "true story," John Ford: John Mack Faragher in Carnes, *Past Imperfect*, 158.

173 Coen Brothers: *Minneapolis Star Tribune*, March 3, 1996, March 23, 1996; *Parade*, March 16, 1997.

173 Theda Bara: Goldberg, *The Book of Lies*, 180–81; *New Yorker*, September 23, 2002.

174 Wayne: Maurice Zolotow, *Shooting Star: A Biography of John Wayne* (New York: Pocket, 1975), 88–89, 96, 120, 134, 304–6; Garry Wills, *John Wayne's America: The Politics of Celebrity* (New York: Simon and Schuster, 1997), 27, 31–32, 35–36, 107–13; *New York Times*, June 13, 1979.

174 Dennehy: *New York Times*, February 22, 1988, April 23, 1989; Burkett and Whitley, *Stolen Valor*, 164.

174 Stallone: United Press International, October 5, 1991; *Bergen* (NJ) *Record*, October 9, 1991; *Star*, February 4, 1992.

174 aspiring actor: *Talk of the Nation*, National Public Radio, December 19, 2001.

175 Gottlieb: *All Things Considered*, National Public Radio, May 14, 2003.

175 Kramer, Walter: *Newsweek*, October 26, 1998.

175 Ball: *Palm Beach Post*, March 18, 1997.

175 name changes: Danny Thomas: *Dayton Daily News*, February 7, 1991; Albert Brooks: *TV Guide*, April 24, 1993; Warren Beatty: *People*, August 22, 1983; Lucille Ball; Lucille Ball, *Love, Lucy* (New York: Boulevard Books, 1997) 1, 4.

175 age discounts: Zsa Zsa Gabor; *People*, November 27, 1989; David Brenner: *Philadelphia Daily News*, December 3, 1979, *People*, September 10, 1990; Carol Lawrence: *Chicago Tribune*, October 4, 1992; Anka Radakovich: *Dayton Daily News*, July 2, 1994, August 20, 1994; Robert Conrad: *Dayton Daily News*, April 2, 2001; Mike Douglas: *Philadelphia Inquirer*, March 9, 1980; Groucho Marx: *New York Times*, August 21, 1977; Marlo Thomas: *Philadelphia Inquirer TV Week* November 23, 1980.

177 Jones: Landon Y. Jones, *Great Expectations: America and the Baby Boom Generation* (New York: Coward McCann and Geoghegan, 1980), 134.

177 Arledge: *Newsweek*, December 16, 2002; Roone Arledge, *Roone* (New York: HarperCollins, 2003).

177 "Liberators": Jeffrey Goldberg, *New Republic*, February 8, 1993; *New York Times*, February 12, 1993; *Washington Post*, February 13, 1993; Harry Stein, *TV Guide*, March 27, 1993; *Current*, September 20, 1993.

178 TV hoaxers: *World Press Review*, October 1992; *Dayton Daily News*, April 26, 1998; *Impact Weekly* (Dayton, Ohio), February 3–9, 2000.

178 Buckwheat: *People*, October 22, 1990; *World Press Review*, October 1992.

178 Freiwald: *Boston Globe*, August 30, 1988; *New York Times*, September 8, 1988; *People*, September 19, 1998.

178 Abel: *World Press Review*, October, 1992; *Dayton Daily News*, April 13, 1994, May 7, 1994.

178 British programs, producer, Edinburgh festival: *Birmingham Post* (England), August 31, 1999; *The Daily Telegraph* (London, England), August 31, 1999; *Daily Mail* (London, England), August 31, 1999; *Guardian* (London, England), August 31, 1999; *Scotsman* (Edinburgh), August 31, 1999.

179 Drescher: *Chicago Tribune*, January 1, 2002.

179 Sky News reporter: *IrelandOn-Line*, December 12, 2003.

179 Rivera: *Baltimore Sun*, December 12, 2001, December 28, 2001; *Washington Post*, December 24, 2001; *The O'Reilly Factor*, Fox News Network, January 3, 2002; *Dayton Daily News*, December 2, 2002.

179 Roberts: *ABC World News Tonight*, January 26, 1994; *Washington Post*, Febru-

ary 14, 1994, February 15, 1994; *Atlanta Journal and Constitution*, February 16, 1994; *Houston Chronicle*, February 16, 1994; *USA Today*, February 16, 1994, February 17, 1994; *Chicago Tribune*, February 27, 1994.

179–80 North, Lear: *New York Times*, July 11, 1987.

180 sitcom husband: teaser, ABC-TV, April 16, 2003.

180 Sullivan: Sullivan, *The Concise Book of Lying*, 131.

181 divorce referred to: *New Yorker*, April 22 & 29, 2002.

181 Middle East: *Newsweek*, May 20, 2002.

181 Didion: *Morning Edition*, National Public Radio, October 26, 2001.

182 taped actors: *San Francisco Chronicle*, March 16, 2004.

182 Bush's visual deceptions: *New York Times*, May 16, 2003.

183 Sulzberger: *Editor & Publisher*, March 22, 2004.

183 "one commentator called Bush": Marjorie Williams, *Washington Post*, July 8, 2001.

12. Peter Pan Morality

184 Jones: Jones, *Great Expectations*, 361.

184 Queenan: Joe Queenan, *Balsamic Dreams: A Short but Self-Important History of the Baby Boomer Generation* (New York: Holt, 2001), 60.

184 Jones: Jones, *Great Expectations*, 2–3.

185 sharing what you felt: See Moskowitz, *In Therapy We Trust*, 244.

185 Barnicle: *New York Times*, September 21, 1998; *Boston Herald*, September 22, 1998.

185 Smith: *Toronto Star*, June 27, 1998.

186 emphasis on being well-intentioned: David Brooks, *Bobos in Paradise: The New Upper Class and How They Got There* (New York: Touchstone, 2001), 250.

187 Jones: Jones, *Great Expectations*, 361.

187 "I don't do nuance": *Washington Post*, February 17, 2004.

187 Queenan: Queenan, *Balsamic Dreams*, 11.

187–88 Klein: *Washington Post*, July 17, 1996.

188 Edwards: *Philadelphia Inquirer*, March 1, 1979.

188 Beasley: *Charlotte Observer*, June 24, 2001.

188–89 Ellis: Joseph Ellis, *American Sphinx: The Character of Thomas Jefferson* (New York: Knopf, 1997), 106; *Boston Globe*, June 18, 2001.

189 Brooks: Brooks, *Bobos in Paradise*, 246, 250; *Newsweek* excerpt, April 3, 2000.

189 neopuritanism: Roger Rosenblatt, *Modern Maturity*, January–February 1996.

189 O'Leary: *Sports Illustrated*, April 8, 2002.

190 Brock: *Newsweek*, July 9, 2001; *New Yorker*, March 11, 2002; David Brock, *Blinded by the Right: The Conscience of an Ex-Conservative* (New York: Crown, 2002), 104, 113–14.

190 Davis: Lanny Davis, *Truth to Tell: Tell It Early, Tell It All, Tell It Yourself* (New York: Free Press, 1999); *New York Times*, December 13, 1996.

190 "God has called me": *Washington Post*, January 8, 2004, citing 2001 profile of Kelley in *Christian Life*.

190 Kelley: *American Journalism Review*, February–March 2004; *USA Today*, January 13, 2004, March 19, 2004; *New York Times*, March 20, 2004; *USA Today*, April 22, 2004.

190–91 Ventura: *St. Paul Pioneer Press*, January 28, 2002; *Minneapolis Star Tribune*, May 9, 2001; www.authentiseal.com.

191 Salisbury: *San Diego Reader*, December 2, 1999; *Hannity & Colmes*, Fox News Network, December 7, 1999; *Minneapolis Star Tribune*, December 14, 1999.

191 Ventura never fired upon: *St. Paul Pioneer Press*, January 28, 2002.

191–92 Fermaglich: Mollie Fermaglich, "Woodstock Envy," *AARP: The Magazine*, February–March 2003.

192 Lewis: *Atlanta Journal and Constitution*, July 15, 2001.

192 Ware: *Cleveland Plain Dealer*, July 19, 1998; *Dayton Daily News*, November 7, 1997; *Newsweek*, November 17, 1997.

192 rock 'n' roll values: *New Yorker*, July 7, 2003.

193 Ventura: *St. Paul Pioneer Press*, January 28, 2002.

193 "with a hair trigger on": *New York Times*, October 6, 2000.

194 Enron trading floor: Click2Houston.com, February 22, 2002, www.click2houston.com/news/1248368/detail.html; *Los Angeles Business Journal*, March 4, 2002; Frank Rich, *New York Times*, March 4, 2002.

194 head of executive recruitment firm: Edwin S. Stanton, Press., E.S. Stanton & Associates, in *Business Week*, September 15, 1986.

194 Waksal: *Dayton Daily News*, October 3, 2003.

194–95 Gates: *Newsweek*, November 12, 2001; G. Paschal Zachary, *Mother Jones*, January–February, 1998.

13. Deception.com

196 Williams: Williams, *Truth and Truthfulness*, 216.

196 Brooks: *Dayton Daily News*, December 12, 2003.

196–97 Blair: *New York Times*, May 11, 2003; *New Yorker*, May 26, 2003; Jayson Blair, *Burning Down My Masters' House: My Life at the* New York Times (Beverly Hills: New Millennium Press, 2004).

197 StairMaster user: Jon Frankel, *People*, May 8, 1995.

197 we lie more by phone: *Boston Herald*, September 21, 1997; Bella M. De-
Paulo, Deborah A. Kashy, Susan E. Kirkendol, Melissa M. Myer, and Jennifer
A. Epstein, "Lying in Everyday Life," *Journal of Personality and Social Psychology*
70 (1996): 992; *Washington Post*, March 7, 2004; ScienCentralNews, April 29,
2004.

198 Romanian company: *New Scientist*, March 5, 2004.

198 phony-degree service: *USA Today*, March 9, 2004; www.easydiploma.com.

199 Salam Pax: *Weekend Morning Edition*, National Public Radio, March 29, 2003.

199 Georgia Tech survey: "GVU's 9th WWW User Survey," www.gvu.gatech./
edu/user_surveys/survey-1998-04/reports/1998-04-use.html.

199–200 Donath: *Yahoo! Internet Life*, May 1999; Judith Donath, "Identity and
Deception in the Virtual Community," in *Communities in Cyberspace*, ed.
Marc A. Smith and Peter Kollock (New York: Routledge, 1999), 29–59; Judith
Donath, "Being Real: Questions of Tele-Identity," in *The Robot in the Garden:
Telerobotics and Telepistemology in the Age of the Internet*, ed. Ken Goldberg
(Cambridge, MA: MIT Press, 2000), 296–311.

200 Marriott: personal communication.

201 customer service reps: *Dayton Daily News*, June 17, 2001; *New York Times*,
May 11, 2003, December 4, 2003; *Newsweek*, May 12, 2003.

201 keyboard-tapping dog: Susan M. Detwiler, "Charlatans, Leeches, and Old
Wives: Medical Misinformation," in *Web of Deception: Misinformation on the
Internet* ed. Anne P. Mintz (Medford, NJ: Information Today, 2002), 28.

202 trolls: Judith Donath, "Identity and Deception in the Virtual Community,"
in Smith Kollock, *Communities in Cyberspace*, 45–49.

202 Feldman: *Southern Journal of Medicine* 93 (2000): 669–72; *Village Voice*, June
27–July 3, 2001.

202 Turkle: Sherry Turkle, *Life on the Screen: Identity in the Age of the Internet*
(New York: Touchstone, 1997, 1995), 44, citing Fredric Jameson on postmodernism, *New Left Review* 146 (1984): 53–92.

202 Donath: *Yahoo! Internet Life*, May 1999, 91.

203 fifteen-year-old: Michael Lewis, "Faking It," *New York Times Magazine*, July
15, 2001.

203 online relationships adolescent: Turkle, *Life on the Screen*, 203–4.

204 Mintz, ed. Anne P. Mintz, *Web of Deception: Misinformation on the Internet*
(Medford, NJ: Information Today, 2002), xvii.

204 Quint and Mintz: Barbara Quint and Anne P. Mintz, "What a Tangled Web
We Weave," in Mintz, *Web of Deception*, 230.

205 SARS virus: ConsumerAffairs.com, May 9, 2003, www.consumeraffairs.com/ news03/fda_sars.html; *Washington Post*, May 10, 2003; *New Orleans Times-Picayune*, May 10, 2003.

205 review of medical Web sites: Susan M. Detwiler, "Charlatans, Leeches, and Old Wives: Medical Misinformation," in Mintz, *Web of Deception*, 23–49.

205 study of sixty Web sites: *Dayton Daily News*, June 4, 1998, citing June 1998 issue of *Pediatrics*.

205 decentralized medium: Goldberg, *The Robot in the Garden*, 3.

205 Rooney: *Trenton Times*, July 26, 2003.

205 Vonnegut: *Dayton Daily News*, August 10, 1997; *Newsweek*, April 5, 1999; *Time*, April 5, 1999.

206 Salinger: CNN, November 10, 1996, March 13, 1997.

206 World Trade Center legends: *New York Times*, September 23, 2001; *Time*, October 8, 2001; *Newsweek Web Exclusive*, October 19, 2001; "Rumors of War," www.snopes.com; Paul S. Piper, "Web Hoaxes, Counterfeit Sites, and Other Spurious Information on the Internet," in Mintz, *Web of Deception*, 10.

206 Mikkelson: *Washington Post*, January 7, 2002.

207 Holmes: *Abrams v. United States*, 250 U.S. 616 (1919).

207 disgusting legends: Chip Heath, Chris Bell, and Emily Sternberg, "Emotional Selection in Memes: The Case of Urban Legends," *Journal of Personality and Social Psychology* 81 (2001): 1029, 1034; *Washington Post*, January 7, 2002.

208 Campanella: Thomas J. Campanella, "Eden by Wire: Webcameras and the Telepresent Landscape," in Goldberg, *The Robot in the Garden*, 39, 41.

208 Goldberg: Ken Goldberg, "Introduction: The Unique Phenomenon of a Distance," in *The Robot in the Garden*, 39, 41.

209 Lindh: *Newsweek*, November 17, 2001; Clarence Page, *Dayton Daily News*, December 14, 2001; *Time*, December 17, 2001, October 7, 2002.

209 Maass: Slate.com, June 2, 2003; *Guardian* (London, England), May 20, 2003; *Publishers Weekly*, July 14, 2003; Salam Pax; *Salam Pax: The Clandestine Diary of an Ordinary Iraqi* (New York: Grove, 2003).

14. The Suspicious Society

213 Augustine: Augustine, *Treatises on Various Subjects*, 78.

214 Ekman: Ekman, *Telling Lies*, 338.

214 Wetzel: *Washington Post*, April 14, 1998.

215 Minsk-Pinsk: adapted from Forrester, *Truth Games*, 48; *Social Research* 63 (Fall 1996): 929.

215 Ansary: *New York Times*, September 23, 2001; Mir Tamim Ansary, *West of Kabul, East of New York* (New York: Farrar, Straus and Giroux, 2002).

216 Arendt: Hannah Arendt "Lying in Politics," in *Crises of the Republic* (New York: Harcourt Brace Jovanovich, 1972), 7.

216 Walters: Stan B. Walters, *The Truth About Lying: How to Spot a Lie and Protect Yourself from Deception* (Naperville, IL: Sourcebooks, 2000).

216–17 Lieberman: David J. Lieberman, *Never Be Lied To Again: How to Get the Truth in 5 Minutes or Less in Any Conversation or Situation* (New York: St. Martin's, 1998), 5.

217 gadgets: *Washington Post*, August 18, 2002.

217 software program: *Financial Post*, February 18, 2002.

217 DePaulo: Carol Toris and Bella M. DePaulo, "Effects of Actual Deception and Suspiciousness of Deception on Interpersonal Perceptions," *Journal of Personality and Social Psychology* 47 (1985): 1071.

218 "Where's the nose?": Bella M. DePaulo and Matthew E. Ansfield, "Detecting Deception from Nonverbal Cues: Pinocchio's Revenge," *Legal Medical Quarterly* 20 (1996): 15.

218 her survey of 120 studies: *New York Times*, May 11, 1999.

218 those with professional need: Gerald R. Miller, Paul A. Mongeau, and Carra Sleight, "Fudging with Friends and Lying to Lovers: Deceptive Communication in Personal Relationships," *Journal of Social and Personal Relationships* 3 (1986): 500.

218 owner of polygraph service: *Palm Beach Post*, February 1, 1995.

218 Chicago company: *Salt Lake City Deseret News*, August 15, 2002.

219 Research on interrogators: Ekman, *Telling Lies*, 284–85, 332; Bella M. DePaulo, "Spotting Human Lies: Can Humans Learn to Do Better?" *Current Directions in Psychological Science* 3 (1994): 83–86; *New Scientist*, March 18, 2002.

219 German psychologist: G. Koehnken, in Ray Bull, "Can Training Enhance the Detection of Deception?" in Yuille, *Credibility Assessment*, 95–97.

219 study in Britain: *New Scientist*, March 18, 2002.

220 Ekman on secret service agents: Ekman, *Telling Lies*, 286–88, 332.

220 "Diogenes sample": *New York Times*, May 11, 1999.

220 Ekman's daughter: Ekman, *Telling Lies*, 288.

220 micro-expressions: *Washington Post*, July 12, 1999; *Times* (London, England), July 21, 2000; *O*, January 2002; *Salt Lake City Deseret News*, August 15, 2002; *Economic Times* (India), February 19, 2003; *Fresh Air*, National Public Radio, May 22, 2003.

220 "spotting them takes an hour": Ekman, *Telling Lies*, 337.

220 "Such a complex, time-consuming approach": *San Diego Union-Tribune*, August 14, 1996.

221 easily spotted cues: *New York Times*, February 12, 1985; Marc D. Hauser, *The Evolution of Communication* (Cambridge, MA: MIT Press, 1996), 606; D. Eric Anderson, Bella M. DePaulo, Matthew E. Ansfield, Jennifer J. Tickle, and Emily Green, "Beliefs and Cues to Deception: Mindless Stereotypes or Untapped Wisdom?" *Journal of Nonverbal Behavior* 23 (1999): 67–89.

221 this cue is a tip-off only: Bella M. DePaulo and Matthew E. Ansfield, "Detecting Deception from Nonverbal Cues: Pinocchio's Revenge," *Legal Medical Quarterly* 20 (1996): 18.

221 nose does get bigger: *Panama City* (FL) *News Herald*, May 23, 1999.

221 spotting small vs. big lies: Ekman, in *San Diego Union-Tribune*, August 14, 2003.

222 early lie-detection methods: Robert Ellis Smith, "The Truth, the Whole Truth, and Nothing But . . . ," unpublished manuscript, 1979; David Lykken, *A Tremor in the Blood: Uses and Abuses of the Lie Detector* (New York: McGraw-Hill, 1981), 25–26; B. Kleinmuntz and J. J. Szucko, "Lie Detection in Ancient and Modern Times," *American Psychologist* 39 (1984): 766–76; Ford, *Lies! Lies! Lies!* 222; Sullivan, *The Concise Book of Lying*, 207, 213–26.

222 two comprehensive studies of polygraph: Ekman, *Telling Lies*, 195–97; Reuters, October 8, 2002; *Dayton Daily News*, October 9, 2002.

222 Bunn: *Psychology Today*, May–June 1997.

222 Lykken: David Lykken, *A Tremor in the Blood: Uses and Abuses of the Lie Detector* (New York: McGraw-Hill, 1981); David Lykken, "Why (Some) Americans Believe in the Lie Detector While Others Believe in the Guilty Knowledge Test," *Integrative Physiological and Behavioral Science* 26 (1991): 214–22.

223 former policeman: *Discover*, March 1986; *Times* (London, England), July 21, 2000.

223 frequency of polygraph use: Ekman, *Telling Lies*, 192.

223 Steinbrook: *New England Journal of Medicine*, July 9, 1992.

223 the way polygraph used: Leonard Saxe, "Lying," *American Psychologist* 46 (1991): 411.

223 Doylestown case: *Privacy Journal*, May 1979.

224 perceived ethics of accountants: *Dayton Daily News*, July 15, 2002.

224 Kintz: *Bulletin of the Psychonomic Society* 10 (1977): 492.

224–25 Kintz's own study: Jo Ann Burns and B. L. Kintz, *Bulletin of the Psychonomic Society* 7 (1976): 87.

225 "Similarly, physicians": Cabot, *Honesty*, 145–48.

225 Media Studies Center survey: *New York Times*, October 19, 1998.

225 Boyd: *Cleveland Plain Dealer*, March 21, 2004.

226 Erwitt: *All Things Considered*, National Public Radio, March 7, 2003.

226 "one of my own nonfiction books": Ralph Keyes, *Chancing It: Why We Take Risks* (Boston: Little, Brown, 1985).

226 Nietzsche: Walter Kaufmann, trans. and ed., *Basic Writings of Nietzsche* (New York: Modern Library, 1992), 283.

227 "Reporters dated the unraveling": *All Things Considered*, National Public Radio, July 20, 2003.

227 "serial fabricator": *Albany* (NY) *Times Union*, June 15, 2003.

227 car dealer: Greg Baszucki of invoicedealers.com, *Dallas Morning News*, January 30, 2002.

227 North: *U.S. News and World Report*, June 6, 1994; *Roanoke Times and World News*, October 23, 1994.

227 Barnicle: *Boston Magazine*, October 1998.

228 Cooke: *New York Times*, November 29, 1981, May 9, 1983.

228 Grubman: Amy Feldman and Joan Caplin, "What Would It Take to Be the Worst Analyst Ever?" *Money*, May 2002.

228 Reid: *Los Angeles Times*, March 11, 2004; *San Diego Union-Tribune*, March 15, 2004.

228 Johnson: Arendt, *Crises of the Republic*, 14; *New Yorker*, September 30, 2002.

229 Broder: Barnes, *A Pack of Lies*, 33.

229 Donnelly: *Boston Globe*, February 21, 1997.

15. The Price of Prevarication

230 Montaigne, *Essays*, 221.

230 Montague: C. C. Montague, *Disenchantment* (London: Chatto and Windus, 1922), 214.

230 Le Carré–Cornwell: *New Yorker*, February 18 and 25, 2002.

231 Farson: personal communication.

231 chronic liar: *Health*, July 1992.

231 Blanton: Brad Blanton, *Radical Honesty: How to Transform Your Life by Telling the Truth* (New York: Dell, 1996); xxv; *Men's Health*, October 1997; *Bergen* (NJ) *Record*, April 26, 1998.

231 Johnson's paranoia: Doris Kearns, *Lyndon Johnson and the American Dream* (New York: Harper and Row, 1976), 314–17; Beschloss, *Reaching for Glory*, 378–79.

231 Shaw: George Bernard Shaw, *The Intelligent Woman's Guide to Socialism, Capitalism, Sovietism, and Fascism* (London: Constable, 1928), 364.

232 Vrij: *Independent on Sunday* (London, England), July 13, 2003.

232 Nietzsche: Nietzsche, *The Will to Power*, 158.

232 one subject in a study: Lucy Fontaine Werth and Jenny Flaherty, "A Phenomenological Approach to Human Deception," in Mitchell and Thompson, *Deception*, 303.

232 brain researchers: *ABC World News Tonight*, December 12, 2001; Associated Press, June 21, 2002.

233 Josephson: Cox News Service, December 14, 2001.

233 Cook: *Bangor Daily News*, September 30, 2003.

233 Cleveland schoolteacher: *Cleveland, Plain Dealer*, July 19, 1998.

233 Wayne-Morrison: Zolotow, *Shooting Star*, 305; Wills, *John Wayne's America*, 27; *New York Times*, June 13, 1979.

233 Reagan, Morris: Morris, *Dutch*, vi.

233–34 Rich: Rich, *On Lies, Secrets, and Silence*, 185–94.

234 Michell: Gillian Michell, "Women and Lying," in *Hypatia Reborn: Essays in Feminist Philosophy*, Azizah Y. Al-Hibri and Margaret A. Simons, ed. (Bloomington: Indiana University Press, 1990), 189.

235 Klockars: *American Behavioral Scientist* 27 (1984): 422.

235 Montaigne: Montaigne, "On Liars," *Essays*, 31.

235 Patterson and Kim: Patterson and Kim, *The Day America Told the Truth*, 45.

235 Bok: *Talk of the Nation*, National Public Radio, December 3, 1996.

235 Soderbergh: screenplay, *sex, lies, and videotape* (Beverly Hills, CA: Leading Artists, 1988), 78.

235–36 Wolfe's subject: Wolfe, *Moral Freedom*, 126.

236 a Tucson caller: *Talk of the Nation*, National Public Radio, December 3, 1996.

236 Pope: *Thoughts on Various Subjects*, in Burton Stevenson, ed., *The Home Book of Quotations* (New York: Dodd, Mead, 1935), 1112.

236 one recovering liar: *Talk of the Nation*, National Public Radio, December 3, 1996.

237 Wittgenstein: Forrester, *Truth Games*, 47; Campbell, *The Liar's Tale*, 249.

237 Nietzsche: Williams, *Truth and Truthfulness*, 12–19.

237 Hemingway: Meyers, *Hemingway*, 47.

237 Le Carré: *New Yorker*, February 18 and 25, 2002.

237 Bergman: Forrester, *Truth Games*, 24.

237 Rousseau: Williams, *Truth and Truthfulness*, 176.

237 Wittgenstein: Campbell, *The Liar's Tale*, 249.

237–38 Pitt-Rivers: Julian A. Pitt-Rivers, *The People of the Sierra* (Chicago: University of Chicago Press, 1954), xvi–xvii.

238 Slater: Slater, *Lying*, 160, 162, 165.

239 on loneliness: Slater, *Lying*, 133.

239 AA meeting: Slater, *Lying*, 205.

239 dialogue with therapist: Slater, *Lying*, 201–2.

240 "fact and truth together": Slater, *Lying*, 204.

16. The Case for Honesty

241 Perkins: John Hall Wheelock, ed., *Editor to Author: The Letters of Maxwell E. Perkins* (New York: Universal Library, 1950), 269.

242 "negative weight": Bok, *Lying*, 32–33.

242 "Mild as this initial stipulation sounds": Ibid.

244 Mencken: Bill Press, *Spin This: All the Ways We Don't Tell the Truth* (New York: Pocket Books, 2001), 51.

245 Nyberg: David Nyberg, *The Varnished Truth: Truth Telling and Deceiving in Ordinary Life* (Chicago: University of Chicago Press, 1993), 3, 5.

246 NPR host: Steve Inskeep hosting Randy Cohen, *Weekend All Things Considered*, National Public Radio, January 25, 2003.

247 Ramotswe: Alexander McCall Smith, *The No. 1 Ladies' Detective Agency* (New York: Anchor, 1998), 210.

247 Bok: Bok, *Lying*, 24–32, 84–85, 91–92, 98, 109.

247 Gaylin: *Medical Economics*, October 11, 1999.

249 Hempel: Amy Hempel, *Tumble Home* (New York: Scribner's, 1997), 20.

249 "benevolent deception": Jennifer Jackson, "Telling the Truth," *Journal of Medical Ethics* 17 (1991): 5.

249 one physician: Cabot, *Honesty*, 15.

249 recent studies: Charles Inlander, *Marketplace*, Public Radio International, December 6, 2001.

250 survey of parents: Patterson and Kim, *The Day America Told the Truth*, 48.

250 Lewis: *Detroit News*, April 1, 1997.

252 Fukuyama: Francis Fukuyama, *Trust: The Social Virtues and the Creation of Prosperity* (New York: Free Press, 1995).

253 Greenspan: *Marketplace*, Public Radio International, September 12, 2002.

255 Bennis: *New York Times*, February 17, 2002.

Index